Better Homes and Gardens®

GIFTS
to make yourself

When you care enough to give a gift, give the best—a gift you've designed, made, and wrapped with your own hands. It is the one sure way to please everyone on your gift-giving list. Study the examples throughout this book, follow the directions, and employ a little of your imagination. You'll be quite amazed at the results.

BETTER HOMES AND GARDENS BOOKS

Editorial Director: Don Dooley
Managing Editor: Malcolm E. Robinson   Art Director: John Berg
Asst. Managing Editor: Lawrence D. Clayton   Asst. Art Director: Randall Yontz
Senior Editor: Marie Schulz
Designers: Julie Zesch, Harijs Priekulis
Contributing Editor: Janice McCord

CONTENTS

INTRODUCTION

Better Homes and Gardens *Gifts to Make Yourself* is a product of the times. With all the push-button appliances, convenience foods, and shorter work weeks, most people have increased leisure time. With this additional free time, along with a growing emphasis on ecology, people are rediscovering nature and realizing some of the advantages of 'The Good Old Days' —fresh-baked bread, hand-crafted afghans, the rich smell and feel of hand-tooled leather, and the charm of intricate stitchery. Suddenly, everyone is interested in the creativity and accomplishment that only crafts can offer.

This book covers a broad spectrum of crafts— knitting, crocheting, decoupage, macrame, needlecraft, candlemaking, leatherwork, and many more. Included are unusual, challenging gift ideas that adults will enjoy making, plus simple craft projects that children from the ages of six to twelve can do. In addition, the book can act as a handy reference guide for youth group leaders who are always searching for new and inexpensive hobby and craft projects.

One of the most appealing things about the book is that a number of the gift items presented are quick and inexpensive to make. In fact, some of the gifts won't cost anything, as they are made of ordinary household items that you probably have around your home.

Make your special gifts by duplicating the designs throughout the book, or simply use the designs as a springboard for your own designs. Always read the directions carefully and completely before beginning a project. Then, follow the directions exactly.

When you are making any of these gifts for a young child, always keep the child's safety in mind. Be sure to use nonflammable, washable, durable fabrics and stuffing. This is particularly important when you are making stuffed dolls and animals. The mothers will appreciate these gifts more if they can be tossed in the washing machine and cleaned. Always take extra care to sew on buttons and trims securely to eliminate the danger of a child chewing and swallowing them. When making wooden toys for children, sand all sharp corners and use only nontoxic paint products.

Another word about safety might also be wise at this point. Throughout the book you will find that some of the gift items are starred. This means that these projects, in addition to those discussed in chapter seven, are suitable for children from the ages of six to twelve to make. Although these are all easy-to-do projects, supervise your child's work—at least until he completes his first project. Let him do the work by himself, but be on hand for extra guidance, encouragement, and praise.

Gifts to Make Yourself is a gift book, an idea book, and a craft book. It was researched and written with you, the reader, in mind. Use it as you will. Read it carefully, briefly scan it, or just look at the pictures for ideas of your own. But, most importantly, start crafting your own gifts and gift wraps now. The sooner you get to work making them, the sooner you will experience the pleasure of creativity and accomplishment that these crafts offer. You'll have a lot of fun at the same time, too.

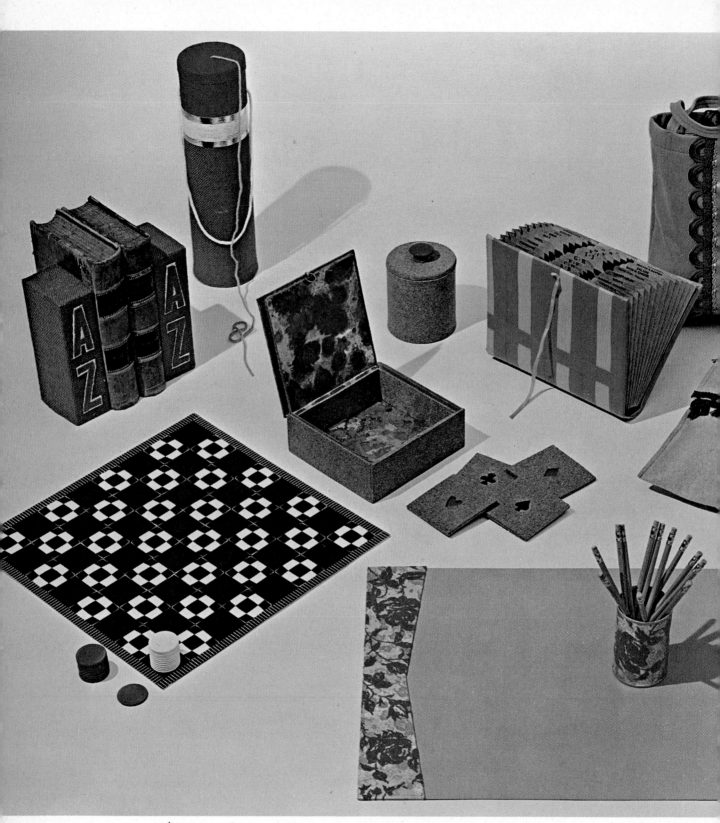

★ Cut-and-paste gifts made of felt, cork, and adhesive vinyl.

chapter 1

EASY AND INEXPENSIVE

You've been making cut-and-paste gifts since you were in the first grade. Paper was probably your first medium because it was readily available and easy to work with. This has not always been the case. Paper, invented in China in the second century, was considered too scarce to be wasted on children until the nineteenth century.

Today's cut-and-paste cult has graduated to new frontiers— fabric, yarn, foil, tape, and cork. Try making the following gifts, and then devise some of your own.

A checkerboard, bookends, and a knitting bag are fun items to make and will be appreciated by anyone on your gift list.

Start with the checkerboard. Mark off 64 squares of black felt 1⅞ inches. Then, cut 128 pieces of white felt, ⅞x½ inch, and glue them onto the black felt. Now you have an instant checkerboard. Use poker chips as checkers.

What about personalized bookends? Try these made from two bricks covered with felt. Cut the initials of the person to whom you are giving the gift, place them onto a white background, and glue them to the felt-covered bricks.

Now, turn your attention to the nifty knitting bags. These are made from felt-covered oatmeal boxes. Tape two cartons together, then cover the bottom and up 9½ inches of the sides with blue felt. Add a strip of metallic tape on which you center white felt. Top with 2½ inches of red felt. For carrycord, punch two holes two inches down on either side, and insert 24 inches of cotton cord. Cover the lid; punch a hole in the top.

Canisters, decorative boxes, and coasters are a cinch to make when you use adhesive cork.

To make a candy canister, wrap the outside of a tin container with adhesive cork. Cut two circles of cork the same size as the can's outer diameter. After the cork has been applied, press adhesive sides together to make two thicknesses.

Next, cut two circles the same diameter as inside rim of canister opening. Center and adhere these to the larger circles. Attach knob to top.

The decorative box is a spruced-up cigar box. Cut adhesive cork the same size as the bottom and sides of the box and apply. Cut the back piece slightly narrower to allow for hinge action. Cut the top piece larger than the original lid to extend flush with the cork-covered exterior. Line the inside of the box with cork and decorative foil paper. Decorate the lid.

The playing-card coasters are made from eight 3½-inch squares of cork. Cut out a center shape in four of the pieces of cork, and insert a piece of vinyl tape behind the opening. To finish, press the adhesive sides together.

Desk sets and desk accessories are fun to fashion from self-adhesive vinyls.

Notice the desk set in the bottom right of the picture. A 16x21-inch sheet of poster board forms the base. To make side pockets, cut two pieces of poster board 16x3 inches wide, with the center angling to two inches. Cover with adhesive vinyl, allowing extra at top, bottom, and sides to attach to back of base. Cut a desk blotter to 15½x21 inches and slip it into side pockets. Cover pencil holder with same vinyl.

The expandable file is simply dressed with a new coat of self-adhesive vinyl.

FABRIC AND YARN

If you are one of the millions of people who have the hoarding tendencies of a pack rat, you'll be able to sit right down to work on any of these projects. Somewhere in your house, you already have boxes of fabric and yarn scraps. But, if you happen to be one of the few people who don't save such would-be treasures, you can purchase your materials and join in the fun. However, be thrifty and buy from remnant tables, since none of the projects require great amounts of fabric, but a variety of patterns.

You will be able to complete almost any idea you dream up with three or four colors each of felt, burlap, vinyl, and cotton print plus a little yarn. If possible, use the self-adhesive fabric; then you have a head start to the finish line.

★ **Felt is a winning material when used to make a handcrafted game board.**

On the other hand, regular fabric can be used and applied with white glue, rubber cement, spray adhesive, or, if you're fusing one fabric to another, try the new iron-on bonding materials found in sewing departments.

Should you choose to do a project using a cotton print fabric or any other fabric that has a tendency to ravel, either hem the edges or prevent the edges from fraying with clear nail polish. Before cutting the fabric, apply a coat of clear nail polish over the line that is to be cut. This seals the edges. Or, if a pinked edge will not distract from your design, you may cut each piece with pinking shears.

Felt wins again on this game board, scoring high because it is easy to work with and because it is inexpensive. To make a handcrafted game, use one of your games or one borrowed from a friend as a pattern or guide for size. Start with a large piece of tightly woven fabric for the backing. Then, cut the design of felt pieces. Set all the pieces in their proper place before gluing with white glue. Construction will be easier if the small pieces are glued to the larger ones before they are attached to the background. To make the playing pieces, stain or enamel spools or decorative knobs. Purchase a pair of dice from the variety store, and type a set of playing rules for the game.

Virtually any game board can be duplicated, particularly if you have a pattern. In most instances, felt works best because the edges do not ravel, and, therefore, do not require any finishing. But, if you are making a game for a small child, perhaps you would prefer to use materials that can be wiped clean with a damp cloth. If so, construct your game board from a piece of vinyl or oilcloth. Then, using different colors of vinyl tape, apply the designs onto the game board. This same idea works well for a permanent, portable, rollaway hopscotch game.

Launch your own anti-litter campaign by giving bright, plastic-lined car litter bags. Cut the pieces from felt; the front and back are 8x10-

inch pieces; the sides are 4x8-inch pieces; and the bottom is also a 4x8-inch piece. Next, cut pieces of polyethelene from plastic bags the same size as the felt, and then glue the plastic to the felt along the edges of the reverse side. Seam the side panels to the front, bottom, and back pieces by using either a straight stitch or a zig-zag stitch close to the edge. Make a handle for the litter bag from a 3x10-inch band of felt. Fold the band in half lengthwise and seam the raw edge. Sew one end of the handle to the center front of the bag, and secure the other end to the back with a gripper snap.

Decorate the front of the litter bags with any design you choose. The designs on the litter bags shown in the picture were cut from felt and glued to the bags, but you may choose to decorate yours with rickrack, braid, beads, yarn, or any number of other things.

This idea makes a thoughtful gift for someone who is about to take a motor trip, especially if you fill the bag with handy articles such as tissues, a flashlight, gum, packaged candy, change for toll roads and bridges, and a road map.

Desk and dresser organizers take on a new look and plenty of new duties when you make them from pint- and quart-size ice cream cartons. Using spray adhesive, rubber cement, or white glue, cover the cartons with a lightweight cotton fabric, spray-paint the top, and secure wooden or ceramic drawer pulls to the lids.

After covering your containers, add more exterior decorations with sewing trims, felt cutouts, yarn motifs, small pictures, or details drawn with marking pens.

When giving this as a desk organizer, fill it with such articles as a letter opener, pens, a typing eraser, stamps, a small stapler and staples, paper clips, scissors, and tape.

Decorate one container for a child and make it a pencil box for his desk at school. Fill it with pencils, a small ruler, and a large eraser.

Or, outfit one of the organizers as a small sewing kit. Fill it with small spools of thread, needles, pins, and scissors.

These handsome bookends would be much appreciated by anyone. Once again, the project requires a couple of scraps of felt and a few wood scraps from the workshop. Cut a pine block to 10½x5x1 inch. Select a variety of decorative moldings and cut them into 10½-inch lengths. If you don't have these on hand, purchase them from a local lumber supply store. Using an epoxy, glue the moldings to the block, starting from the center. When the glue is dry, saw the block in half. With a rag, rub on a walnut stain and allow it to dry overnight. Finish the wood with two coats of matte medium or liquid sealer. From X.020-inch heavy gauge aluminum, cut two pieces 3½x7¼ inches with tin snips. Round off the corners and smooth the edges with a file. In a vise, bend the aluminum at 2⅝ inches to a right angle. Spray the aluminum with flat black enamel, and when dry, attach it to the blocks with ¾-inch nails or strong epoxy glue. Cut two pieces of felt 5¼x5 inches to cover inside of bookends. Attach with glue.

★ **Litter bags, desk organizers, and bookends made with fabric and yarn.**

★ Stylized rooster felt scroll.

★ Fruit design felt wall hanging.

On these two pages, you'll find a collection of the quickest, easiest gifts you could ever imagine. And, if that's not enough to inspire you, they are also real money savers. Each gift is made by simply gluing a small amount of fabric or yarn to some other inexpensive item.

Make this rooster felt scroll in less than an hour. Cut the rooster sections from felt, using a predrawn stylized pattern, then attach them with white glue to the 24x44-inch felt background panel. So that the scroll will hang properly, fold over two inches along the top edge and glue along the edge. Insert a rod and attach a cord at each end. Or apply double-faced pressure-sensitive tape to the top and bottom of the panel. Then, mount the panel on the wall.

The fruit felt wall hanging makes a quick and easy shower or house-warming gift. It is made of a 30x48-inch piece of felt. Cut apple and pear shapes in colored felt, making stylized sections, stems, and leaves. Glue the pieces to each other, then to the felt background.

For hanging, fold over the top two inches and glue the edge to the background. Insert a rod or window-shade bar through the casing, and tie a cord on each end of the rod.

Coordinated desk sets are always people pleasing gifts. Buy an inexpensive desk set, or make your own from heavy cardboard and tin cans. (See page 7 for complete directions on how to make a desk blotter.) Whichever way you do it, give the desk set a custom look by trimming it with leftover yarn. Paste the yarn to the objects by spreading a thin line of white glue about three or four inches at a time; lay the yarn down on the glue and pat the yarn down firmly. The design that you make is up to you. Try stripes, chevrons, or just wavy lines.

Picture frame jewelry cases make lovely gifts for every lady on your list. To duplicate these, drill a hole in the center top of a small picture frame and attach a drapery ring. Refinish the frame with acrylic paints. Finish the frames with highlights of rub-on antiquing gold.

Next, cut a piece of ½-inch foam rubber to fit the inside of the frame and back it with a piece of cardboard cut to the same size. Cut velvet or any other rich-looking fabric one inch larger than the foam rubber; stretch it over the rubber and glue the fabric to the cardboard. Cut another piece of cardboard to fit the back of the frame. Spray it with gold paint and glue it to the back of the frame.

The mini note board, bottom right, is a perfect gift for children to make for Mom or an older sister. Simply glue a 12-inch carpet tile to a 14-inch burlap-covered cardboard square. Trim it with felt cutouts and pompons.

★ **Picture frame cases to hold jewelry.**

★ **Decorative mini note board.**

★ **Coordinated desk accessories.**

★ Nutcracker finger puppets, a delightful gift for any child.

9   10   11   12   13 14 15   16   17   18

★ Re-create a favorite fantasy with felt, glue, and assorted trims.

14

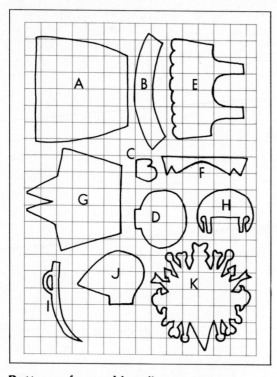

Patterns for making finger puppets.

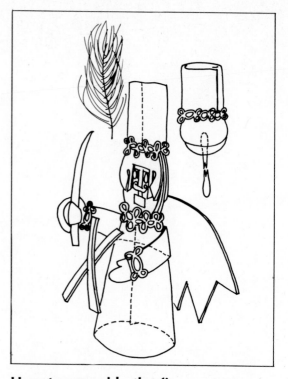

How to assemble the finger puppets.

THE NUTCRACKER FINGER PUPPETS

Long before the Russian composer Tchaikovsky wrote the music for the Nutcracker ballet, generations of boys and girls had been captivated by the legend of the wonderful nutcracker.

Now you can re-create this fantasy world for the children you love. Make the cast of characters from felt, trims, and scraps of fabric.

To make a stage, cover a dress box or grocery store carton with gift wrapping paper or fabric. Then, make a stage curtain from velvet.

When everything is completed, put on the production for the children. Run through it a couple of times and then let the children do their own version. It may not resemble your version, but you'll be amazed at just how many times the plot twists and turns.

Before long, they'll be asking you to help them make more finger puppets to act out their favorite fairy tales, television programs, children's records, and even their own families.

Assemble all the materials they will need and show them step by step how to make the finger puppets. At the same time, explain how you

change the character by changing its costume or hair color. Then, turn them loose with blunt scissors, white glue, felt, sewing trims, yarn, and scraps of fabric. Offer suggestions, but let each child make his own creature.

After each child has made several of the finger puppets for himself and staged the production, complete with an audience, you might suggest that they make a stage and cast of characters for a friend. A gift such as this will delight any child, especially one who is confined at home with measles, mumps, chicken pox, or even a common cold.

GENERAL INSTRUCTIONS

For each puppet, cut the basic body shape (A), as shown in the top left line drawing, from felt. Scale this to fit the finger. These puppets are 3½ inches tall, 2½ inches wide at the top, and 3¾ inches wide at the bottom. Overlap the sides of the body slightly and glue firmly with white glue. Leave the top and bottom open. Unless specified otherwise, cut two of B (arms), two of C (hands), and two of D (head). Glue the arm pieces together with the hands in place between. Then, glue the arms to the back of the body. Next, place a cotton swab between the head sections and glue all together. Insert the protruding end of the swab into the neck opening and glue the head to the body. See the second line drawing for assembly.

1. Arab Dancer, Coffee. Assemble the basic body. Add yellow circles for the top, black pompons for hair, and lace trim for the veil and skirt.

2. Tea the Chinaman. Assemble the basic body, using yellow felt. Trim with sequin braid and make hair from bunches of black sewing thread.

3., 9., and 13. Flowers. Assemble the basic body from bright green felt. Glue the tops of bodies closed and add flower shapes. Finally add petals, and trim with sequins and beads.

4. Sugar Plum Fairy. Assemble the basic body, using pink felt. Wrap layers of lace trim around the body. Make hair from small red pompons. Scatter beads and sequins in the hair, and add a small pink felt crown.

5. Sugar Plums. Assemble the basic body and glue the top closed. Glue pompons of different sizes and colors all over the bodies and scallop the bottom edge of the felt body.

6. Snowflake. Assemble A and glue the top closed. Cut snowflake shape (K) and glue it to the body. Add sequins or beads for eyes.

7. and 8. Snow King and Queen. Assemble the basic bodies. Glue on yellow felt hair for the queen and brown felt hair for the king. Wrap the bodies in white fur and trim with sequins. Add hats from fur and crowns from felt.

10. Nutcracker Soldiers. Assemble the basic body. Cut hair (H) from brown felt. Cover the back of the head with felt. Add a moustache and white felt bands on the cuffs of the coat.

11. and 14. Mouse King and Soldiers. Make the heads, using pattern J. Add round ears and, for the king, a yellow crown. Glue on black pom-

pons for the nose. Glue arms to the sides instead of the back. Add silver cardboard swords, braid to the cuffs, and tassels to the shoulders.

12. Clara. Assemble the basic body. Cut an apron (E) and buttons from white felt and glue them to the body. Braid 12 strands of yarn 12 inches long and glue this to the head. Add short yarn strips tied together in the center for bangs. Cover the back of the head with yarn. Tie bows on the ends of the braids and on the top of the head. Cut and glue felt eyes and draw a mouth and a nose with a felt-tip pen.

15. Nutcracker Prince. Assemble the basic body. Using pattern G for a guide, but cutting the sides parallel, cut out the yellow coat. Trim the coat with gold braid and sequins. Cut hair and crown out of felt and glue in place.

16. Nutcracker. Assemble the basic body. Cut and glue on the cape, using G, but making it smaller at the top. Cut hair (H) from white felt. Cover the back of the head with felt. Cut sword (I) from stiff gold cardboard. Glue on gold braid trim, white stripes across the coat front, and a silver cardboard sword. Add a hat and plume.

17. Dr. Drosselmeyer. Assemble the basic body. Cut coat and collar according to pattern F. Gather and glue a small amount of lace at the neck. Add hair cut from white felt and make one eye and one eye patch from blue felt.

18. Franz. Assemble basic body. Cut a shirt, using the top half of pattern A. Glue this to the assembled body, and add a collar and buttons. Glue 10 strands of yarn three inches long to head.

NOTE: These 18 characters make up the cast of the Nutcracker production. The directions for making and dressing the various characters are just guidelines. They are not given as rules. You may dress and trim your cast any way you like. If you don't have a lot of felt scraps, substitute other fabrics. Cotton, oil cloth, vinyl, wool, and doubleknits may also be used. If the fabric is likely to fray, cut it with pinking shears rather than straight-edged scissors. You may have to do this for your child.

FOIL AND TAPE

Cloth, vinyl, and metallic tapes and aluminum foil—herein lies an untapped resource of gift-making materials. Transform coffee cans into canister sets, ordinary cardboard boxes into silvery treasure chests, or pieces of mailing tubes into instant napkin rings. The possibilities are practically limitless.

The cloth and vinyl tapes are available in a rich rainbow of colors and come in ¾-inch or 2-inch widths. The metallic tapes, which look like ribbons of silver and gold, come in a 2-inch width. All of these inexpensive tapes are sold in hardware, variety, discount and department stores, and supermarkets.

Buy a couple of rolls of these tapes and begin experimenting. Try covering orange juice containers to make desk organizers or pretty planters, add racy stripes to an old flowerpot, or make an ultramodern wall hanging.

Or, improve on an inexpensive ready-made item by adding a smart design. For example, make an inexpensive bath scale stand out by applying stripes or chevrons. Buy an ordinary alarm clock, and dress it up to match the bedroom with designs cut from the colorful tapes. Or, make personalized lunch boxes for your children with initials made from these tapes.

With just a little practice, you'll soon get the feel of using tape and will then be turning out your own tape-trimmed specialties.

The tape-trimmed bathroom ensemble shown in the two photos below is a good example of what can be done to dress up ready-made merchandise. The inexpensive plastic hamper, wastebasket, tissue box, and soap dish become eye-catchers when they are trimmed with strips of black vinyl and aluminum metallic tape.

★ **Decorator hamper and wastebasket.**

★ **Tissue box and soap dish.**

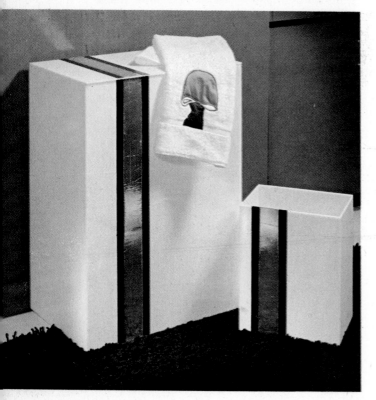

★ A handsome antique foil box.

The handsome antique foil box pictured above is a great gift for someone on your list. You can make it easily from inexpensive materials. All you need is the box, aluminum foil, cardboard, household string, black enamel, and glue.

Paint the inside of the box first and allow it to dry. Next, draw a variety of flowers, leaves, and flower centers in an assortment of sizes on lightweight cardboard, and cut them out. Glue the shapes in place, putting some smaller flowers on top of the larger petals. Draw curlicues on the top and the sides of the box, then spray these outlines with adhesive. Lay lengths of cord onto the pattern and press firmly in place. Remove hinges and closure. Tear off a strip of lightweight aluminum foil the length and width of the lid. Crumple the foil gently and lightly flatten it out, but don't smooth it. Spray the box with adhesive. Press the foil around the raised patterns. Continue in this manner until the box is completely covered with foil, placing the overlapping edges on the bottom side of the box. When the box is dry, brush it completely with black paint. When the paint is just dry, rub the box with a clean, soft cloth to remove the surface paint. Spray over the finished box with a clear plastic or clear varnish. Replace the hinges and the closure.

1. Cut and glue on cardboard motifs. 2. Glue on cording. 3. Cover box with crumpled foil. 4. Antique with enamel.

Decorator boxes take on a different look when they are adorned with aluminum or gold tape. Team the tape with prints, antiquing foam, India ink, shoe polish, or vinyl and cloth for gifts that will intrigue and surprise nearly everyone on your gift-giving list.

Choose any type of box you like—wood, metal, plastic, or cardboard. Then, begin planning your design. Cover the box with smooth, shiny foil tape, or cover just the lid and reserve the bottom for vinyl or cloth tape. Or, glue string, buttons, or paper doilies onto the box, cover the box with foil tape, and with an orange stick, press the tape down and around the objects.

Or, try putting an applied texture on the foil tape. Create a freehand design on the tape with an orange stick or small knitting needle after the tape has been applied to the box.

Decorator boxes made of foil tape.

If freehand is hard for you, trace a design onto the shiny side of the tape and then apply the tape to the box. If you wish, try another tracing technique: simply pick up the raised texture of a planter, a carved molding, or a tooled leather belt. Leave the paper backing on the tape. Lay the tape, shiny side up, over the object and rub with an orange stick or knitting needle to pick up the design. When you've completed the pattern, peel off the backing and apply the tape to the box. The tape is strong, so it will hold the design motifs well. The design will not smooth out as the tape is applied. For an embossed effect, lay the tape, shiny side down, over the object and rub over the paper side. By doing this, the design will be raised.

The antiqued recipe box, top, is simply a metal box covered with aluminum tape. After the box is covered, trace a design onto the tape. Then, antique the box with an antiquing foam glaze, India ink, or shoe polish. After the glaze is dry, rub off the glaze with a clean dry cloth. The design will be darker, as some of the glaze will stay in the indentations.

The decorator box, middle, was made from a plastic sandwich box. Cover the bottom of the box with black vinyl tape. Cover the lid with aluminum tape. Then, cut a print from a greeting card to fit the indentation in the center of the lid. Glue the print in place with white glue. Then, brush on several coats of liquid gel medium from an artist supply store. Let it dry thoroughly between coats. This will give the print a muted texture. Finally, line the inside of the box and the lid with black velvet.

The woven silver box, bottom, is the richest looking cardboard box you'll probably ever see. Cover the bottom half of the box with aluminum tape. Then, leaving the paper backing on the tape, cut the tape into ½-inch strips. Weave the strips to fit the top of the box. Trim the woven tape to exactly fit the top of the box. Attach the woven tape to the top by framing the four edges with pieces of aluminum tape that overlap ½-inch of the top edges and cover the sides of the lid. Line the inside of the box and the lid with red velvet.

Picture frames make great gifts. They seem to be one item people just never have enough of. Here are some new ideas for every style of picture frame. Try your hand at one of these works of art, and see how easy it is to make.

The contemporary frame, top, is an inexpensive way to frame a canvas. Buy lath stripping from the lumber supply company. Cut four pieces to frame the canvas. Cover these pieces with black vinyl tape. Cover each piece individually, and then nail them into the edges of the canvas. Cut four more pieces of the lath stripping to frame the black frame. Cover each piece individually with aluminum tape, and nail these pieces on top of the black vinyl tape-covered frame. When finished, the frame closely resembles expensive polished aluminum strip frames.

The mock silver frame, center, is an expensive-looking imitation. Purchase an inexpensive narrow wood or metal frame from the variety store. Cut the aluminum tape to fit each of the four sides of the frame, carefully mitering the corners. Begin by covering the inside edge of the frame, then the front, and finally the outside edge and back of the frame. If the frame has any grooves, carefully run a knitting needle or orange stick over the tape, following the grooves. When finished, the frame will look very much like an expensive sterling silver frame.

The richly carved frame, bottom, is easier to make than its looks might suggest. Purchase an unfinished frame from a variety store. Glue pieces of sewing trim to the unfinished frame, mitering the corners. Then, cover the frame with foil tape and press out the design with an orange stick or knitting needle, being careful not to tear tape. (For details, see page 21.)

The ornate frame, left, also is made from an unfinished frame. Since the frame is wider than the two-inch tape, the tape must be overlapped and applied in sections. Along the outer edge of the frame, apply tape that has a rubbed design. On the back and inside of the frame, leave the tape unadorned. When the frame is completely covered, finish it with an antiquing foam or India ink. (See page 20 for complete details.)

The heavily embossed frame, right, is a real masterpiece. Either buy an unfinished frame or pick up a wide frame at a garage sale and begin playing silversmith. Cover the inside portion of the frame with aluminum tape, mitering the corners. For the outside portion of the frame, cut strips of metal tape to fit the frame. Lay the tape, shiny side down, over a raised design. (Tape the edges down to keep the tape from slipping.) Using a knitting needle, rub over the design. When the design is completed, pick up the tape, carefully remove the paper backing, and apply the strips to the outer edge of the frame. Cover the back of the frame with smooth aluminum tape. When the frame is completely covered, antique it with antiquing foam glaze or India ink. Let this dry and then rub off the excess with a clean dry cloth.

Elegant, handcrafted picture frames.

When styling a picture frame with aluminum or gold tape, you can do so as simply or as ornately as you wish. For contemporary frames, use the tape just as it comes from the roll. For more formal or traditional frames, simulate a hand-tooled effect by tracing various textures.

To duplicate the frame below, use foil tape on which you have embossed the texture you wish to duplicate—the molding around a door, the intricate pattern on a wire screen, the design on a planter, for examples. Avoid textures more than ⅛ inch high, as these may tear the tape.

Once you've located the texture you want to duplicate, lay the premeasured strip of tape down on the texture, shiny side up. Using an orange stick or knitting needle, rub over the tape, being careful not to tear the tape. As you rub, you will mold the tape over and around the design. When you've completed rubbing the design, pick it up and peel off the paper backing. Lay the tape on the side of the frame, being careful not to wrinkle the tape. Lightly smooth the tape in place. Continue the same process all around the frame until all four sides are covered. Then, turn frame over and cover back side of frame. When finished, antique the frame if you wish. Use regular antiquing glaze or try one of the new foam antiquing glazes. Spray out a small amount and rub it on the frame. Let it dry completely. When it is dry, take a small, clean dry cloth and rub gently over the glaze. This will pick up the glaze from the smooth portions of the tape. The glaze will remain in the indentation. Shoe polish, India ink, colored nail polish, and enamel may also be used as an antiquing media. Finish with a coat of clear lacquer, either sprayed or brushed on.

Cover each side of frame individually.

When all sides are covered, antique.

To duplicate this richly carved frame, purchase an unfinished wood frame and some sewing trim from the notions department of your local department store. For best results, use a heavy trim that has lots of cutouts. Delicate lace will not show up very well. On this picture frame, a metallic gold braid was used.

Cut the trim to fit each side of the frame. Cut the ends of the trim at a 45-degree angle. Glue the trim to the picture frame with white glue. Now, cut four strips of tape the length of the sides of the frame. Cut the ends at a 45-degree angle so that the corners will miter and not overlap one another. Remove the paper backing from the tape and lay it in place on the frame. Press the tape down and under the inside edge of the frame. Now, press the tape down and smooth it with your thumb until you reach the bottom edge of the sewing trim. Then, take an orange stick or small knitting needle and begin working the design into the tape. Press hard enough to pick up the design but not so hard that you tear or cut the tape. Occasionally, check the point on your knitting needle or orange stick. With use, they can become rough and cause the tape to tear. First, mold the bottom edge of the trim. When you have this finished, use your fingers to smooth the tape along the top of the frame and over the edge. Finish one side and then go on to the next. When all four sides are completed, turn the frame over and do the back of the frame. Antique the frame with an antiquing glaze or India ink. Then, spray it with a clear lacquer.

If your frame is very wide, you may want to add several rows of sewing trim. Use a wide braid at the outside edge, then drop to narrower braids as you move into the center.

Cover the sewing trim with foil tape.

The finished frame looks like this.

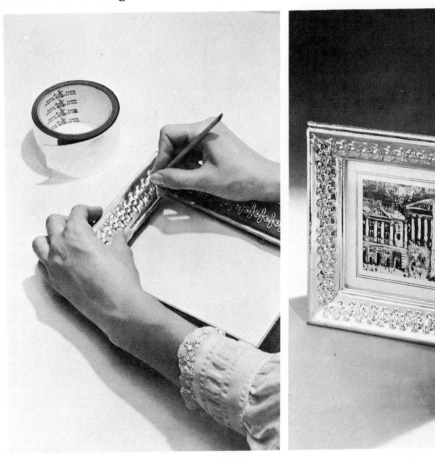

PAPER PROJECTS

Paper is easy to work with and is probably the least expensive, most readily available craft material. For these and other reasons, it has long been used in connection with gifts.

Think of all the forms of paper you already have around your home—tissue paper, gift wrap paper, crepe paper, shelf paper, paper bags, paper napkins, facial tissues, paper towels, cardboard, old magazines, and newspapers.

Join the ranks of the ecology movement and try recycling some of this paper into gifts. Actually, you've been doing this for years, though on a smaller scale. Remember the paper plate pictures you made for your mom in the first grade or the papier-mâché piggy bank you made in Scouts or the paper-covered ice cream tub wastebasket you made for your grandmother? They were fun to make and fun to receive.

On the next few pages, you'll find some really great paper gifts, all of which have a little more style and permanence, though maybe not the charm of your childhood gifts.

Handcrafted boxes made to order can solve some of your gift-giving problems. Decorative boxes to hold everything from jewelry to paper clips make very popular gift items. But, finding all these little wooden boxes in just the right size and price range can be a time-consuming and expensive venture. Eliminate these obstacles by making your own boxes.

One of the simplest ways to accomplish this is to tear apart a small cardboard box such as the kind jewelry comes in. Flatten it out, then, using the cardboard from dress boxes, draw and cut out your own pattern. Fold it up, creasing

These handcrafted boxes are made from recycled cardboard and aluminum.

Metamorphosis blocks provide entertainment for people of all ages.

the edges sharply, and tape the corners securely. Do the same for the lid. Finally, cover, line, and decorate your box with printed gift wrapping paper, wallpaper, colorful shelf paper, adhesive-backed paper, fabric, or tape.

You may also make these boxes from aluminum. Go to a printing shop and ask for a sheet of aluminum that has been used as an offset printing plate. This aluminum may be scored with a sharp instrument and is easily cut with a pair of sharp scissors.

Metamorphosis blocks, or six-for-the-price-of-one, offer endless amusement for people of all ages. The ones above are made from wooden blocks covered with magazine illustrations.

For each set of blocks, it takes six illustrations — one for each side of the block. The number of blocks you will need depends on the size of your illustration. Lay the blocks closely together in a square or rectangle. Next, cover the blocks with spray adhesive, lay the illustration on top of the blocks, and then press down firmly. When the glue is dry, use an artist's knife to cut through the illustration, separating the blocks. Turn the blocks and do another side. Continue until all sides are covered.

If you don't like the look of antiquity, try using mod posters, program covers, road maps, sheet music, calendar prints, or whatever you happen to have handy. Key the illustrations to the recipient's special interests.

PAPIER-MÂCHÉ

Weathered mission bells made of papier-mâché and suspended from a gnarled wooden branch will please almost anyone who likes the Spanish or Mediterranean decor.

To duplicate these, use an existing bell or a plastic foam bell for a form. Cover the bell with two layers of aluminum foil. Then, tear paper bags into 1x2-inch strips, dip in diluted white glue, and cover the bell with two layers of overlapping strips. Allow to dry thoroughly. Remove the papier-mâché shell from the bell. Trim the edges. Next, take a 6-inch piece of wire and bend it into the shape of an M. Cut a

★ **Mission bells for a Spanish decor.**

slit in the top of the bell. Push the wire into the slit, bending the ends out against the inside of the bell. Now, secure the wire with masking tape. Coat the bell and wire with a ¼-inch layer of papier-mâché, add trims, and let dry. When dry, gesso and paint with acrylics.

To make the clapper, form a wire loop and wrap with an aluminum foil ball. Bend the ends of the wire up to hold the ball securely and cover with papier-mâché. Tie a piece of thread through the loop on the ball and to the wire inside the top of the bell. Hang the bell to a weathered branch by tieing a leather thong through the wire at the top of the bell.

This novel serving dish will be the hit of any party. Make one for your favorite hostess by molding several thicknesses of wadded newspaper or heavy paper toweling that has been thoroughly saturated with glue. While shaping, use masking tape to hold the body parts in position. To make the legs, use 6-inch lengths of paper towel cores, sloped at the top to fit the body. When all the parts have been assembled, give the entire object another layer of papier-mâché. Let dry and paint with acrylics. If you wish, apply detailed decorations with an assortment of felt-tip pens. Glue a straw basket to the back and it's ready to give.

Make a coordinated desk ensemble from papier-mâché covered odds and ends. Use bricks for bookends, round containers for pencil and mail holders, a cardboard box for extra memo paper, plastic foam for the hand blotter, and cardboard for the desk blotter holder. Papier-mâché all the pieces with a ⅛-inch thickness of commercial papier-mâché. Paint on designs with bright poster paints, leaving some areas white for contrast. Finish with several coats of acrylic glaze; let dry between coats.

For unique candleholders, once again set to work with several thicknesses of glue-saturated newspaper. Form the bodies of the giraffe and the crane. Attach coat hangers cut to the de-

★ A novel, decorative serving dish.

★ Colorful, coordinated desk set.

★ Unique animal candleholders.

★ Clever bathroom vanity accessories.

sired lengths for legs, bill and the giraffe's neck. Let dry, then give one more coat of papier-mâché. When dry, paint with acrylics. Attach a candle cup to the backs of the animals with glue.

Give clever bath accessories made from papier-mâché. To make the jewelry holder, weight a detergent bottle with plaster of Paris. Then, wire the fingers and thumb of a garden glove and stuff with cotton. Put the glove over the top of the bottle, stuffing cotton into the opening around the neck of the bottle. For the soap dish, glue an inverted egg cup to the bottom of a saucer.

Use a handleless cup or tumbler for the comb holder. For the lipstick tote, use half of a foam ball. Press shallow holes in the ball, making them large enough to hold lipstick tubes. Cover all of these pieces with a ⅛-inch-thick layer of commercial papier-mâché. Let the papier-mâché dry thoroughly. Make a glue solution by mixing one part water to two parts white glue. Soak cotton fringe trim in the glue solution, squeeze out excess glue, and apply the trim to the individual accessories at the top or bottom edges. Paint each item with two coats of poster paint and apply several coats of acrylic glaze.

A beguiling rag doll that will delight any young miss.

chapter 2

NEEDLECRAFT

The word 'sewing' means many things to many people. But, to most of us, it means replacing lost buttons and raising or lowering hems. Not a very exciting pastime, to say the least.

That is why this chapter is entitled 'Needlecraft.' Within this chapter are many mind-boggling gift ideas that will challenge you to take up creative stitchery. Try your hand at the many embroidery, crewel, and needlepoint projects, make a variety of children's toys, or create stunning gifts for the home. There's a wide variety from which to choose.

CHILDREN'S GIFTS

The beguiling rag doll, reminiscent of Becky Thatcher days, is dressed in carefully contrived oddments of fabric, complete with poke bonnet, high-laced boots, and a freckled face.

Material for body: 1 yard of 36-inch pink flannel, ⅓ yard of blue checked cotton, 2 7x19-inch pieces yellow velvet, an 8x8-inch piece white velvet, 2 skeins brown yarn, 3 yards black yarn, and 3 pounds chip foam.

Cut all pattern pieces. (See page 28 for pattern.) Sew shoes to bottom of legs. Sew leg seams. Attach soles. Stuff to within two inches of top and stitch closed. Sew arm seams, stuff to within two inches of top, and sew closed.

Attach back of head to back of body. Sew front head pieces together; attach to body front.

Set legs into the bottom of the body and sew front and back body pieces, right sides together, at the bottom. Sew up sides, setting arms in place on inside. Turn to the right side through the slit in back; stuff. Close opening.

For hair, mix two skeins of different-colored brown yarn. Cut 30-inch lengths. Divide into 10 sections, tie a knot four inches from top, and braid. Tie at bottom, leaving 3 inches free. Hand-stitch the sections to the head, using the top 4 inches for the bangs.

Sew black yarn laces in shoes.

Dress materials: ¾ yard of 45-inch red fabric, 4 inches of 45-inch fabric (dress band), ⅗ yard of 36-inch fabric (ruffle).

Sew the collar in two sections. Sew the dress front and back at the shoulders and the sides, attaching the band at the same time. Close the sleeves and attach to armholes, gathering excess into top four inches. Hem sleeves.

Gather dress top into collar. Gather ruffle into dress bottom. Add snaps.

Apron and hat materials: One yard of white pique, 60 inches of ribbon, fabric scraps, one package wide red bias tape, ½ yard 36-inch fabric, and 50 inches ⅔-inch-wide ribbon.

For apron, cut one piece of 9x29-inch pique. Cut out top of apron. Sew bias tape around top and on sides of bottom. Put a 2-inch hem in bottom. Gather the top of the bottom section into the waist of the top, and sew 30 inches of ribbon to each side of the apron.

Draw a patchwork design lightly on the apron front, and glue the scraps in place. Zigzag stitch.

Cut out the hat pieces. Gather the curved edge on the large piece to fit the straight side of the brim. Sew the brim sections together on the curved side and turn. Work the gathers of the top into the brim; sew closed. Gather the bottom edge into the center 10 inches of the ribbon. Fold the ribbon in half; stitch closed.

28

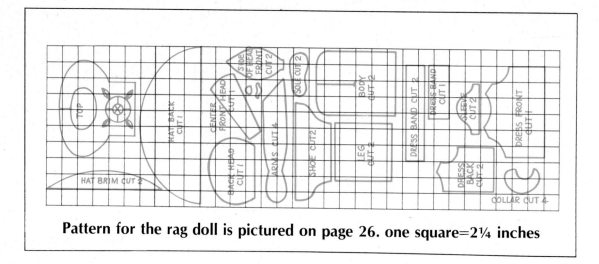

Pattern for the rag doll is pictured on page 26. one square=2¼ inches

Stuffed toys, opposite page, delight children of any age—from toddlers to teen-agers.

To cut the various pieces, see the pattern sketches at the bottom of the opposite page.

All of these dolls require such small amounts of fabric that you probably will be able to construct many of them from fabric you have left over from other sewing projects. So, before you run out to buy the various materials needed for the dolls, check your sewing supplies for leftover fabric, spare buttons and buckles, small pieces of lace and braid, and partially used skeins of different colors of yarn.

Cowboy: Cut body, using gingham fabric for pattern piece B and plain fabric for pattern piece C. Sew heads to bodies at the neckline and body top B to body bottom C at waistline. With right sides together, seam around doll, leaving a 3-inch opening at top of head. Trim seams, turn right side out, and stuff. Stitch closed by hand. Cut felt facial features and hair; stitch or glue in place. Cut out the hat, then with right sides together, seam around the top of crown; turn right side out. With right sides together, seam the brim to the crown. Turn right side out; tack to head. Cut out kerchief. Turn right side out and stitch closed. Tie around neck. Add a vest cut from felt.

Clown: Cut body from printed fabric, using pattern piece A. Cut two pieces, sew together, and stuff as for cowboy. Make hat, following sketch. For bow tie, cut 4x4-inch square of striped fabric. Fold in all raw edges; tack. 'Pinch'

center by wrapping fabric around it. Hand-stitch in place. Cut felt facial features; stitch or glue in place. Add pompons for hair and suit buttons.

Baggy-pants clown: Cut the body, using gingham fabric for pattern piece B and solid-color fabric for pattern piece C. Construct as for cowboy. For hair, cut short lengths of heavy yarn. Fold them in half; tack through center to doll's head. Cut felt facial features, and stitch or glue in place. Spread yarn to form 'fluffy' hair.

Santa Claus: Cut the body, using red fabric, from pattern piece A. Cut two. Construct like cowboy. Then, fluff yarn for hair and beard, and sew or glue in place. Cut and glue the facial features as above. Trim edge of the hat and the body (to simulate jacket) with white yarn.

Dutch boy: Using solid-color fabric for B and striped fabric for pattern piece C, cut the body. Construct like cowboy. Cut hat like sketch; cut the two headbands 10x1 inches. Gather circular crown to fit headband. Then stitch, with right sides together. Seam peaks of cap together on outside curve; turn right side out. Press. Seam inner headband to outer headband, sewing cap peak between them at center front. Turn inner headband to inside; hand-tack to top of outer headband. Hand-tack cap to head. See baggy pants clown for instructions on face preparation. Cut kerchief as in sketch. With right sides together, seam, leaving open a little on inside edge. Turn right side out; hand-tack closed. Press. Tie around neck. Sew on four brass buttons as shown in photo.

Humpty Dumpty beanbag: As indicated in sketch, cut pieces, using a good-quality felt. Join the body section to the head on front and back. Glue felt hands and cuffs to the arm sections. Sew shoes and buckles to leg sections. With the right sides together, seam the upper section of the body and head, catching in arms at the proper location. With the right sides together, seam one side of the base to the body front, catching in legs. Turn right side out; add beans. Stitch opening closed. Glue on felt facial features and a piece of lace at the neck.

Soldier beanbag: From scraps of red, blue, pink, and black felt, cut the pieces as indicated in the sketch. Join the hat to the head, the head to the upper body, and the upper body to the lower body on the front to the back, catching in arms at proper location. With right sides together, seam one side of the base to the body front, catching in the legs. Cut facial features, shoes, and chin strap from felt. Glue these and the visor in place. Add cord and braid trim to the hat and jacket. Cut hands and shoes from felt; glue in place on arms and legs. Fill with beans; stitch opening closed.

Use the patterns and the designs given here, then experiment with other designs. By adapting the doll's body and clothing, you can make many other interesting characters.

When making the dolls, always consider the age of the child who will be using them. If the child is very young, be sure that the buttons and the trims are sewed on very securely.

Stuffed toys that will delight children of all ages — from toddlers to teen-agers.

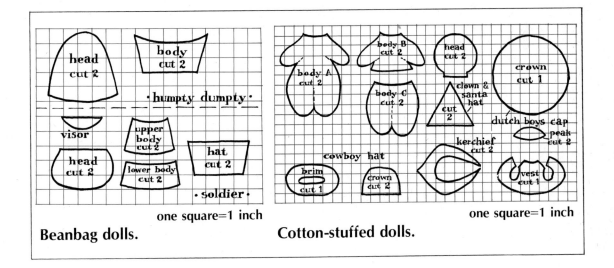

one square=1 inch

Beanbag dolls.

one square=1 inch

Cotton-stuffed dolls.

These beanbag animals are made with felt, thread, and yarn.

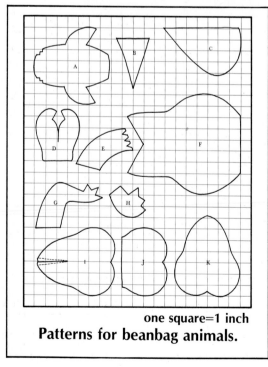

one square=1 inch
Patterns for beanbag animals.

These colorful beanbag animals are fun to watch, play with, and even toss in the air.

To make the frog, use pattern pieces G, H, I, J, and K. Cut two each of G and H for back and front legs, and two of J. Cut two half-dollar-size circles and small white circles for eyes. With light yarn that contrasts with the body, stitch legs to the bottom piece K. Stitch eyes to I. Pleat I at the back with a sewing machine.

Stitch K to I, leaving the front half open. Machine-stitch the two J pieces together along the straight edge, right sides together, then sew the bottom half to the top of K. Fill the frog with beans and complete stitching around the upper mouth on the I piece.

For the whale, cut one A, B, and D and two Cs, plus two pieces the size of the front of A cut across from fin to fin. Stitch bottom edges of C pieces to each side of A from the back to in front of fins. Do not knot off yarn. Machine-stitch two mouth pieces, right sides together.

Sew the bottom half to the front of A with thread from the A and C connection. Sew the front and the top of the side head pieces together to an inch beyond the curve. Add B and stitch to the back edges of the C pieces. Insert beans and add tail D to the back; sew shut. Sew up the tail about one inch along the cut.

For the owl, sew two round eyes and a pointed beak to the front piece F. Sew two wings E to the back piece F. Stitch around the top and the sides; add beans and sew the bottom shut.

Make the pig, the hippo, and the cow from two identically cut felt pieces. First, stitch the pieces of felt on the wrong sides, leaving an opening for the stuffing. Then, stuff the body and hand-tack the opening shut. Add felt and stitchery decoration before sewing the creatures shut. Do this with zigzag stitching. Yarn, a pipe cleaner, and rolled felt form the tails.

> The gingham dog and the calico cat
> Side by side on the table sat...
> There was going to be a terrible spat.

If you remember this childhood poem, you'll remember what happened next.

> The air was littered, an hour or so,
> With bits of gingham and calico.

Make the gingham dog and calico cat fly by stitching this pair of toys for someone special.

For the gingham dog, you'll need ⅓ yard of gingham fabric. Cut the pieces from the pattern, placing the ears on the bias. Stitch a dart for the hind legs on the front section only. With right sides together, seam the front and back, leaving a few inches open at the bottom. Clip the seams, turn, and stuff firmly. Hand-tack the opening closed. Seam around the ears, leaving the top edge open. Trim, turn, and press. Turn under ¼ inch at the top and hand-tack to each side of the head. Seam the tail, clip, turn, and stuff. Tack the tail to the lower center back. Cut felt features and sew in place. Tack on collar.

Assemble the calico cat the same way as you did the gingham dog, catching the ears as you sew the front to the back. Cut felt features and sew or glue them in place. Embroider whiskers and tie on a perky ribbon bow.

The calico cat and gingham dog.

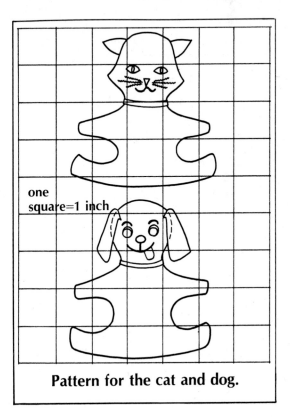

one square=1 inch

Pattern for the cat and dog.

★ These felt animals make friends easily. Introduce some child you know to an octopus pajama bag, a turtle tote, a pet book cover, or a clever beanbag.

Begin this octopus pajama bag by drawing a large circle on a piece of graph paper. Fold ½ yard of felt in half, and place the pattern so that the head is in a corner. Cut out two bodies, three hair bows, and two ¾x8-inch handle strips. Do the same for the hair from a 9x12-inch piece of pink felt, snipping out points for strands, and cut two felt eyes.

Place a 6-inch zipper, face down, vertically in the center of the wrong side of the body back. Baste; sew in place, enclosing top end of zipper. Cut a slit on the right side of back body piece over the length of the zipper so the right side will be open. Outline the mouth with embroidery floss; glue on eyes.

Pin two bodies together with wrong sides in. Topstitch the handle pieces near edges. Fold in half and position inside body pieces at top center. Baste octopus together, then topstitch entire body and arms. Stuff the arms with tissue, and put a new pair of pajamas inside the head. Make a bow from 1-inch-wide ribbon and tack to head under handle. Glue on felt bows. Then, glue down hair points around the face.

For the turtle tote, you'll need four 9x12-inch pieces of felt: two yellow, one orange, and one green. Cut out two shells and heads, four feet, two tails, and two green strips ¾x8-inches for handles. Place a 6-inch zipper in back as directed for octopus. Glue or stitch head pieces, tails, and feet together. Stuff. Glue eyes on head and six yellow spots on shell.

For a handle, topstitch strips together along the outside edges. Fold in half. Following the illustration, place the turtle's head, tail, and feet between shells, with handle on top. Baste entire turtle first, then machine-stitch.

These book covers are special because they provide a place to hold a pencil, too. To make the cover, place an open book on felt. Trace around outside; then add ½ inch to the top and bottom and 1½ inches on either end for overlap. Cut with pinking shears. Fold overlap inside and baste. Topstitch ½ inch from edges.

Puppy: Using your own freehand sketches, cut the following: one yellow body, two orange legs, one orange face, one orange ear, six large orange circles, two large black circles, three small black circles, one black butterfly body, one black nose, one piece of light and one dark green grass, and two pink wings. Apply glue to legs and ears. Attach to the body. Glue on rest of body; dot in whiskers with marking pen. Put glue along outside edges of cutout, omitting top of head so as to leave an opening for a pencil. Glue on dog, butterfly, and grass.

Kitten: Cut one red body, one large red circle, two pink ears, two pink legs, six large pink circles, one white face, two large black circles, one black nose, one black tongue, one yellow flower, two yellow eyes, one yellow bow, one piece of light and one dark green grass, one green stem, and one green leaf.

Glue as for the dog. Fold bow in half and glue together at center, then to kitten. Dot in whiskers with a marking pen.

Each of these clever beanbags has a stump, an egg, or a nest to call home.

To make the bear, cut two bear bodies, four large yellow circles, one yellow stomach, two black tree trunks, two small black circles, two pink flowers, one pink circle, one bright pink flower, two bright pink circles, and two green leaves. Outline stitch mouth to face and satin stitch the nose. Decorate, following picture.

Topstitch on the outside edges. Leave an opening on bottom to insert birdseed. Close opening. Topstitch tree trunk together, leaving an opening at the top. Insert the bear.

For the duck, cut two yellow bodies, two white eggs, one large white circle, one white wing, one gold wing, two gold duck bills, two large, bright pink flowers, two green leaves, and one medium black circle. Assemble as you did for the bear, gluing decorations to egg and duck. Fill with birdseed. Glue second bill to back of first. Topstitch egg, leaving top open.

To assemble bird, cut two dark blue bodies, one medium blue wing, one light blue wing, one light blue tail, one large white circle, one medium black circle, one yellow beak, one large, light pink flower, two small, light pink flowers, one bright pink breast, one large, bright pink circle, one large, bright pink flower, two small, bright pink circles, two green leaves, and two beige nests. Insert tail between bodies; topstitch. Add trim. Fill. Blanket stitch nest.

Hobby dolls inspire the creative child to greater accomplishment.

These hobby dolls will please a wide range of children. Make a freehand sketch of the pattern pieces. With right sides together, stitch up the body. Turn and stuff. Using two circles for the head, put right sides together and stitch, leaving an opening at the bottom. Turn and stuff. Now, stitch the head to the body. Add yarn hair and felt facial features. Tack or glue in place. Equip each doll with a different craft. Miss Michelangelo will delight the young artist with her crayons, poster paints, and paint brushes. Sewing Sam, complete with a pair of scissors, pin cushion, thread, and tracing wheel, will help a child enjoy sewing.

This patchwork floor pillow undoubtedly will become the most prized possession of any child. In fact, as a parent, you'll have quite a time trying to convince your child that it was not given as a replacement for his bed.

To make this larger-than-life-size pillow, sew a wild assortment of washable prints together with a double zigzag stitch. Since the pillow is about 5x6 feet, save time by using large patchwork pieces. Line the pillow with about five yards of heavy cotton fabric and insert a zipper down the middle of the back. This zipper will make stuffing the pillow a great deal easier. Stuff the pillow with shredded foam.

A 5x6-foot patchwork floor pillow of multi-patterned washable fabric.

Fanciful felt arm puppets.

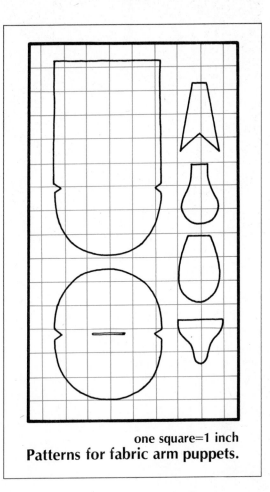

one square=1 inch
Patterns for fabric arm puppets.

A whimsical cast of arm puppet characters can be made from scraps of felt, corduroy, and velvet. Cut out two long shapes according to the scaled pattern. Cut one shape for the mouth. Glue or stitch the faces to the bodies and sew on button eyes and other trims.

With the outsides together, stitch from the ends to the notches on each side. Cut a slit for the tongue and stitch the tongue to the mouth inset. Still on the wrong side of the fabric, pin mouth inset to matching notch on the base of the puppet. Then, stitch the finished top with rickrack and turn right side out. Add earrings and pirate rings of shiny metal.

A wide variety of materials can be used for these hand puppets, providing that the materials are fairly stiff. The features can be made of felt, heavy cotton, iron-on tape, buttons, beads, yarn, braid, pompons, ribbon, and rickrack. See your notions department for other trims.

Velvet and corduroy arm puppets.

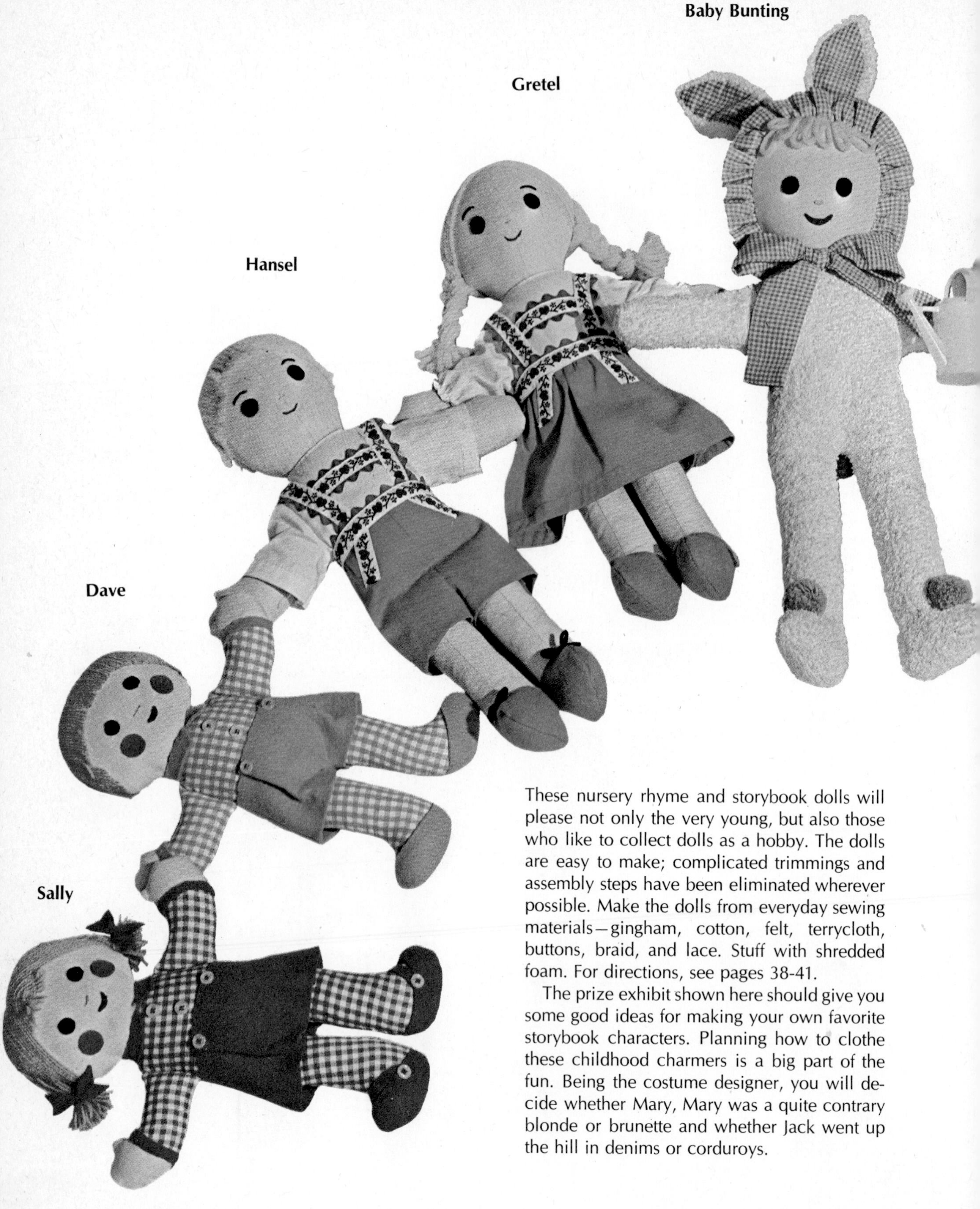

Baby Bunting

Gretel

Hansel

Dave

Sally

These nursery rhyme and storybook dolls will please not only the very young, but also those who like to collect dolls as a hobby. The dolls are easy to make; complicated trimmings and assembly steps have been eliminated wherever possible. Make the dolls from everyday sewing materials—gingham, cotton, felt, terrycloth, buttons, braid, and lace. Stuff with shredded foam. For directions, see pages 38-41.

The prize exhibit shown here should give you some good ideas for making your own favorite storybook characters. Planning how to clothe these childhood charmers is a big part of the fun. Being the costume designer, you will decide whether Mary, Mary was a quite contrary blonde or brunette and whether Jack went up the hill in denims or corduroys.

Mary, Mary

Jack

Humpty Dumpty

Jill

Willie Winkie

DOLLS
ON
PARADE

BASIC CONSTRUCTION

The basic construction is the same for each doll, with variations in costuming and trims. A ¼-inch seam allowance is included in all of the patterns shown for these dolls.

For each doll, you will need ⅓ yard pale pink cotton fabric (36 inches wide), thread, kapok or shredded foam, ½ ounce heavyweight wool yarn for girls or ¼ ounce for boys, a scrap of black felt, and a few inches of pale pink, red, and black embroidery floss.

Body: Cut the doll body from pink fabric according to the pattern at the bottom of the page. With right sides together, seam the two head fronts together, then the two head backs together. Join the front head to the front body at the neckline. Repeat for back. Join the front to the back, leaving the lower body open. Clip

the curves and turn the body right side out. Stuff the arms firmly with shredded foam; stitch from each armpit to the top of its respective shoulder. Seam the legs together, leaving the top open. Clip the curves; turn. Stuff the legs firmly and stitch closed by matching the front seam to the back seam at the center. Seam the legs to the lower body front. Stuff the head and body firmly. Turn under ¼ inch on the body back and hand-tack the doll closed.

Face: Cut black felt eyes, and sew or glue the eyes in place. Embroider a pink nose, a red mouth, and black eyebrows, using an outline stitch and three strands of embroidery floss.

Hair: For the boys' hair, cut several lengths of wool and place them from front to back over the top of the head to form hair. With matching

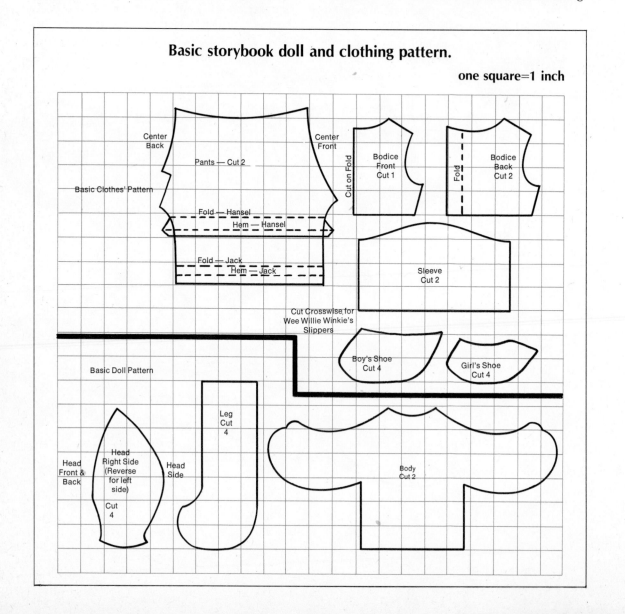

Basic storybook doll and clothing pattern.

one square=1 inch

thread, sew each strand to the head over the seam of the head from one side over the top to the other side. Trim, and tack ends in place.

To make the hair for Sally and Gretel, cut long lengths of wool and place them from side to side over the top of the head. With matching thread, sew each strand in place down the center like a part. Pull hair to the sides and tie.

To make Jill's hair, cut long lengths of wool and place them from front to back over the top of the head to form hair, letting more wool hang down in front than in back. (The hair should hang about 1½ inches below the nape of the neck in back.) With a matching color thread, sew each strand to the head about 1¼ inches in front of the top head seam in the center, and taper over to meet the head seam halfway down the sides. Flip the hair back, and tie.

For Mary, Mary, Quite Contrary's hair, cut long lengths of wool and place them over the head center section only from front to back, letting some of the wool hang down over the face. With matching thread, sew each strand in

place over the top seam of the head. Trim the front to look like bangs. Cut long lengths of wool, and fold in half. With matching thread, sew through the folded strands just forward the head side seams to form hair at the sides.

Clothes: (For all but Wee Willie Winkie) *Bodice:* Cut bodice as shown in the top pattern on page 38. Join the front bodice to the back at the shoulder seam. Turn under ¼ inch on the bodice back facing and stitch. Press the facing to the wrong side along the line indicated on the diagram. Turn under ¼ inch at the neckline and topstitch. With the right sides together, sew the sleeve to the shoulder. For boys, make a ½-inch hem at the wrist. For girls, turn under ¼ inch at the wrist. Cut two 4-inch pieces of elastic and sew to the wrists, on the inside, stretching to produce a gathered cuff. Stitch the underarm seams. *Skirt:* Cut skirt 21x5½ inches. Make a ½-inch hem on one long side; sew. Seam two shorter edges together, leaving open 2½ inches at top. Press the seam open.

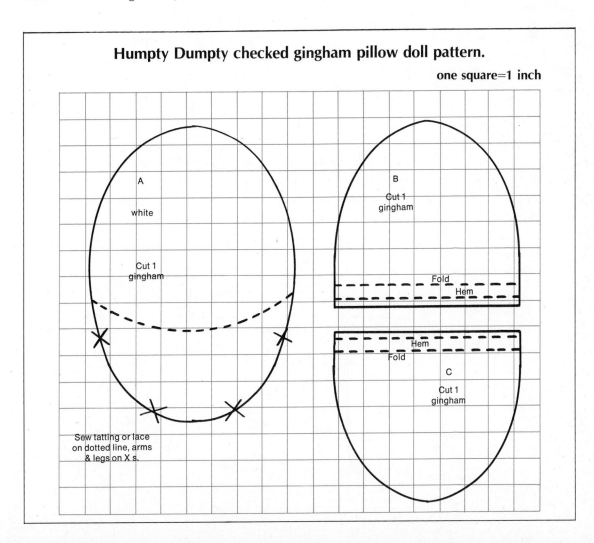

Gather the top of the skirt to fit the bodice, and sew the top of the skirt to the bodice at the waistline. *Pants:* Join the center front seams together. Join the center back seams together below the extension tab. Turn under ¼ inch on the extension tab and topstitch. Make a ½-inch hem at the bottom of the pants. Sew the inside leg seams, joining the back to the front. Join the pants to the bodice at the waistline. *Closure:* For both girls' dresses and boys' outfits (except for Wee Willie Winkie) sew three gripper snaps at the back. *Shoes:* Cut according to pattern on page 38. Seam, clip the curves, and turn. For girls' shoes, cut two felt strips 3½x¼ inch. Place the strips over the top of the foot. Hand-tack the strips to the shoe on the inside edges, and sew a button over the outside edges of each of the shoes.

DETAILED INSTRUCTIONS

Humpty Dumpty requires ⅓ yard white cotton, ⅓ yard pink or blue gingham, a ½-ounce skein pink or blue wool, 36 inches yellow wool, a small piece of blue felt, scraps of pink, red, and black felt, ¼ yard lace, shredded foam, thread, and three gripper closures.

To make the doll, cut two pieces of white fabric from pattern A (page 39). With right sides together, seam, leaving open a few inches at bottom. Clip curves, turn right side out, and stuff

with foam. Stitch the end closed. From gingham fabric, cut one piece each of A, B, and C. On right side of A, sew a row of lace as indicated in diagram. Cut bow and features of felt, and appliqué in place. Make loops of yellow wool across top of head for hair.

From pink yarn, cut 60 lengths of 7½ inches and 60 lengths of 10½ inches. Separate into equal-length groups of 10 strands each. Taking three groups of equal length at the same time, braid to form arms and legs. Secure braids at top and bottom with matching wool. Line up tops of arms and legs with edge of face at points indicated on diagram and sew to face ¼ inch from edge. Make a ½-inch hem on straight edge of B and C, and sew. With right sides together, place C over lower part of A and seam around curved edges. B will overlap C along straight edge. Clip curves, turn, and press. Insert a white pillow into the gingham cover and sew gripper snaps to close opening at back of doll.

The Baby Bunting doll requires ⅜ yard white terry cloth, 6 inches pink and white gingham fabric (36 inches wide), a small amount of pale pink broadcloth, felt scraps, 18 inches yellow wool, 3 pink pompons, foam, and thread.

To make this doll, cut fabrics as indicated in the diagram on the opposite page. Seam the center back of the head, and sew dart in head

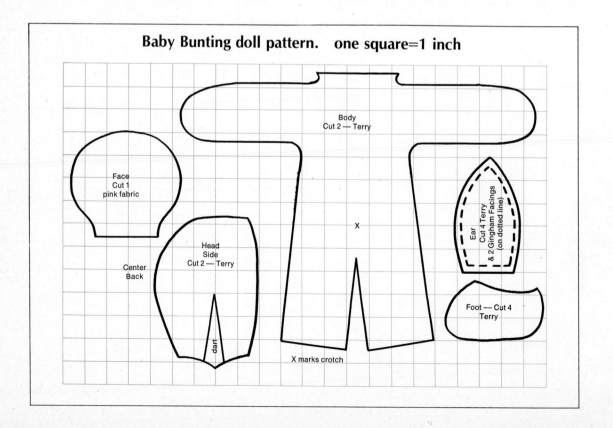

Baby Bunting doll pattern.   one square=1 inch

Body
Cut 2 — Terry

Face
Cut 1
pink fabric

Ear
Cut 4 Terry
& 2 Gingham Facings
(on dotted line)

Center
Back

Head
Side
Cut 2 — Terry

Foot — Cut 4
Terry

dart

X marks crotch

side. Cut a gingham strip 24½x2½ inches and fold in half lengthwise. Gather the cut edges to fit around the head side, and sew to the right side of head side. With the right sides together, sew face to head side (with ruffles in between the two). Clip the curves and turn the material right side out. With the right sides together, seam the ears, leaving the lower edges open. Clip the curves and turn, and appliqué gingham facing to inside of ears. Turn raw edges to inside and sew ears closed. 'Pleat' ears by folding edges to meet in center; hand-tack.

Seam body front to body back, leaving an opening at the neck and the bottom of each leg. Clip the curves and turn right side out. Seam the feet, leaving the upper edges open. Clip the curves and turn. Turn under ¼ inch on the open edges of the feet, and tack to bottom of legs around ankle. Stuff the head, body, and feet firmly. Turn ¼ inch under at the neckline and sew the head to the body by hand, being sure to stuff in enough foam to keep the head erect.

Cut a strip of gingham check 23x3½ inches. Fold the material in half lengthwise; seam, leaving one short end open. Turn right side out; stitch the opening closed. Press and tie to form a bow. Hand-tack the bow to the center front of the neck. For the hair, tack loops of yellow wool across the top of the face, just below the ruffle. Cut felt features; glue or sew them in place. Hand-tack a pink pompon on top of each foot and one at the back like a tail.

To make the Dave and Sally gingham dolls, use the pattern at the bottom of this page. You will need ¼ yard pink fabric (enough for both of the dolls), ⅓ yard gingham, a 12-inch square pink or blue felt, red and black felt scraps, foam, thread, 6 buttons for boy, 10 for girl (⅜-inch diameter, 4-way, sew-through type), gold wool, a few inches of pink embroidery floss, 4 inches pink ¾-inch-wide ribbon, and white glue. Construct these dolls in the same way you would make the other dolls.

Wee Willie Winkie is constructed the same as the other dolls, but to clothe him, use the pattern below. Cut the night shirt and cap from ⅓ yard cotton flannelette, and trim the doll with red ball fringe or some pompons.

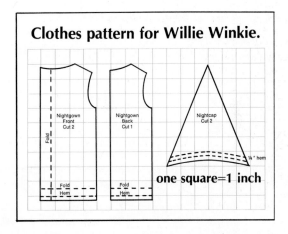

Clothes pattern for Willie Winkie. one square=1 inch

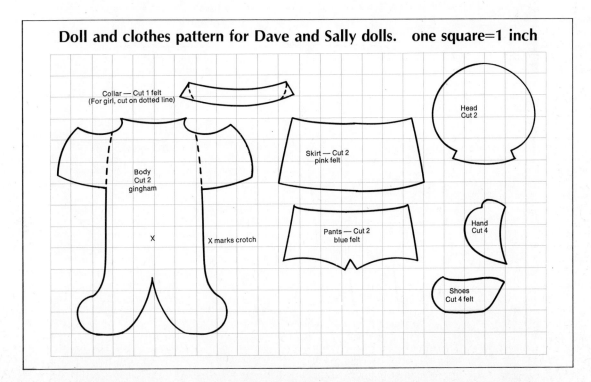

Doll and clothes pattern for Dave and Sally dolls. one square=1 inch

NOVEL GIFTS TO SEW FOR ADULTS

If sewing is your bag, try your hand at making one of these tote bags. Any season of the year, one of these totes is sure to be welcome.

The owl tote bag requires two burlap pieces 14½x13¾ inches, two pieces 2½x20 inches, and one oval 5¼x11⅝ inches. Machine-baste interlining to sides. The lining is 13¾x12½ inches. Sew bottom at seam edges and through the middle. Sew strap seams, press, and turn. Thread two ½-inch cords through straps, and seam down the center. Stitch the straps to the bag.

Assemble felt owl and leaves, press onto iron-on material, and appliqué to the bag. Sew side seams and bottom of bag. Turn down 2-inch hem at top and slip-stitch to interlining. Cut lining for bag; cut a double thickness for bottom. On one bottom turn under an end 2½ inches for a slot for cardboard stiffener. Stitch side seams and bottom of lining. Press down ½-inch hem on top edges, and turn lining right

side out. Slip lining over bag, wrong sides together. Slip-stitch lining to bag. Turn and slip in cardboard stiffener for bottom.

For the sun tote bag, cut one burlap piece 31x11¾ inches and mark across it, beginning at one end at 2 inches from the edge, 3 inches from edge, and 13¾ inches from edge. Repeat beginning at opposite end. Cut one burlap piece 22x4½ inches and one 25x4½ inches, rounding corner for the pocket. For the lining, cut one felt piece 25x11¾ inches, one 11¼x4½ inches, one 14x4½ inches, one to match pocket, and one 11½x4½ inches for the pocket piece.

Machine-baste interlining (27x11¾ inches) to large burlap piece at seam edges and down center, placing material two inches inside ends.

Cut a sun from yellow and orange felt, place on iron-on tape, and press. Outline features with embroidery thread and appliqué to pocket. Add piping, line, and sew pocket to bag.

Owl, sun, and fish tote bags made of inexpensive burlap.

Tiger, fish, and elephant beach bags with unique design features.

Line the handles with felt, leaving the lower two inches unsewed. Stitch the side seams to the gusset-handle pieces, allowing ½ inch over from the bottom seam. Sew the bottom seam. Stitch the 2-inch hem of the bag to the free 2-inch edge of gusset-handle lining. Slip-stitch hem to the interlining along the raw edge. Line the same as for the owl tote bag.

The fish tote bag requires two burlap pieces 14x18½ inches, four pieces 3½x10½ inches, and one piece 4½x15 inches. Cut two interlining pieces 11x12x18½ inches, one 4½x15 inches, and one 4½x14½ inches for the pocket.

Stitch the interlining to the sides and to the bottom of the bag. Appliqué felt fishes assembled on iron-on tape.

Stitch straps (fold in half lengthwise and stitch; turn right side out). Turn in one end; edgestitch. Fold strap in half and stitch to bag. Sew bottom to sides. Sew side seams. Sew bottom side seams. Fold down top 2-inch edge of bag and slip-stitch to interlining.

Line the bag the same as for the owl tote. Edgestitch the bag, press, and slip in bamboo handles. Stitch below bamboo.

These beach bags are made in the same way as the tote bags on the opposite page. Draw a pattern for each bag and then, following the directions for the totes, assemble a beach bag.

This tiger beach bag travels well to the beach or pool. It has a separate sunning cloth with a tiger head attached for a pillow. Buy the tiger print (either cotton or terrycloth), and trim it with felt and yarn features.

Make this fish bag for someone who is about to go on vacation. The bag is made from easy-to-sew sailcloth. Use a plastic interlining for the bag. Make a zippered fin pocket to hold loose change, a comb, sunglasses, sun tan lotion, and other beach gear. As a final touch, trim the fish bag with rows of yarn fringe.

This jumbo elephant bag is a guaranteed crowd pleaser. It stands 18 inches high and is fashioned from pink felt. The bag has a 16-inch zipper closure and covered cord handles. Both sides of the bag are trimmed with black piping and contrasting felt, which also is used for the eyes, tusks, toes, and flowers.

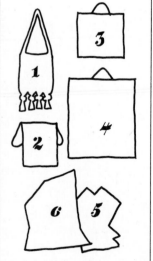

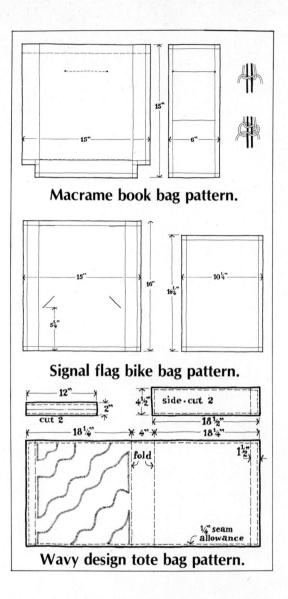

Macrame book bag pattern.

Signal flag bike bag pattern.

Wavy design tote bag pattern.

Rows 3 and 4: Repeat rows 1 and 2. *Row 5:* Set aside 4 cords; pull next 8 through orange bead, making square knot below bead; thread on yellow bead on same 8 cords plus 4 yellow cords from each side. *Row 6:* Tie overhand knots below beads; trim ends. Braid yarn for side trim and decoration on bag flap.

2. Sew a simple bike bag from solid-color fabric. This bag is worn on the back and holds books or other gear while cycling. Stitch straps to top and back sides long enough to fit over each shoulder. Signal flags (these signify 'onward') are cut from iron-to tape. (See the middle sketch on the opposite page.)

3. and 4. For a colorful tote bag, follow the measurements on the third sketch. Cut the bag from heavy orange duck. Cut wavy design strips from red and yellow duck (two from each color). Appliqué the designs by machine-stitching around the outside edges. Make the colorful family tote (No. 4) to measure 25x21 inches.

5. Cut place mats 13x9 inches from drip-dry fabric. Cut freeform flower shapes; position on mats. Then, stitch with tight zigzag stitches, working from the center outward. Fold the edges under ½ inch; zigzag-stitch hems.

6. To make this reverse appliqué rug, you will need four pieces of felt measuring 2x3 feet each. (Use a good-quality part-wool or all-wool felt for making the rug so that it will withstand normal wear. When it is finished, treat it to a coat of soil-resistant spray.) Use red, magenta, yellow, and green felt.

First, cut away the green felt where the yellow felt is to show through, doing the area around the border and center medallion. Stitch the yellow felt and the green felt onto the magenta felt, not including the two side areas or the center area. Then, cut out the yellow felt and the green felt for the side panels; position so that the yellow felt is atop the green felt on the magenta. Next, cut the center green felt, position on the magenta felt, and stitch. Finally, cut out the magenta felt; position red felt behind it, and stitch down. Trim the ends of the rug with ball fringe. Zigzag the fringe to the rug.

1. To make the macrame book bag, make a pattern by following the first sketch. The bag takes ½ yard orange velveteen, ½ yard interfacing, ½ yard lining, 1 yard belting (used around top edge between lining and velvet), beads, and yarn. For macrame trim, begin with 12 lengths yellow yarn and eight orange, all 30 inches long. Thread yarn through needle; pull through front edge of bag's bottom, eight cords to a group. Even yarn so each double strand is 15 inches. *Row 1:* Square knot 4 cords together, continue across row (10 knots). *Row 2:* Skip first 2 cords; square knot alternate groups of 4 together (9 knots), ending with 2 extra cords.

Assorted gifts that you can make with help from your sewing machine.

Happy aprons will help to make everyday chores a little more pleasant for you.

These happy aprons will help every lady of any house. They will brighten her day and protect her from spots and spills as she goes about her daily work. Make these aprons from the brightest-colored material you can find, preferably using a double-thickness of fabric.

These wide-awake aprons are easy to make. Cut the front and back pieces of the apron according to the pattern above, using the simple designs that are shown or making your own. Machine-appliqué these designs to the front of apron, using a wide zigzag stitch. Press after sewing each section to prevent puckering. When possible, use an embroidery hoop as you stitch. Then pin front and back together with right sides facing. Position the ties at the sides and top. (A two-yard package of twill tape is enough for one apron.) Stitch around the pieces, taking a ⅜-inch seam. Leave a 6-inch opening at the center bottom. Turn the apron right side out through the opening in the bottom. To finish, hand-stitch the bottom closed.

For an added, extra-special bonus gift, use the same appliqué technique for other kitchen items. Use the bright flower, snowflake, or sunburst design on hotpads, kitchen towels, and appliance covers. Give one or two of these items along with the apron for a coordinated gift set. You'll be giving a kitchen full of surprises that offer year-round usefulness and a touch of gaiety.

All of these items are so quick and easy to make that you'll probably want to make a few extra items just to add a cheerful atmosphere to your own kitchen.

Make a smashing bandanna table runner by sewing five bandannas together, end to end. Fold the corners of the end bandannas into the center, making certain that both sides are even. Whipstitch in place and machine-stitch cotton fringe to the sides and edges.

For the matching napkins, trim off the edges of the bandannas, and make a ¼-inch hem around the edges.

You can make these patio-geared accessories in just a few hours. The tray is a picture frame with a bandanna mounted inside. Use an unfinished picture frame that has a pane of glass cut to fit, and glue ½-inch bead molding around the edge. Paint the frame and molding black. Attach handles to the ends and cover the tray's back with a piece of hardboard.

For the porch pillow, cut a ⅛-inch foam the same size as a bandanna. Sandwiching the kerchief, foam, and a piece of muslin together, quilt the top, following the general design of the bandanna. Sew fringe around the edge of one bandanna. Lay the second bandanna on top and machine-stitch around three sides. Insert the pillow form and sew the opening closed.

To make the fanciful flowers, cut 12 petal shapes from a bandanna. Stitch two petals together, turn, and press. Attach six petals to a stem and wrap with floral tape. Glue a black pompon in the center of each flower. Holding the flowers upside down, spray with starch.

Here, four bandannas become a perky poncho —a clever cover-up from sun and breezes. Sew two pairs together, then pin the two sets together to create a large square. Cut out a center square that's large enough to slip over the head. Allow a ½-inch seam. Finish inside with bias tape. Stitch cotton fringe around outside edge.

For the notable tote, choose blue denim that's been cut into two pieces measuring 13½x17½ inches each. Pockets to hold sunglasses and other paraphernalia measure 10½x13½ inches and 5x6½ inches. Cut bandanna linings from two kerchiefs the same size as the bag and the pockets. Stitch the lining to the bag. Cut two handles 14x2½ inches from denim; line the bag with bandanna print. Make five double petal shapes for the bandanna flower trim.

Bandanna table runner and napkins.

Patio-geared accessories.

Bandanna poncho and tote.

★ **Weed and flower wall hanging.**

To begin this weed and flower wall hanging, sketch designs on paper until you find a pleasing one. Then, transfer the design to fabric with a marking pencil or a tracing wheel.

To duplicate this wall hanging, purchase one 3x2¼-foot length of green burlap; two brass curtain rods; a variety of weights and colors of yarn; red, white, and yellow felt remnants; and white glue. Stitch along long sides one inch from edge. Fringe-in to stitching.

Starting at left, use a stem and crewel stitch for weed stems and straight stitch, French knots, and a couching stitch for the head.

For the second weed, use braided yarn couched down for stem and French knots and one row of chain stitching for the head of the flower and also for leaves.

The large flower has a stem of thick chain stitching with slant-stitch couching. The head is formed from red, yellow, and white felt that is attached with glue and edged with an outline stitch. Outline this flower with a satin stitch.

To form the center flower, use a scroll stitch for the stem and couched loops of heavy yarn for the head. The tall flower is a repeat of the small plant with massed French knots and leaves of clustered chain stitches.

Turn the ends under and stitch down for casings at top and bottom. Insert brass café curtain rods. Attach a cord for hanging. The cord may be purchased in a fabric shop, or use several strands of yarn braided together.

Stylized sandpipers on a 17½x39-inch burlap background peck away on this novel wall hanging. The panel hangs from a wood dowel rod laced through burlap loops made by folding 3-inch-long burlap bands in half. You may also use a brass curtain rod.

Fasten the loops to the panel with heavy-duty thread. Stitch a hem around all the edges. Line the panel with muslin. Cut the birds from burlap, then appliqué them to the backing with yarn. Chain-stitch the beaks, legs, and the butterfly onto the burlap. Then, outline the bird's wings and tails with a couching stitch.

Both of these wall hangings are very simple in design and construction. Even young girls who are just beginning to learn stitchery will find these gift items easy enough to make.

★ **Stylized sandpiper wall hanging.**

Birds on parade decorate linens.

Bunnies scamper across linens.

'Birds on parade' and 'scampering bunnies', above, are designer linens for the bed and bath. Custom-made linens are good gifts—especially when they are designed and made by the giver. The only things that you need to have to make these one-of-a-kind linens are plain-colored sheets and towels, some design ideas, and an idea of what the recipient will like. Whatever design you choose, designer linens are a perfect gift for a youngster on your gift list.

The above two design motifs were traced onto a soft cotton fabric, cut out, and machine-appliquéd, using a satin stitch, to good-quality towels, washcloths, sheets, and pillow cases.

To duplicate these motifs, expand the design patterns on the opposite page to full size. Or, create your own designs. Draw a simple design freehand, or borrow a design from a printed fabric. Either cut the design from the fabric and appliqué it, or redraw the design, simplifying it for easier appliquéing.

Materials needed: For a twin bed, purchase one pillowcase, one fitted sheet, one flat sheet (to appliqué), one washcloth, one hand towel, and one bath towel. For a larger bed, purchase two pillowcases and two sheets in the correct size. Purchase the linens in any solid color.

Cut the designs to be appliquéd from a contrasting color. Any soft fabric, such as cotton, appliqués well. Use iron-on interfacing under the appliqué fabric for easier machine stitching. This will hold the motif in place and will prevent the motif from puckering as the machine is satin stitching. Use a mercerized thread that matches the color of the appliqué.

Directions for appliquéing: Expand designs to full size for patterns. For each of the articles, use the following designs in this order. *Birds:* Pillowcase—designs 1, 2, 3, 4, 5; twin sheet—for left half, use designs 1, 2, 3, 4, 5, 2, 3, 4. For right half, use designs 5, 4, 3, 2, 1, 5, 4, 3; bath towel—designs 1, 4, 3, 5; hand towel—de-

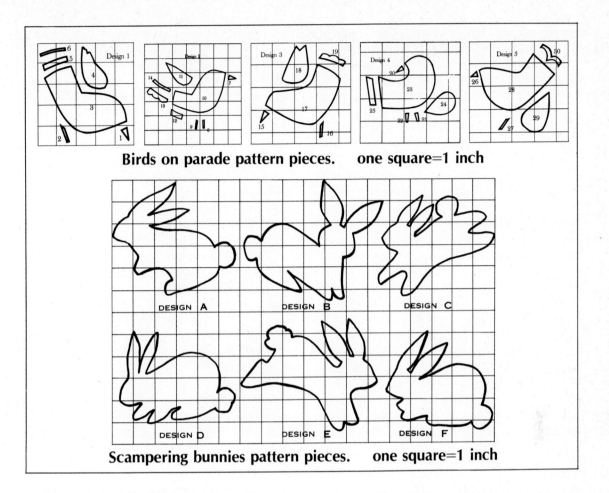

Birds on parade pattern pieces.   **one square=1 inch**

Scampering bunnies pattern pieces.   **one square=1 inch**

signs 2, 5, 4; washcloth—design 1. *Bunnies:* Pillowcase—designs B, C, F, A, E, F; sheet— for the left half, use designs C, D, A, E, F, C, F, E. Center, A. Right half use designs B, C, A, B, C, E, D, C; bath towel—designs A, E, D, C; hand towel—designs A, D, B; washcloth—de- sign E. Center each design along the hem area of the pillowcase and sheet. Center each design along the edge of the towels. On the wash- cloth, put the design just above the border.

The designs face both right and left. Cut the designs as the pattern indicates. When cutting, be sure to place the appliqué patterns on the right side of the fabric you use.

Apply iron-on interfacing to the wrong side of the fabric to be appliquéd. The added stiffening will make machine appliquéing easier.

Cut out the appliqué patterns as needed for each article. Keep each of the design units to- gether when using the bird motifs.

Place the patterns on the appliqué fabric. Draw around the patterns. Cut out each motif, following the drawn line and keeping the pieces of each design together. NOTE: All of the ap- pliqué pieces are numbered or lettered, and they must be applied to the fabric in the order that is given above in directions for appliquéing.

Pin each motif onto the sheet, pillowcase, towel, or washcloth, following the order that is given. Pin all of the pieces of one design care- fully in place before proceeding to the next one. Be sure that each design is aligned and evenly spaced before you begin stitching.

With thread that matches the color of each appliqué piece, machine-stitch around each piece, using a satin stitch. If you so desire, you may use a single line of satin stitching to make the birds' legs. When all of the appliqué designs are stitched in place, press them with an iron until they are wrinkle-free.

The bridge table cover, below, is an unusual, but highly welcomed gift. Make a couple of these card table covers and give them to a friend who belongs to a bridge club. She'll enjoy using them to match her card tables the next time she entertains the group.

To make this design, first cut vinyl or oilcloth fabric to the size of the table, leaving a ⅝-inch seam allowance on each side. For the inverted scallop pattern on each side, draw a rectangle the width of the side of the table (plus the ⅝-inch seam allowance) and 6½ inches deep. Mark off a 2½-inch depth exactly in the center and then draw an inverted scallop from each side of the rectangle bottom to the center spot. Cut the fabric and lining to this size for each side of the table cover.

Topstitch the side fabric pieces to the top of the table cover. Then, stitch the corner sections together. Sew the lining pieces together at the corners. Baste the lining to the table cover. Bind the bottom edges with bias tape; fold under and slip-stitch the top edges of the lining to the table cover. Make large tassels for each corner from rug yarn. Tie the tassels together with the extending yarn ends, and pin them in place in each of the four corners.

To make the tassels, begin by winding cotton rug yarn around a 4½-inch card. Then, slip out the card. Tie the yarn at one end by slipping a piece of yarn under the loops, bringing it back up over the loops, and tieing a knot. Cut the other end of the carded loops to allow the tassels to spread and hang free. Trim each of the yarn strands evenly. Using yarn, sew a tassel to each corner of the table cover.

Decorator pillows, below, make a great gift idea for someone who seems to have everything. These pillows are made of felt and burlap and can be made in all shapes, sizes, and colors.

Cut felt to the desired shape. Lightly sketch a design on the front. For the yarn designs, use a large needle. Knot the yarn in the back of the material after every stitch when making the loops on the bird and the flower. Catch the individual felt petals forming the breast of the bird with a running hand stitch, and knot at the back after each completed stitch. Machine-stitch the felt designs in place. For an additional three-dimensional effect, use the movable celluloid eyes that can be purchased in variety and fabric stores. The flower stem is simply an embroidery chain stitch sewed to the pillow top.

★ **Checkered bridge table cover.**

★ **Decorator pillows of felt and burlap.**

Cut a matching back piece the same size as the front. Machine-stitch three sides of the front and back together, right sides together. Stitch a lining of muslin or cheesecloth on three sides and fill with shredded foam. Now, machine-stitch the fourth side of the lining closed. Put the foam pillow into the decorated cover and hand-stitch the fourth side closed. When using tassels, attach the tassels to the corners of the cover before inserting the inner pillow. Using yarn, attach the tassels to the corners of the pillow cover by sewing them in place securely.

This calico 'flower' wall hanging, right, can make you a big hit at the next bridal shower or house warming you attend. To duplicate this charming 'antique' wall hanging, clean and rub an old pine board, about 18x30 inches, with brown umber pigment. Wrap a 6-inch-wide strip of hemmed calico over the left part of the board as shown in the picture. Then, wire a reproduction of a Meissen Blue Onion trivet to a nail in the upper portion of the board and hang a reproduction of a Meissen salt box by the handle from a second nail. A needle holder placed inside the salt box will securely hold the calico flowers, greenery, and stems of flocked dried weeds. For a longer-lasting arrangement, use artificial or dried fillers.

For the flowers, cut circles of calico in many sizes. Gather the circles around the outside edges, fill the center with cotton padding, and draw the gathered fabric together tightly. Wind blue yarn around a 2-inch card several times. Remove the yarn, tie it in the middle, and cut the loops, forming a pompon. Sew these pompons to the top of the flowers. Insert a length of heavy wire into the underside of the flowers for stems. Cover the wire with green florist tape, if you wish. Crochet a small cap, similar to a calyx, slip it on the wire, and secure it to the bottom of the flower to hide the gathers.

For variety, you can make a different pattern of flower by using rectangular pieces of calico fabric instead of the calico circles. Fold the rectangular piece of fabric lengthwise, fill it with cotton padding, and gather with needle and thread, sewing the open edges together. Attach heavy wire stems; fashion the centers and the cap as before.

A calico 'flower' wall hanging with Meissenware decorator accents.

Colorful needlepoint trivets.

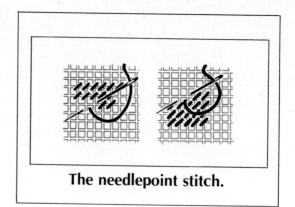

The needlepoint stitch.

Colorful needlepoint trivets, above, are specially geared for girls to make for their mothers. The canvas with large stitches is made quickly, even by unskilled hands. Use the brilliant colors of gift-wrap yarn currently available in the party favors section of most stores, and delight both yourself and the person to whom you give the gift. A child may need a little help the first time, but not thereafter!

Use a 10-inch square canvas with 3½ stitches per inch, a large tapestry needle, felt for backing, white glue, and colorful yarn.

The patterns sketched below have the following yarn requirements: Blue flower requires 1 yard green, 5 yards navy, 8 yards blue, and 12 yards lime; Ladybug requires 2 yards black, 4 yards red, and 12 yards yellow; Pink flower requires 1 yard lime, 4 yards magenta, 8 yards pink, and 10 yards olive; Geometric design requires 6 yards magenta and 13 yards orange. **NOTE:** To do the needlepoint stitch, always start at the upper right-hand corner. Cut the yarn into 24-inch lengths for easiest handling, and work each row from right to left; turn the work upside down and return row from right to left. (See the sketch above.)

After the design and background are worked, trim the corners at a 45-degree angle, leaving about ½ inch at the corners. Fold edges under and glue. To ensure that the trivet will look finished from both sides, glue a piece of felt of a complementary color to the bottom in order to cover the turned-under edges and to protect tabletops from possible scratches. You may wish to apply a coat of soil-resistant spray when finished to help the yarn repel unexpected spills. The yarn will stay brilliant longer, too.

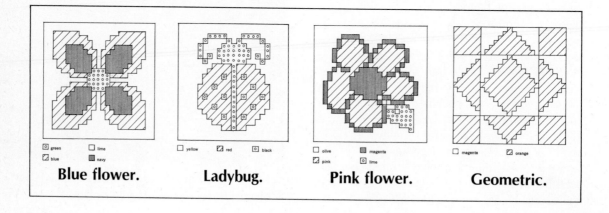

| ⊡ green | ☐ lime | | ☐ yellow | ☑ red | ⊡ black | ☐ olive | ■ magenta | ☐ magenta | ☑ orange |
| ☑ blue | ■ navy | | | | | ☑ pink | ⊡ lime | | |

Blue flower. **Ladybug.** **Pink flower.** **Geometric.**

NEEDLECRAFT KITS

Prepackaged needlework kits can be an instructional tool for beginners or a convenience product for those experienced in needlecraft. These kits can give all the knowledge, experience, and courage a novice needleworker needs to later graduate to designing her own projects. Or, they can simply be a time-saver—saving any needleworker from having to run all over town selecting the necessary materials.

Whatever your degree of skill, you'll radiate with pride when you complete one of these easy-to-make needlecraft kits from Better Homes and Gardens. They are relaxing to do and fun, too. And what a lovely gift.

The cares of the day will vanish when you work on one of the kits shown on the next four pages. Each absorbing needlecraft kit comes with easy-to-follow instructions, illustrated stitchery charts, yarn, and a needle. These kits do not include frames, pillow forms, or stuffing.

'Words of Wisdom' is a touching sampler that expresses a timely sentiment. It contains a thought we too often forget in our busy modern world. Perhaps you'll want to embroider one for a special child you know. The classic design is stamped on Belgian linen and will fit into any decor. The kit (No. 00442) includes easy-to-follow instructions, an illustrated stitchery chart, pure wool yarn, and the proper needle. When finished, the sampler fits a 14x18-inch frame. For more information, write Better Homes and Gardens, Reader Service Dept. 1A9, P.O. Box 374, Des Moines, Iowa 50336.

'Dancing Butterflies' (see next page) is a gorgeous ecru pillow featuring beautiful, exotic-colored butterflies adorning a leafy background. This kit is an easy, fun way to create an exciting addition to any decor. This big 16x16-inch pillow kit (No. 00475) includes an easy-to-understand diagram with instructions, cording, zipper, needle, and embroidery yarn. For more information regarding this kit, write Better Homes and Gardens, Reader Service Dept. 1A9, P.O. Box 374, Des Moines, Iowa 50336.

The 'Pansy Pillow' (see next page) is a round pillow that is 14 inches in diameter by 2 inches deep. Easy and enjoyable to make—a treasure to own. The kit (No. 00453) comes complete with design stamped on lime-colored linen for entire pillow, 2-inch-wide boxing strip, matching piping, crewel embroidery yarns, zipper for easy cover removal when cleaning, needle, and detailed instructions. The pillow contains an array of colors that will make it fit into any room beautifully. Patient purples, yummy yellows, and gracious greens combine to make a versatile, do-it-yourself pillow. For more information, write Better Homes and Gardens, Reader Service Dept. 1A9, P.O. Box 374, Des Moines, Iowa 50336.

'Words of Wisdom' sampler.

The 'We Two' pillow kit, a 14x14-inch knife edge pillow, pairs well with the 'Family Outing' pillow. The kit (No. 00455) comes with stamped design on natural linen, crewel yarn, cording, zipper, needle, and instructions. For more information, write Better Homes and Gardens, Reader Service Dept. 1A9, P.O. Box 374, Des Moines, Iowa 50336.

The 'Family Outing' pillow kit features a mother, father, and baby quail nestling in a meadow. It creates a handsome 14x14-inch knife edge pillow for the den or family room. The kit (No. 00456) includes the design printed on linen, wool yarn, cotton cording, zipper, easy-to-follow instructions, and a needle. For more information, write Better Homes and Gardens, Reader Service Dept. 1A9, P.O. Box 374, Des Moines, Iowa 50336.

'Three Wise Owls' in a tree that is just beginning to turn to fall colors make up this needlework design. You'll be amazed at how easy this crewel picture is to create. The kit (No. 00443) includes the design printed on cotton fabric, pure wool yarn, step-by-step instructions, an illustrated stitchery chart, and the needle. When completed, the picture may be framed in a 14x24-inch frame. (The frame is not included in the kit.) For more information, write Better Homes and Gardens, Reader Service Dept. 1A9, P.O. Box 374, Des Moines, Iowa 50336.

The 'Serenity Prayer' sampler contains an ageless thought that you can stitch for yourself or for others. And it's easy to make. Kit (No. 00302) includes design stamped on Belgian linen, cotton embroidery floss, and instructions. Sampler fits a 14x18-inch frame. For more information, write Better Homes and Gardens, Reader Service Dept. 1A9, P.O. Box 374, Des Moines, Iowa 50336.

These needlepoint vegetable designs, opposite, are cross-section views of a tomato, avocado, mushroom, and green pepper.

The designs are intriguing and yet simple and easy to live with. The foursome pictured here would complement nearly every kitchen decorating scheme and would become something of endearing and enduring quality to enjoy for many years to come.

Each design comes in an individual kit that contains yarns, needle, stamped canvas, and complete directions. The finished designs each fit easily into a standard 8x10-inch frame. For more information about the kits, write Better Homes and Gardens, Reader Service Dept. 1A9, P.O. Box 374, Des Moines, Iowa 50336.

'Dancing Butterflies' and 'Pansy.'

'We Too' and the 'Family Outing.'

'Wise Owls' — 'Serenity Prayer.'

Needlepoint vegetable kits make charming and unique gifts.

Perpetual four-season calendar — a gift of lasting beauty and usefulness.

The perpetual four-season calendar pictured above was inspired by an old-fashioned sampler. The colorful flower designs are not complicated; each one is a practical lesson in stitchery and introduces a simple embroidery stitch in each flower of the month, plus one for each of the four seasons of the year.

The months and numbers are held in place securely by hook and nylon tape, which, at the same time, also permit you to move them easily to make way for the coming month, making your calendar one that is always up to date.

This handsome calendar kit includes two stamped pieces of 100 percent natural-colored linen to embroider, enough nylon tape for changing the months and days around as needed, embroidery thread, and complete directions for the embroidery stitches and for assembling and mounting the calendar.

The kit can be purchased with the frame (No. 064-01), or without (No. 062-01). For complete information about this kit, write Better Homes and Gardens, Reader Service Dept. 1A9, P.O. Box 374, Des Moines, Iowa 50336.

The square clock below, with its face decorated with crewel embroidery of Scandinavian design, is a rare beauty. This could very well be the answer for someone on your gift list.

The crewel embroidery stitches are simple to embroider, and it requires very little expertise to mount the clock works and the completed crewel embroidered face in the 15½-inch-square decorator frame. The handsome gold-edged frame comes assembled and finished.

This clock is available in two models: with an electric movement (No. 073-01), or a battery-operated movement (No. 074-01). Both versions contain everything you will need: the clock face design stamped on cotton and linen fabric, a walnut-finished wooden frame, a mounting board, a sufficient quantity of 100 percent crewel wool and embroidery cotton, a crewel needle, and complete directions.

The D-cell battery for the movement is not included, but you can buy them almost anywhere. For more information, write Better Homes and Gardens, Reader Service Dept. 1A9, P.O. Box 374, Des Moines, Iowa 50336.

If you make this octagonal-shaped wall clock for someone on your gift list, you can be sure that the lucky recipient will treasure it as a conversation piece as well as a timepiece. And, it may be a family heirloom in the future.

The cordless, battery-operated decorator clock mechanism is simple to mount in its completely assembled, prefinished octagonal frame once you have finished the embroidery pattern on the clock face. The design looks intricate, but actually it is made up of simple stitches. The kit (No. 879-01) includes everything that you will need to complete your clock. There is the face design stamped on luxurious cotton and linen fabric, an ample supply of crewel wool and embroidery cotton, a crewel needle, the handsome octagonal-shaped frame, the battery clock movement, a Masonite mounting board, and complete easy-to-follow instructions. The clock operates on one standard D-cell battery, which is not included.

For additional information, write Better Homes and Gardens, Reader Service Dept. 1A9, P.O. Box 374, Des Moines, Iowa 50336.

Gaily decorated square clock.

Octagonal-shaped wall clock.

A colorful granny afghan made of 124 crocheted blocks.

chapter 3

KNITTING & CROCHETING

You can personalize your gift giving by presenting items that require both time and skill to make. Knitting and crocheting, two very old forms of needlecraft, require both the mastery of basic techniques and patience. But the net result is a gift that says 'I love you' more clearly than many others.

There are new yarns in a veritable rainbow of hues and new patterns, in both knit and crochet items, constantly emerging and opening up further possibilities for the gift giver who is a knitting and crocheting enthusiast.

CROCHETING

This colorful granny afghan measures 49x70 inches and is made of 124 blocks.

MATERIALS: 4 ply knitting worsted; 19 ounces of White, 9 ounces of Tangerine, 8 ounces of Yellow, and 5 ounces of Atomic Pink.

Crochet Hook, Size H.

GAUGE: Each of the squares measures five inches across; each square measures seven inches diagonally from corner to corner before they are joined together.

Square: Starting at center with Pink, ch. 6. Join with sl st to form ring. *1st rnd:* Ch 3, 3 dc in ring, (ch 2, 4 dc in ring) 3 times; ch 2. Join with sl st to top of ch-3—4 groups. Break off, fasten. *2nd rnd:* Attach Yellow to any ch-2 sp, ch 3, in same sp where yarn was attached make 2 dc, ch 2 and 3 dc—**first corner made,** * ch 1, skip next 4 dc group, in next sp make 3 dc, ch 2 and 3 dc—**corner made.** Repeat from * 2 more times; ch 1. Join to top of ch-3—4 corners. Break off, fasten. *3rd rnd:* Attach Tangerine to any corner ch-2 sp, ch 3 and complete first corner as before; * ch 1, skip 3-dc group, 4 dc in next ch-1 sp, ch 1, skip dc group, make corner as before in corner ch-2 sp. Repeat from * 2 more times; ch 1, 4 dc in next ch-1 sp, ch 1. Break off, fasten. *4th rnd:* Attach White to any

corner ch-2 sp, ch 3 and complete first corner as before; * (ch 1, 3 dc in next ch-1 sp) twice; ch 1, make corner as before in corner sp. Repeat from * 2 more times; (ch 1, 3 dc in next ch-1 sp) twice; ch 1. Join. Break off, fasten.

Block squares to measurement. Arrange squares in a diamond pattern. Using a darning needle and White, sew squares together from corner sp to corner sp, working through back loop only of each st, thus leaving front loops of sts free to form a ridge on right side.

Crochet abbreviations

ch	chain
sc	single crochet
dc	double crochet
sl st	slip stitch
sp	space
rnd	round
st(s)	stitch(es)
inc	increase
dec	decrease
beg	beginning
hdc	half double crochet

* or ** Repeat whatever follows the * or ** as many times as specified.
( ) Do number indicated in parentheses.

Edging: With the wrong side facing, attach White to dc preceding the first free corner ch-2 sp on a corner square, ch 1, ** 4 sc in the next corner sp, (sc in each of the next 3 dc, sc in next ch-1 sp) 3 times; sc in each of the next 3 dc, * 4 sc in the next corner sp, sc in each dc and in each ch-1 sp to within the next inner corner sp, draw up a loop in the next (joined) corner sp on this square, draw up a loop in corner sp on the next square, yarn over the hook and draw through all 3 loops on hook, sc in each dc and in each ch-1 sp to within the next free corner ch-2 sp. Repeat from * across to within the first free corner sp on the next corner square. Now repeat from ** around. Join to the first sc. Break off and fasten.

This helmet and mittens set is a perfect gift for any little girl, especially on cold, winter days. (The directions are given for the small size. Changes for medium and large sizes appear in parentheses that follow.)

MATERIALS: 4 ply, knitting worsted; 4 (5,5) ounces of Burnt Orange, 1 (2,2) ounces of Medium Gold, and ½ ounce of Tangerine.

Crochet Hook, Size H.

GAUGE: 4 dc=1 inch; 2 rnds=1 inch. Be sure to check your gauge before starting. The helmet will fit a 16-17 (18-19, 20-21)-inch head. The measurement around the Palm of Mitten: 4-4½ (5-5½, 6) inches.

DIRECTIONS FOR HELMET

Starting at the center top with Burnt Orange, ch 6. Join with a sl st to form a ring. *1st rnd:* 12 sc in ring. Join with sl st to the top of ch-3. *2nd rnd:* Ch 3, dc in the same ch as joining, 2 dc in each dc around—24 dc, counting ch-3 as 1 dc. *3rd rnd:* Ch 3, 2 dc in the next sc—**inc made;** * dc in the next sc, 2 dc in the next sc. Repeat from * around. Join to the top of the ch-3 —36 dc, counting ch-3 as 1 dc. Hereafter always count ch-3 as 1 dc. *4th rnd:* Ch 3, dc in the next dc, * 2 dc in the next dc, dc in each of the next 2 dc. Repeat from * round, ending with a 2 dc in the last dc. Join—48 dc. *5th rnd:* Ch 3, dc in each of the next 2 dc, * 2 dc in the next dc, dc in each of the next 3 dc. Repeat from * around, ending with a 2 dc in the last dc. Join —60 dc. Joining of rnds is at the center back.

For Medium and Large Sizes Only—6th rnd: Ch 3, dc in each of the next 4 dc, * 2 dc in the next dc, dc in each of the next 5 dc. Repeat from * around, ending with a 2 dc in the last dc. Join—70 dc. *For Large Size Only—7th rnd:* Ch 3, increasing 7 dc evenly spaced around, dc in each dc. Join—77 dc. *For All Sizes—Next rnd:* Ch 3, dc in each dc around. Join—60 (70—77) dc. Repeat last rnd 7 more times. *Following 2 rnds:* Ch 1, sc in the same place as joining, sc in each st around. Join to first sc. At end of last rnd, break off and fasten.

Motif (Make 2): Starting at center with Burnt Orange, ch 5. Join with sl st to form ring. *1st rnd:* Ch 4, (dc in ring, ch 1) 9 times. Join the last ch-1 with sl st to the 3rd ch of ch-4—10 sps. *2nd rnd:* Sl st in the next sp, ch 4, dc in the same sp as the last sl st, * ch 1, dc in the next ch-1 sp, ch 1, in the next ch-1 sp make a dc, ch 1 and a dc. Repeat from * around, ending with a ch 1, dc in the last ch-1 sp, ch 1. Join to the 3rd ch of ch-4—15 sps. Break off and fasten. *3rd rnd:* Attach Gold to any sp on last rnd, ch 3, holding back on hook last loop of each dc, make 3 dc in the same sp where the yarn was attached, yarn over hook and draw through all 4 loops on hook—**starting cluster made;** * ch 2, holding back on hook the last loop of each dc, make a 4 dc in the next sp, yarn over hook and draw through all 5 loops on hook—**cluster made.** Repeat from * around, ending with a ch 2. Join to the top of first cluster—15 clusters. Break off and fasten. *4th rnd:* Attach Tangerine to any ch-2 sp between clusters on last rnd, 2 sc in same sp where yarn was attached, * ch 3, 2 sc in next ch-2 sp. Repeat from * around, ending with a ch 3. Join to first sc. Break off; fasten.

Leaving 2¾ (3, 3½) inches at the center back between motifs, sew motifs over the lower section of the helmet as shown.

Tie String (Make 2): Cut 6 strands of Burnt Orange, each 1 yard long. Hold the strand together and fold in half to form a loop. Insert crochet hook through sp at center of the lower edge of a motif and draw the loop through; draw the loose ends through the loop and pull tightly to form knot. Divide strands into three parts and braid strands to within last 5 inches. Tie knot at end of braid. Trim ends to form tassel.

DIRECTIONS FOR MITTENS

LEFT MITTEN: Starting at lower edge of hand (at base of cuff) with Burnt Orange, ch 19 (23, 27) loosely to measure 5 (6, 7) inches. Join with sl st to first ch to form a circle. *1st rnd:* Ch 3, skip joining, dc in each remaining ch. Join with sl st to top of ch-3 — 19 (23, 27) dc, counting ch-3 as 1 dc. *2nd rnd:* Ch 3, dc in each dc around. Join to top of ch-3 — 19 (23, 27) dc, counting ch-3 as 1 dc. Hereafter always count ch-3 as 1 dc. Repeat 2nd rnd 0 (1, 2) more times.

Thumb Gore: 1st rnd: Ch 3, dc in each of the next 5 (7, 9) dc, 2 dc in the next dc — **inc made for the thumb gore;** dc in each of the next 2 (3, 3) dc, 2 dc in the next dc — **another inc made for the thumb gore;** dc in each of the remaining 9 (10, 12) dc for the back of the hand. Join — 21 (25, 29) dc. *2nd rnd:* Ch 3, dc in each of the next 6 (8, 10) dc, 2 dc in the next dc, dc in each of the next 2 (3, 3) dc, 2 dc in the next dc, dc in each of the remaining dc. Join — 23 (27, 31) dc. *3rd rnd:* Ch 3, dc in each dc to within next 2-dc group, ch 2 (3, 3), skip next 6 (7, 7) dc for Thumb Opening, dc in each of remaining dc. Join. *4th rnd:* Ch 3, dc in each dc and in each ch st around. Join — 19 (23, 27) dc. Repeat 2nd rnd of Mitten (not Thumb Gore) until length is 2 (2½, 3) inches from opening.

Tip Shaping: 1st rnd: Ch 3, * holding back on hook the last loop of each dc, dc in each of the next 2 dc, yarn over hook and draw through all 3 loops on the hook — **dec is now made;** dc in each of the next 2 dc. Repeat from * around, ending with dec over the last 2 dc. Join — 5 (6, 7) decs now made. *2nd rnd:* Ch 3, * dec over the next 2 sts, dc in the next dc. Repeat from *

Little girl's cozy, warm crocheted helmet and mittens set.

around, ending with dec over 2 sts, dc in each of next 2 sts. Join—10 (12, 14) sts. *3rd rnd:* Ch 3, * dec over next 2 dc. Repeat from * around, ending with dc in last dc. Join. Leaving a 6-inch length of yarn, break off. Thread a darning needle with this end of yarn, gather top of sts closely together and fasten securely.

Thumb (1st rnd): With right side facing, attach Orange to first dc of skipped sts for Thumb, ch 3, dc in each of next 5 (6, 6) dc, holding back on hook last loop of each dc, dc in same st where next dc of hand was made and in center loops of same next dc, yarn over and draw through all 3 loops on hook, dc in each of next 2 (3, 3) ch sts, holding back on hook last loop of each dc, dc in center loops of next dc on hand and in same st where same dc of hand was made, complete a dec as before. Join—10 (12, 12) dc. Repeat 2nd rnd of Mitten 2 (3, 3) times.

Tip shaping (next rnd): Repeat the 3rd rnd of the Tip Shaping of the Mitten; then finish it the same as for the Tip of the Mitten.

Cuff: For Small Size Only—Motif (1st rnd): Starting at center with Burnt Orange, ch 5. Join with sl st to form ring. *1st rnd:* Ch 4, (dc in ring, ch 1) 10 times. Join with sl st 3rd ch of ch-4— 11 sps. Break off and fasten. *2nd and 3rd rnds:* Work same as 3rd and 4th rnds of Motif for Helmet—11 clusters on 2nd rnd and 11 ch-3 loops on 3rd rnd. *For Medium and Large Sizes Only:* Make one Motif same as for Helmet. *For All Sizes:* Holding mitten with joining of rnds at side fold and thumb to the front, mark center back ch st on starting chain of mitten. *1st row:* Working along opposite side of starting chain with right side facing, attach Burnt Orange to marked ch st, sc in same ch where yarn was attached, holding motif in back of work with wrong side facing, sc in any ch-3 loop on last rnd of motif, sl st in each of next 3 ch sts on starting chain of mitten, ch 3, with wrong side of motif facing, sc in next ch-3 loop on motif, (dc in each of next 3 ch on mitten, 2 dc in next ch) 3 (4, 5) times; dc in next ch st on mitten, sc in next free loop to the right on motif. Break off and fasten. *2nd row:* Attach Burnt Orange to next free ch-3 loop to the left on motif, sc in same loop, skip first 2 dc on last row, dc in each dc to within last 2 dc, sc in next free ch-3 loop to the right on motif. Break off and fasten. *For*

Medium and Large Sizes Only—3rd row: Repeat last row. *For All Sizes—Next row:* Attach Burnt Orange to next loop to the left on motif, sc in same loop, ch 2, dc in each dc on last row, ch 2, sc in next loop to the right on motif. Break off and fasten. *Following row:* Attach Burnt Orange to next loop to the left on motif, sc in same loop, ch 2, dc next 2 ch sts on last row, dc in each dc and in each of next 2 ch sts, ch 2, sc in next loop to the right on motif. Break off and fasten. Repeat last row until all ch-3 loops on motif have been used; do not break off at end of last row. *Next rnd:* Ch 3, with right side facing, make 2 dc in same loop where last sc was made, dc next 2 sc on motif 3 dc in next loop, dc in each of next 2 ch sts on last row, dc in each dc, dc in each of next 2 ch sts. Join to top of ch-3 at beginning of this rnd. Break off; fasten yarn.

Tassel: Cut 6 strands of Burnt Orange, each 8 inches long. Hold strands together and fold in half to form a loop. Insert hook through a dc at center back of last rnd of cuff and draw loop through; draw loose ends through loop and pull tightly to form a knot. Trim evenly.

RIGHT MITTEN: Work same as for Left Mitten until the 2nd rnd has been completed. Repeat 2nd rnd 1 (2, 2) more time.

Thumb Gore (1st rnd): Ch 3, dc in each of next 8 (9, 11) dc for back of hand, 2 dc in next dc, dc in each of next 2 (3, 3) dc, 2 dc in next dc, dc in each remaining dc. Join—2 dc inc for thumb gore. *2nd rnd:* Ch 3, dc in each of 9 (10, 12) dc, 2 dc in next dc, dc in each of 2 (3, 3) dc, 2 dc in next dc, dc in each remaining dc. Join. Starting with 3rd rnd of Thumb Gore, complete same as for Left Mitten.

The butterfly afghan shown on the opposite page measures 49x66 inches and consists of 12 squares, each 16 inches square, joined together. You can follow the same design and make two extra squares that can be mounted and framed for use as wall hangings.

MATERIALS: Washable sport yarn, 2 ounce skeins, color A—Periwinkle Blue—5, color B— Grape Punch—9, color C—Cyclamen—2, and color D—White—1.

Crochet Hook, Size E.

GAUGE: Center-5 dc=1 inch; 3 rows=1 inch.

DIRECTIONS

*Square—Center—*With A, ch 44 for the lower edge. Each of the 23 rows of center is worked in dc. *Row 1 (wrong side):* Work 1 dc in the 4th ch from the hook and in each remaining ch; 42 dc. NOTE: Ch 3 at the beginning of each row counts as 1 dc. *Row 2:* Turn, sl st into the first st, ch 3, 1 dc in 2nd st and in each remaining st, end with a last dc in top of ch 3; 42 dc. *Row 3:* Same as row 2. Leaving an end of about 10 yards, break yarn. Wind this end around a small bobbin. Wind another small bobbin with about 10 yards of A. Cut a few strands of A, B, C, and D, in one-yard lengths.

To change colors or add new strands, draw a loop of a new color or strand through the last two loops, completing the last dc of the previous color. *Row 4 (right side):* With A work first 12 sts as before, joining a B strand by drawing it through the last two loops of the last A st, drop A to the wrong side; 6 B, joining a new A strand through the last B st as before; 2 A over last B strand, drop B; 4 more A, joining a new B strand through the last A st, drop A; 6 B, joining a bobbin of A through the last B st, 2 A over the last B strand, drop B; 12 A. *Row 5 (wrong side):* With A work first 10 sts, changing to B by picking up a B strand from row below and drawing it through the last 2 loops of the last A st, drop A to the wrong side; 2 B, joining a C strand through the last B st as before, drop B; 6 C, joining a new B strand through the last C st, 2 B over both the C strand and the A strand from row below, changing to this A strand through last B st as before, drop B and C; 2 A, changing to B strand from row below through last A st, break A; 2 B, joining a new C strand through last B st, drop B; 6 C, joining a new B strand in last C st, drop C; 2 B over the A strand from row below, changing to this A strand through last B st, drop B; 10 A to end. *Row 6:* With A, work first 10 sts, changing to B as before, drop A; 2 B, change to C, drop B; 2 C, joining a D strand through last C st, 2 D over C, 2 C over D, drop D, 2 more C over B strand from row below, changing to this B strand, drop C; 2 B, change to C, drop B; 4 C, joining a new D strand through last C st, 2 D over C, drop D, 2 C, change to B, drop C; 2 B, change to A, drop B; 10 A to end.

Crocheted butterfly-design afghan.

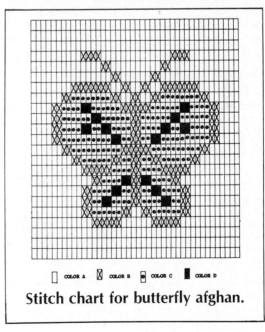

☐ COLOR A ☒ COLOR B ▣ COLOR C ■ COLOR D

Stitch chart for butterfly afghan.

Beginning with row 7, follow chart until 23 rows have been completed; end on wrong side.

*Border—Round 1—*Ch 4, turn, 1 dc in 2nd st, * ch 1, skip 1 st, 1 dc in the next st; repeat from * 18 times, ch 1, 1 dc in the space under ch 3 at end of the row; 21 spaces across the upper edge of the square; ch 3, 1 dc in the same space for the corner, skip base of last row of the square, ** ch 1, 1 dc in base of end dc of next row; repeat from ** 19 times ending with last dc in base of 2nd row from end, ch 1, 1 dc in space under end st of last row of square, ch 3, 1 dc in same space for corner; 21 spaces along left edge of square plus corner spaces; ch 1, 1 dc in next st, continue around working lower and right side edges to correspond to opposite edges, end with ch 3, join with sl st in 3rd ch of ch 4 at beginning of rnd; 21 spaces on each side plus 4 corner sps. *Round 2:* Turn, sl st into corner space, ch 3, turn, 1 dc in same space for half of corner, * 1 dc in each dc and in each space to within next corner, 2 dc, ch 3, 2 dc all in corner space; repeat around from *, end with 1 dc in last dc, 2 dc in corner, ch 3, join with sl st in top of ch 3 at beginning of round to complete 4th corner; 47 dc on each side. Fasten off. *Round 3:* From right side, with loop of B on hook, sl st into any corner space, ch 6, 1 dc in same space for corner, * ch 2, 1 dc in next dc, ch 2, skip 1 dc, 1 dc in next dc, ** ch 2, skip 2 dc, 1 dc in next dc; repeat from ** 13 times—to within 2 sts of corner—ch 2, skip 1 dc, 1 dc in next dc, ch 2, 1 dc, ch 3, 1 dc all in corner space; repeat around from *, end with 1 dc in last dc, ch 2, join with sl st in 3rd ch of ch 6 at beginning of round; 18 spaces each side plus corners. *Round 4:* Sl st to center of corner space, ch 6, turn, 1 dc in same space for corner, ** ch 2, 1 dc in next dc; repeat from * to next corner, ch 2, 1 dc, ch 3, 1 dc all in corner space; repeat around from *, end with 1 dc in last dc, ch 2, join with sl st in 3rd ch of ch 6 at beginning of round. Repeat round 4, 6 times. *Round 11:* Sl st to center of corner space, ch 8, turn, work same as for round 4, working 5 ch instead of 3 in each corner space. Fasten off the yarn.

*Finishing—*Block. Darn in all ends. Arrange squares as illustrated. With care to match sts and keep seams elastic, sew squares together.

Crocheted gypsy shawl.

Crochet a colorful circular gypsy shawl for the young lady in your house. Use eight balls of Bucilla Multi and a Size H crochet hook.

GAUGE: 3 spaces=2 inches, 6 rows=3 inches.

DIRECTIONS

With loop on hook, ch 6, join with sl st in first ch to form ring. *1st rnd:* sl st in ring, ch 6, 1 dc in ring, * ch 3, 1 dc in ring; repeat from * 3 times, ch 3, sl st in 3rd ch of ch 6; 6 sps. *2nd rnd:* sl st in next space, ch 6, 1 dc in same sp, * ch 3, 1 dc in next sp, ch 3, 1 dc in same sp; repeat from * around, end ch 3, sl st in 3rd ch of ch 6; 12 sps. *3rd rnd:* sl st in next sp, ch 6, 1 dc in same sp, * ch 3, 1 dc in next sp, ch 3—1 dc, ch 3, 1 dc in next sp—**an inc made;** repeat from * 4 times, ch 3, 1 dc in last sp, ch 3, join with sl st in 3rd ch of ch 6; 18 sps. Continue inc 6 spaces in each rnd, having inc directly over those of previous rnds until 30 rnds in all. To round out shawl—*31st row:* Inc 6 sps evenly spaced, with care not to have inc directly over previous incs. *32nd row:* Inc 12 sps evenly spaced with care not to have incs directly over previous incs. Repeat last 2 rows once. Fasten off. Steam lightly with steam iron.

Fringe: First, wind the yarn around a 7-inch length of cardboard, cutting the yarn at one end. Then, knot a 4-strand fringe in the spaces around the edge.

KNITTING

Knitting abbreviations

st(s) . . . . stitch(es)
k . . . . knit
p . . . . pearl
dec . . . . decrease
inc . . . . increase
tog . . . . together
beg . . . . beginning
rnd . . . . round
sl . . . . slip
psso . . . . pass slipped
stitch over
sp . . . . space
yo . . . . yarn over
dp . . . . double-pointed (needle)
* or ** Repeat whatever follows the * or
** as many times as specified. ( ) Do
what is in parentheses the number of
times indicated.

Knitted Victorian sampler afghan.

This Victorian sampler afghan is a patchwork of various stitches. The afghan measures 51x65 inches, including the border. Each strip measures 7 inches wide.

MATERIALS: 4 ply Knitting Worsted; 24 ounces each of Baby Aqua and Deep Rose, and 10½ ounces of Safari.

Knitting Needles, No. 6.

Crochet Hook, Size G.

GAUGE: 5 sts=1 inch; 7 rows=1 inch.

DIRECTIONS

First Strip: (PATTERN No. 1) Starting at the lower edge with Rose, cast on 35 sts. *1st row (right side):* Knit. *2nd row:* K 1, p 33, k 1. *3rd row:* K 4, p 7, (k 3, p 7) twice; k 4. *4th row:* K 1, (p 3, k 7) 3 times; p 3, k 1. *5th row:* Repeat 3rd row. *6th row:* Repeat 2nd row. *7th row:* K 1, p 5, k 3, (p 7, k 3) twice; p 5, k 1. *8th row:* K 6, p 3, (k 7, p 3) twice; k 6. *9th row:* Repeat 7th row. *10th row:* Repeat 2nd row. Repeat the last 8 rows (3rd through 10th row) until the length

is 7 inches, ending with a wrong-side row. Break off and fasten. Attach the Safari and knit 2 rows. Break off and fasten. Attach the Aqua. NOTE: Hereafter work 1 pattern with Aqua and the following pattern with Rose, knitting 2 rows between the patterns with Safari. Each pattern should measure 7 inches, and each pattern should end with a wrong-side row.

PATTERN No. 2—1st row (right side): With Aqua, knit. *2nd row:* K 1, p 33, k 1. *3rd and 4th rows:* Repeat first and 2nd rows. *5th row:* K 4, p 2, (k 3, p 2) 5 times; k 4. *6th row:* K 1, (p 3, k 2) 6 times; p 3, k 1. *7th and 8th rows:* Repeat 5th and 6th rows. Repeat last 8 rows until length of this pattern is 7 inches, ending with a wrong-side row. With Safari, k 2 rows.

PATTERN No. 3—1st row: With Rose, knit. *2nd row:* K 6, p 5, (k 5, p 5) twice; k 4. *3rd row:* K 1, p 4, k 5, (p 5, k 5) twice; p 4, k 1. *4th row:* K 4, p 5, (k 5, p 5) twice; k 6. *5th row:* K 2 (p 5, k 5) 3 times; p 2, k 1. *6th row:* Repeat 5th row. *7th row:* Repeat 4th row.

8th row: Repeat 3rd row. *9th row:* Repeat 2nd row. *10th row:* K 1, p 2, (k 5, p 5) 3 times; k 2. *11th row:* Repeat 10th row. Repeat last 10 rows (2nd through 11th row) for pattern. Work in pattern until length of pattern No. 3 is 7 inches, ending with a wrong-side row.

PATTERN No. 4 — 1st row: With Aqua, knit. *2nd row:* K 7, (p 7, k 7) twice. *3rd row:* K 11, k 2 tog, yo, k 9, yo, sl 1, k 1, psso, k 11. *4th and all even rows:* Repeat 2nd row. *5th row:* K 10, k 2 tog, yo, k 11, yo, sl 1, k 1, psso, k 10. *7th row:* K 9, k 2 tog, yo, k 13, yo, sl 1, k 1, psso, k 9. *9th row:* K 8, k 2 tog, yo, k 15, yo, sl 1, k 1, psso, k 8. *11th row:* K 7, k 2 tog, yo, k 17, yo, sl 1, k 1, psso, k 7. *12th row:* Repeat 2nd row. Repeat the last 10 rows (3rd through 12th row) to complete pattern No. 4.

PATTERN No. 5 — 1st row: With Rose, knit. *2nd row:* K 1, p 33, k 1. *3rd row:* K 2, * insert needle in next st as if to k, (yo) twice and draw through st on left-hand needle, slip st off left-hand needle — **long st made;** k 4, long st in next st. Repeat from * across, ending with k 3. *4th row:* K 1, p 2, (with yarn in front of work and dropping the 2nd loop of the long st, slip next long st as if to p, p 4, slip next long st as before) 5 times; p 1, k 1. *5th row:* K 2, (slip long st onto a dp needle and hold in front of work, k 2, k long st from dp needle, slip next 2 sts onto a dp needle and hold in back of work, k long st, k 2 sts from dp needle) 5 times; k 3. *6th row:* Repeat 2nd row. *7th row:* (K 4, long st in next 2 sts) 5 times; k 5. *8th row:* K 1, * p 4, (slip long st, dropping the second loop as before) twice. Repeat from * across, ending with a p 3, k 1. *9th row:* K 2, (slip next 2 sts onto a dp needle and hold in the back of the work, k next long st, k 2 sts from dp needle, slip next long st onto a dp needle and hold in front of work, k next 2 sts, k the long st from dp needle) 5 times; k 3. *10th row:* Repeat the 2nd row. Repeat the last 8 rows (3rd through 10th row) to complete pattern No. 5.

PATTERN No. 6 — 1st row: With Aqua, knit. *2nd row:* K 1, p 15, p 2 tog, p 16, k 1 — 34 sts. *3rd row:* K 4, (yo, k 1, k 2 tog, sl 1, k 1, psso, k 1, yo, k 4) 3 times. *4th and every even row:* K 1, p 32, k 1. *5th row:* K 5, (yo, k 2 tog, sl 1, k 1, psso, yo, k 6) 3 times, ending with k 5 (instead of k 6). *7th row:* K 2, (sl 1, k 1, psso, k 1, yo, k 4, yo, k 1, k 2 tog) 3 times, ending with a k 2. *9th row:* K 2, (sl 1, k 1, psso, yo, k 6, yo, k 2 tog) 3 times, ending with a k 2. *10th row:* Repeat the 4th row. Repeat the last 8 rows (3rd through 10th row) for pattern, inc one st on the last row — so there are 35 sts.

PATTERN No. 7 — 1st row: With Rose, knit. *2nd row:* K 1, p 33, k 1. *3rd row:* K 2, p 1, k 2, p 1, (k 2, p 4, k 2, p 1) 3 times; k 2. *4th and 6th rows:* Repeat 2nd row. *5th row:* K 2, p 1, (k 2, p 4, k 2, p 1) 3 times; k 2, p 1, k 2. *7th row:* K 2, p 4, (k 2, p 1, k 2, p 4) 3 times, k 2. *8th row:* Repeat 2nd row. Repeat the last 6 rows (3rd through 8th row) for pattern, dec one st on the last row — so there are 34 sts.

PATTERN No. 8 — 1st row: With Aqua, knit 34 sts. *2nd row:* K 1, p 2, k 1, (p 6, k 1, p 2, k 1) 3 times. *3rd row:* K 3, (p 1, k 6, p 1, k 2) 3 times; k 1. *4th, 5th, and 6th rows:* Repeat 2nd, 3rd, and 2nd rows. *7th row:* K 3, (p 1, slip 3 sts on a cable holder and hold in back of work, k next 3 sts, k the 3 sts from holder, p 1, k 2) 3 times; k 1. *8th, 9th, and 10th rows:* Repeat 2nd, 3rd, and 2nd rows. Repeat last 8 rows (3rd through 10th row) for pattern, inc one st at end of last row — 35 sts.

PATTERN No. 9 — 1st row: With Rose, knit. *2nd and 4th rows:* K 1, p 33, k 1. *3rd row:* K 3, (yo, k 2, slip the yo over the 2 k sts, k 2) 8 times. *5th row:* K 1, yo, k 2, slip the yo over the 2 k sts, (k 2, yo, k 2, slip the yo over the 2 k sts) 8 times. *6th row:* Repeat 2nd row. Repeat last 4 rows (3rd through 6th row) for pattern. Work in pattern until length is 7 inches, ending with a wrong side row. Bind off. NOTE: Always k 2 rows with Safari between patterns and bind off at end of last pattern of each strip.

Second strip: With Aqua, cast on 35 sts. Work Pattern No. 2 through Pattern No. 9, then work Pattern No. 1.

Third strip: With Rose, cast on 35 sts. Work Pattern No. 3 through Pattern No. 9 then Patterns No. 1 and 2.

Fourth strip: With Aqua, cast on 35 sts. Work Pattern No. 4 through 9, then Nos. 1, 2, and 3.

Fifth strip: With Rose, cast on 35 sts. Work Pattern No. 5 through 9, then No. 1 through 4.

Sixth strip: With Aqua, cast on 35 sts. Work Pattern No. 6 through Pattern No. 9, then Pattern No. 1 through Pattern No. 5.

Seventh strip: With Rose, cast on 35 sts. Work Pattern No. 7 through 9, then No. 1 through 6.

Block each strip to measure 7x63 inches. With right side of work facing, using Safari, sc closely along the 4 sides of each strip, making 3 sc in each corner st and being careful to keep work flat. Join with sl st to first sc. Break off and fasten. Leaving the back loops free, sew strips neatly together.

Border: With right side facing, attach Safari to sc following any corner. *Next 4 rnds:* Ch 1, working in the back loop of each sc, sc in each sc around, making 3 sc in each corner sc. Join. *5th rnd:* Ch 1, * working from left to right, insert hook through both loops of next sc to the right and complete an sc. Repeat from * around. Join, break off and fasten.

Block to measurements.

This diamond and cable pattern knitted afghan measures 48x58 inches, excluding the fringe. It knits up faster than you would think because it is done on large size (No. 10) needles. Choose a lively color for the afghan.

MATERIALS: 4 ply Knitting Worsted; 40 ounces of Deep Turquoise.

Circular Needle No. 10 (29-inch length).

Crochet Hook, Size G.

One double-pointed needle.

GAUGE: Each diamond panel (40 sts) = 10 inches; each cable panel (22 sts) = 4 inches.

NOTE: Circular needle is used to accommodate the large number of sts. Work is done in rows.

DIRECTIONS

Starting at the lower edge, cast on 218 sts. *Row 1 (right side):* K 5, for the border, place a marker on the needle; p 2, k 3, p 2, k 8, p 2, k 3, p 2,— last 22 sts from the cable panel; place a marker on the needle; * k 19, skip next st, from the front of the work, k in back of the next st, pull out this st to measure 3/8 inch, then k skipped st and drop both sts from the left-hand point of the needle—**twist made;** k 19—last 40 sts made form diamond panel; place a marker on the needle; p 2, k 3, p 2, k 8, p 2, k 3, p 2, place a marker on the needle. Repeat from * twice more; k 5 for the border. There are 4 cable panels, 3 diamond panels, and a 5-st border at each end. *Row 2:* K 5 for border, k 2, p 3, k 2,

Knitted diamond and cable afghan.

p 8, k 2, p 3, k 2, * p 40, k 2, p 3, k 2, p 8, k 2, p 3, k 2. Repeat from * twice more; k 5 for the border. *Row 3:* K 5, * p 2, k 1, in the next st k, p and k; turn; p 3, turn; k 3 tog—**picot made;** k 1, p 2, k 8, p 2, k 1, make picot in next st, k 1, p 2, k 18, (twist over the next 2 sts) twice; k 18. Repeat from * across to within the last 5 sts, k 5. *Row 4 and all even rows:* Repeat 2nd row. *Row 5:* K 5, * p 2, slip the next 2 sts on dp needle and hold in back of the work, with the yarn in back slip the next st as if to p, k 2, sts from dp needle—**picot-cable twist made;** p 2, k 8, p 2, make picot-cable twist over the next 3 sts, p 2, k 17 (twist over 2 sts) 3 times; k 17. Repeat from * across to within the last 5 sts, k 5. *Row 7:* K 5, * p 2, k 1, picot in the next st, k 1, p 2, k 8, p 2, k 1, picot in the next st, k 1, p 2, k 16, (twist over 2 sts) 4 times; k 16. Repeat from * across to the last 5 sts, k 5. *Row 9:* K 5, * p 2, picot-cable twist over 3 sts, p 2, slip the next 4 sts on dp needle and hold in the back of the work, k next 4 sts, k 4 sts from the dp needle—**back cable made;** p 2, picot-cable twist, p 2, k 15, (twist over 2 sts) 5 times; k 15. Repeat from * across to the last 5 sts, k 5. *Row 11:* K 5, * p 2, k 1, picot, k 1, p 2, k 8, p 2, k 1, picot, k 1, p 2, k 14 (twist over 2 sts) 6 times; k 14. Repeat from * across to the last 5 sts, k 5. *Row 13:* K 5, * p 2, picot-cable twist, p 2, k 8, p 2, picot-cable twist, p 2, k 13, (twist over 2 sts) 7 times; k 13. Repeat from * to within the last 5 sts, k 5. Last 12 rows (2nd through 13th rows) form the pattern for the cable panel only. *Row 15:* K 5, * work in pattern (as for 3rd row) across the cable panel only, k 12, (twist over 2 sts) 8 times; k 12. Repeat from * across to within the last 5 sts, ending the last repeat with work across the cable panel, k 5. *Row 17:* Repeat 13th row. *Row 19:* Repeat 11th row. *Row 21:* K 5, * work in pattern as for 9th row (back cable row) across the cable panel, k 9, twist over 2 sts to start a new diamond, k 4, (twist over 2 sts) 5 times; k 4, twist over 2 sts, k 9. Repeat from * across to the last 5 sts, k 5. Hereafter, in working in the cable panel pattern, be very careful to make the back cable (as on 9th row) on every 12th row. *Row 23:* K 5, * work in pattern across the cable panel, k 8, (twist over 2 sts) twice; k 4 (twist over 2 sts) 4 times; k 4, (twist over 2 sts) twice; k 8. Repeat from * across to the last 5 sts, k 5. *Row 25:* K 5, * work in pattern across the cable panel, k 7, (twist over 2 sts) 3 times; k 4, (twist over 2 sts) 3 times; k 4, (twist over 2 sts) 3 times; k 7. Repeat from * across to last 5 sts, k 5. *Row 27:* K 5, * work in pattern across cable panel, k 6, (twist over 2 sts) 4 times; k 4, (twist over 2 sts) twice; k 4, (twist over 2 sts) 4 times; k 6. Repeat from * across, ending with k 5. *Row 29:* K 5, * work in pattern across cable panel, k 5, (twist over 2 sts) 5 times; k 4, twist over next 2 sts, k 4 (twist over 2 sts) 5 times; k 5. Repeat from * across, ending with k 5. *Row 31:* K 5, * work in pattern across the cable panel, k 4, (twist over 2 sts) 6 times, k 8, (twist over 2 sts) 6 times; k 4. Repeat from * across, ending with k 5. *Row 33:* K 5, * work in pattern across cable panel, k 3, (twist over 2 sts) 7 times; k 6, (twist over 2 sts) 7 times; k 3. Repeat from * across, ending with k 5. *Row 35:* K 5, * work in pattern across cable panel, k 2, (twist over 2 sts) 8 times; k 4, (twist over 2 sts) 8 times; k 2. Repeat from * across, ending with K 5. *Rows 37 through 47:* Repeat 33rd row through 23 rd row back in reverse order. *Row 49:* K 5, * work across the cable panel, k 9, twist over 2 sts, k 4, (twist over 2 sts) 5 times; k 4,

twist over 2 sts k 9. Repeat from * across, ending with k 5. *Row 50:* Repeat 2nd row. The last 40 rows (11th through 50th rows) form the pattern. Repeat 11th through 50th rows 5 times more. *Next 3 Odd Rows:* Repeat 11th, 13th, and 15th rows. *Following 7 Odd Rows:* Keeping the continuity of cable panel pattern, for diamond panels, starting with 13th row, work same as for 13th through first row back in reverse order. Bind off in pattern.

Border: Row 1: With the right side facing and crochet hook, sc evenly along the cast-on edge. Ch 1, turn. *Rows 2 and 3:* Sc in each sc. Ch 1, turn. At the end of the 3rd row, omit the ch-1. Break off and fasten.

Fringe: Wind yarn about 50 times around a 7-inch piece of cardboard; cut at one end, thus making 14-inch strands. Hold two 14-inch strands together and double them to form a loop. With the right side facing, from wrong side, insert a hook in the first sc on the last row of the border and draw a loop through. Draw the loose ends through the loop and pull up tightly to form a knot. Tie two 14-inch strands to each sc across the last row of the border. Make the border and tie the fringe along the opposite edge in the same way. Trim evenly.

This cloud-soft afghan is a blend of fluffy coral mohair and rust wool that knits up quickly. The finished afghan measures 48x65 inches.

MATERIALS: Mohair, Castilian Coral, 16 1-ounce balls. Twist knitting worsted, Rust, four 4-ounce skeins.

29 inch round needle, No. 11.

GAUGE: 2½ sts=1 inch.

DIRECTIONS

Cast on loosely 176 sts on a rnd needle. 29 inches long, size 11, or size to get the correct gauge. Using Twist worsted k 1 row. P 1 row. Change to mohair. *1st row:* (preparation row only) * yo, sl 1 (purl-wise), k 1, * repeat. *2nd row:* * yo, sl 1 (purl-wise), k 2 tog * repeat. *3rd and 4th rows:* Same as 2nd row. Change to Twist worsted and repeat the 2nd row, four times. Repeat the above until 13 balls of Mohair are used, save the other 3 for the fringe. K 1 row, p 1 row with Twist worsted and cast off. To make a firm edge for the fringe loosely pick up

176 sts with Twist worsted and cast off. Do this at the beginning and end of the blanket. At the other two edges pick up sts with Twist worsted, 4 sts for every 8 rows of pattern (2 sts in the Mohair row, 2 sts in the Twist worsted row). K 1 row, p 1 row 3 times. K 3 rows, p 1 row, k 1 row, p 1 row, k 1 row, p 1 row, k 1 row, p 1 row, cast off. Turn back and hem the edges.

Block: The fringe goes down the sides. It is made with 3 strands of Mohair and 1 strand of Twist worsted 12 inches long.

The handsome wall hanging in the background of the photo is knitted from synthetic straw. Upon completion, it measures 21x76 inches. With these generous measurements, this novel wall hanging can also do double duty as a room divider. When it is used as a wall hanging, hang it over a plain-colored piece of fabric. You can omit the fabric liner when you are using it as a room divider.

MATERIALS: Yarn, ½ pound wide raffia.
Knitting needles, No. 11.
GAUGE: 2½ sts=1 inch, 3 rows=1 inch.

DIRECTIONS

Cast on 46 sts. K 1 row, P 1 row. The next two rows are repeated 90 times for a panel without any wooden end pieces that measures 19x72 inches. *Row 1:* K 2, * lift the 4th st over the 3rd st and knit it, then knit the 3rd st * repeat * to *, k 2. *Row 2:* P. Cast off knitting.

To Block: Use fiberboard or any other surface that is possible to pin into. Mark heavy wrapping paper off in one section 20x74 inches. Use heavy 'T' pins, which are sold in stationery stores. Put the raffia into water. Remove and roll in a towel until damp-dry.

Before beginning to pin, pull the knitted piece lengthwise and a little widthwise. Using 'T' pins, pin the wall hanging to the wrapping paper-covered fiberboard. Pin every inch at each end and then every inch down the sides. The more pins that you use the straighter the panel will be. Be exceptionally careful not to pin into the straw or it will tear. To give the hanging more body, spray the hanging with a satin finish spray or any plastic spray. (This is also a good pattern for place mats, using a plain edge on each side.)

Mohair afghan and raffia wall hanging.

How to make mounting frames: Cut four pieces of ¼-inch hardwood to 21x1⅝-inch strips. Lay the two boards one on top of the other, and drill ten holes with centers 2 inches apart, using a ½-inch drill bit, starting 1½ inches in from the edge of the wood. Make sure that you drill through both pieces of wood.

Cut a ½-inch dowel rod into ten ¾-inch pieces. On the back board, glue a dowel into each of the ten holes. Carefully place the wall hanging onto the ten dowel pieces before adding the front piece. Now, push the front board onto the dowel pieces. (The front board is removable so that the back piece can be nailed to the wall easily.) Repeat the same process to make a bottom mounting frame for the synthetic straw wall hanging.

Try making this macrame necklace trimmed with fishing sinkers.

chapter 4

MACRAME

Macrame is simply knot tieing. It is a craft that originated many years ago when sailors whiled away the hours on long sea voyages by practicing their marlinspike seamanship. They not only tied the basic nautical knots (see pages 74-76), they arranged them in various groupings.

Today, macrame is the center of much interest. Hobbyists have adapted the basic knot-tieing techniques for use in making wall hangings, belts, purses, and jewelry.

At first glance, macrame looks impressively complicated, but it isn't. It is done with a few knots tied in any kind of cording. *Learn the knots and abbreviations on pages 74-76, and soon you'll be making your own macrame designs.*

To make this necklace, use three colors of crochet-cotton—orange (O), maroon (M), and purple (P)—two large beads, 10 small beads, 48 fishing sinkers, and a wire choker. Cut the cords eight times the desired finished length.

Double the cords. Starting with P, attach four cords to the choke with LHK. (See abbreviations on page 74.) Attach four M cords, eight O cords, four M cords, and finish with four P cords.

Work four rows of HDHH. Make four SK in P and M cords on left side. For two rows, make ASK and follow with four SK. Work one row of HDHH in P and M cords, two rows of VDHH, and one row of HDHH. Repeat the above instructions for the P and M cords.

With outside O cords, work two rows of DDHH downward toward the center. With four center cords, tie one SK. Slip large bead over the two center cords, bring the two outer cords around the bead, and tie a SK below the bead. With the single cord closest to the bead on either side of the center, alternate a bead and an OK until each cord has five beads. With the remaining five O cords on either side, make LHB. Use the two outside cords to tie 12 LHK

over the three innermost cords. Use the two centermost O cords on each side to make two rows of DHH downward.

Make two rows of HDHH. With the center O cords, make two rows of DDHH downward toward the center. With the four center O cords, make four SK.

With the P cords on the outside edges, make four rows of DDHH downward toward the center. With four center P cords, make four SK. Alternate cords and make four SK. Alternate back and make four SK with the four center cords. Alternate the cords for four SK. Alternate back and make four more SK. Slip large bead over two center cords, and bring two outer cords around and tie SK. Finish with OK.

Move back up to body of work and with two innermost O cords make LHB of eight knots. Use these two O cords to make a LHK over outside group of four P square knots on either side. Repeat with eight more LHK on O cord and one LHK over second group of four square knots. Using the four center cords, tie eight square knots. Finish with OK. Move back up and with innermost O cord, tie one row of DDHH downward toward outside edge. Repeat with remaining three O cords.

Tie an OK in the pairs of the two cords. Leave ½-inch space and alternate cords. Tie second row of OK. Trim cords, and attach a fishing sinker to the end of each cord.

BASIC KNOTTING KNOW-HOW

All of the basic macrame knots are discussed here and on the following pages. Actually, just two simple knots are used in combinations to create all macrame designs—the half knot and the half hitch. Once these knots and their variations have been mastered, you can create to your heart's content. Tie every knot close to the previous knot unless directed otherwise. Keep cords straight, untangled, and in proper sequence. Use T-pins to pin your work down to a knotting board (made from an 18x24-inch piece of heavy cardboard or fiberboard).

Macrame abbreviations

LHK	—Lark's Head Knot
LHB	—Lark's Head Braid
HH	—Half Hitch
HDHH	—Horizontal Double Half Hitch
DDHH	—Diagonal Double Half Hitch
VDHH	—Vertical Double Half Hitch
CDDHH	—Crossing Diagonal Double Half Hitch
HK	—Half Knot
SK	—Square Knot
ASK	—Alternate Square Knot
OK	—Overhand Knot
HHB	—Half Hitch Braid
JK	—Josephine Knot
HKL	—Half Knot Loose

Lark's Head Knot. Fold cord in half, then bring top of loop down over cords to form two loops. Fold new loops back so they touch each other. Slide over the holding line and tighten.

Lark's Head Braid. This series of knots is one of the easiest sinnets to do because it uses only two cords—the knot-bearer and the knotting cord—and the basic Lark's Head Knot. The first cord is the knot-bearer; the second, the knotting cord. Take second cord over and behind knot-bearer. Bring second cord up through loop created by second cord. Now, take second cord under knot-bearer and back up through loop created by this step. Pull tightly and repeat the process as many times as instructed.

Half Hitch. Learn this knot by following the illustration below. It is the most useful knot in macrame, as it has a number of variations.

Horizontal Double Half Hitch. Begin this knot at either the right edge or the left. This cord will be the knot-bearer. While knotting, keep cord taut and held horizontally over the other cords. Loop the adjacent cord in a clockwise direction over the knot-bearing cord if it is the far right cord and counterclockwise if the knot-bearer is the far left cord. Make two loops with each cord and knot firmly.

Diagonal Double Half Hitch. Divide cords in two groups, and use far right and far left cords

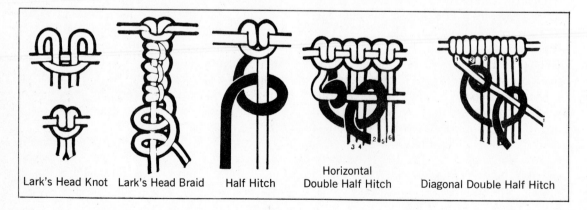

Lark's Head Knot   Lark's Head Braid   Half Hitch   Horizontal Double Half Hitch   Diagonal Double Half Hitch

as knot-bearers. Hold knot-bearer taut and at a 45-degree angle over cords. Make double loops over it on each cord (loops go clockwise in right group and counterclockwise in left group). At intersection of cords, double-loop left knot-bearing cord over right cord. Continue double half hitches until X is completed.

Vertical Double Half Hitch. Place a pin inside the far left cord. Slide that cord under the next one and loop around it twice in a clockwise direction. Reverse the process when you reach the far right side by using the right outer cord to knot, looping counterclockwise.

Crossing Diagonal Double Half Hitch. This knot looks like double Xs when completed. Divide cords in half and make a left and right diagonal double half hitch. To make second X, take the second cord from the left and use it as your knot-bearer, double-looping all left-hand cords onto it. Then, when you reach the center, take the first right cord (should be the far right cord that is now in the center position), and double-loop it over the same knot-bearer. Continue to do the same with each adjacent cord.

Half Knot. Create this from four cords that have been looped around the holding line. The two center or 'filler' cords should remain stationary while you knot outer cords around them. (Secure the filler cords with pins or tape while working.) Then, bend the right outer cord over the filler cords. Bend the left outer cord over the right one, under the filler cords, and out over the right cord. A series or 'sinnet' of half knots results in a spiral design.

Square Knot. This knot is made in two steps. First, make a half knot as previously described. Then, bend right outer cord under filler cords. Bend left outer cord under right cord, over filler cords, and under right cord. Tighten resulting knot of each step before continuing.

Alternate Square Knot. These knots require groups of four cords to complete. Make a row of square knots (total number of square knots must be a multiple of four). Allow some extra cord space between it and the row above. To alternate, let the two far left cords remain unused while you knot the next four cords together in a square knot. The third row should look just like the first. This time, you will include the two outer right and left cords that row two did not use. (Illustrated on page 76.)

Overhand Knot. This simple knot is often used to start cords, or to end cords so they won't fray. To position the knot exactly, put a large pin through the loop and tighten the cords around it. Take out the pin. To make the knot, bend the cord up into a loop. Take end of cord behind and through loop, and tighten. (Illustrated on page 76.)

Half Hitch Braid. The half hitch braid is simply a series of single half hitches. When working from the left to the right, hold the knot-bearing cord (the second cord) vertically taut. Loop the first cord over the knot-bearer. Then, bring it around behind the knot-bearer and up through the loop created by the first cord. Pull the knot tightly and repeat the process to form the braid. (Illustrated on page 76.)

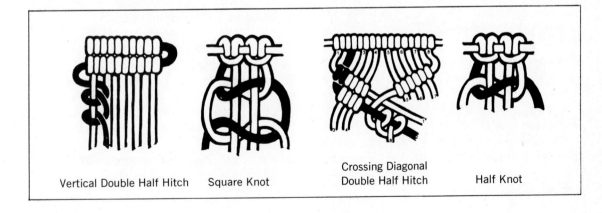

Vertical Double Half Hitch   Square Knot   Crossing Diagonal Double Half Hitch   Half Knot

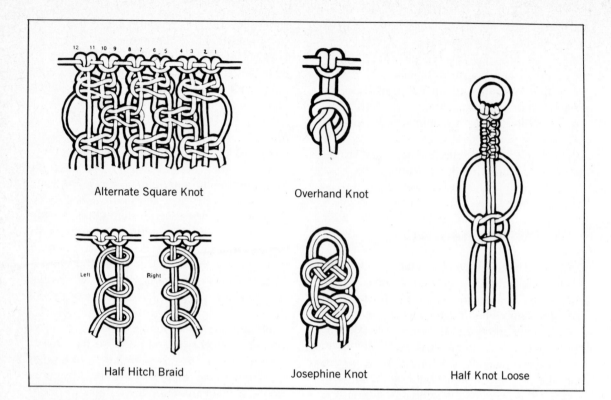

Alternate Square Knot

Overhand Knot

Half Hitch Braid

Josephine Knot

Half Knot Loose

Josephine Knot. This is the prettiest and most decorative of all the macrame knots. It is a large knot and requires lots of space and cording. Study the diagram closely to see exactly when and where the various cords go over and under the various loops. To begin, make a counterclockwise loop, bringing the ends behind the starting cord and down. Now, with an adjacent cord, make a clockwise loop, going over the counterclockwise loop, under the ends, and over the first loop's starting cord. The ends of the second loop should now go down through the intersection of the two loops and behind the first loop. Repeat the process, beginning with the counterclockwise loop, and your first Josephine Knot is completed.

Half Knot Loose. This is just a simple variation of the half knot as previously described. Make a half knot, leaving the filler cords straight and stationary. Knot the outer cords around the filler cords, but this time do not pull the outer cords tight. Let them form a circle around the filler cords instead. If you're making a series of these knots, make sure you keep the circles uniform in size and spacing.

Knotting knacks

You can use cords of cotton, seine twine, string, mod yarn, nylon twine, rattail, rope, hemp, or ribbon straw. These cords vary in thickness and pliability; therefore, your knots may not look exactly like those shown.

The length of the cord needed to tie a particular design varies, too. A good rule is to cut each cord eight times the desired length of the finished project. End cords or knot-bearers should be twice as long as filler cords.

If your cord breaks or isn't long enough to finish the project, splice the cords together with white glue. Unravel both ends to be spliced, coat with glue, retwist, and allow to dry. If the cord has a center core, pull it out and cut off ½ inch of the core from one end. Cut off ½ inch of the cord covering of other piece. Coat core with glue and push covering onto core.

MORE KNOTTY GIFT IDEAS

To make the macrame handbag below, cut nylon braided cord in 32 pieces, each 70 inches long; one piece 20 inches long; one piece 26 inches long; and five pieces, each 30 inches long. You'll need 38 large and 31 smaller beads.

Tie knots in end of the 20-inch cord and pin to the board. Fold the 70-inch cords in half and attach to holding-cord with LHK. Tie one row of SK. Tie holding cord together with SK.

Make one row of ASK. Alternate cords for row three. Tie three SK, using same four cords. Make one ASK and follow with four SK, using same four cords. ASK one row. Slide large bead on center two cords of SK; bring outer two around bead. Tie SK. Tie one row of ASK. Add bead to center cords of SK, and SK. Tie ASK and three SK. Finish with one row of ASK.

Fold the bag in half, with the SK of the beginning holding-cord in the center. Tie a knot in the remaining 26-inch cord, ten inches from the end. Pin the bag to your knotting board, and pin the knot of the holding-cord to the knotting board at the left-hand side of the bag. Tie HDHH on the holding-cord. Turn and knot HDHH on the remaining 32 cords. SK the holding-cord together, allowing ends to become fringe. Trim the fringe to eight inches, and slip a small bead on every other cord. Tie OK at bottom of cords. To make the handle, tie five 30-inch pieces together with loose OK (to be removed later). Tie two outer cords over three center cord fillers in five SK. Slide a bead on three filler cords, tie five SK—and repeat four times. Untie OK and run the ends of the handle into knots at the sides of the bag. Trim handbag. (Line bag if you wish.)

The headband below is made of maroon, orange, and purple wool. Cut two lengths of each color eight times the finished length.

★ **A sophisticated fringed handbag.**

★ **Stylish Swedish wool headband.**

Fold each piece in half and tie knots in the folded ends. Pin the cords to the knotting board, with four maroon cords in the center, two purple cords on either side, and two orange cords on the outside. Five inches from the ends, begin knotting by taking the right center maroon cord and tieing a row of DDHH on it. Move downward toward the left. Do the same with the center maroon cord on the other side.

With remaining center maroon cords, work another row of DDHH. Make a third row on innermost purple cords. With left and right outside cords, work toward center with CDDHH, crossing at center. Repeat for length desired. Finish with three rows of DDHH. Trim.

The cinch belt below is made of orange and fuchsia braided cord. Cut four cords of each color seven times your waist measurement, and four 5-foot cords of each color for fringe.

Pin the center of one orange cord to your board. Fold the remaining cords in half, and tie to the first orange cord with LHK. With the left-hand orange cord, tie two rows of HDHH. For the third row, tie SK. For fourth row, tie ASK. Repeat rows three and four until the desired length is reached. Finish with two rows of HDHH over the outside right cord. Trim the fringe to 2½ feet and tie OK. To finish, lay one orange cord along the starting edge. Fold the remaining fringe cords in half, pull through the starting row, and tie in LHK. Tie an OK in orange cord close to the knots on either side.

The macrame belt shown below is made by cutting four lengths of braided nylon cord (two white and two black), each 156 inches long (for a 26-inch belt), or six times the desired belt length. (You can use any kind and color of cording.) Measure 26 inches (or ⅙ the length of the cord) from one end and make a SK, knotting the two outside cords over the two inside cords. Make a JK ½ inch from the square knot. Continue making JKs at 1-inch intervals until the belt is the desired length. Leave ½-inch space; make a SK. Finish ends with OK.

★ **A cinch belt for the adventurous.**

★ **Easy-to-make Josephine-knot belt.**

Here's a wall hanging that really lets you express your skill in macrame, as well as your imagination. It can be used as either a wall hanging or a room divider, so its versatility and uniqueness are bound to please even the most problem person on your gift list.

The materials required are: two ⅜-inch brass curtain rods or ¾-inch dowel rods, rubber bands, white glue, and ten 500-foot balls of 30# weight carpenter's chalk thread (also known as mason line or seine twine).

Fold 62 cords (48 feet long) in half and fasten over the rod with LHK. It is a good idea to butterfly the cords for easier handling.

Pull the far right cord horizontally across the other cords and hold it taut. Then, make a row of HDHH over this knot-bearing cord.

For the next several inches of the hanging, this same type of knot is used, but not straight across. Only portions of the cords are used, some in diagonals and some in curves. Occasionally, leave spaces where the cords are open, and pull some cords across or twist them around into a series of half hitches. Use rubber bands to hold cords you aren't working on.

Remember, this wall hanging is free-form. This means that you can improvise as you go along. No two of them look the same, so whatever design you come up with is fine.

The vertical flat braids that appear intermittently in the design are a series of double half hitches. Hold one or more vertical cords taut and alternately loop double half hitches around the vertical cord.

The twisted braids are simply half hitch series. As you knot, the series naturally twists.

Loop all the cords around the bottom rod. Then, add three rows of ASK. Trim off the fringe as evenly as possible at the bottom.

When doing any project this large, the cords are so long that they often become tangled as you work. To minimize tangles, loop each cord into a butterfly before beginning the project. Start the butterfly 12 inches from your project. Loop each cord in a figure-8 fashion between your thumb and little finger, working down the cord to the end. Wrap a rubber band around the middle of the butterfly. This shortens the long cords, making them easier to work with, and the cords will easily pull longer as you work.

An intriguing free-form wall hanging.

An unusual decorative wall hanging.

This two-toned decorative wall hanging looks quite complicated, but if you've 'learned the ropes' of knotting, you'll have absolutely no trouble making it yourself.

You will need the following materials to make the wall hanging: two 1½-inch wooden dowels cut in 19½-inch and 17½-inch lengths, two wooden finials, one ⅜-inch dowel 17½ inches long, fuchsia and orange dye, some orange paint, and a 3/16-inch pulley cord.

The central part of the hanging requires 14 pieces of cord 45 feet long (dyed orange), 14 pieces of cord 45 feet long (dyed fuchsia), and 2 pieces of cord 71 feet long (dyed fuchsia).

Tassels require 43 feet of orange cord for the top, 75 feet of orange cord for the bottom, and 85 feet of fuchsia cord for the bottom. The tassels are optional.

The hanging-cord (optional) requires two pieces of orange cord 161 inches long and two pieces of orange cord 80 inches long.

Glue the knobs to the long rod and paint the knobs orange. Let the paint dry thoroughly. This rod serves as a holding rod for the entire design. Then, fold the cords and fasten them to the rod with an LHK. Alternate colors, each with eight cord lengths (four strands that have been folded). You now should have eight groups of fuchsia and seven groups of orange. The outer cords should be 43½ feet long.

Cut the cord. Then, dye it according to the instructions on the package of all-purpose dye.

The finished length of the macrame wall hanging is approximately six feet. *Row 1-6:* Work each group of four cords into square knot sinnets. *Rows 7-10:* HDHH, using the right outer cord as the knot-bearer. *Rows 11-15:* ASK in groups of four cords. *Rows 16-19:* HDHH, using the left outer cord as the knot-bearer. *Rows 20-23:* Square knot sinnets of eight cords knotted over four center filler cords. *Rows 24-27:* HDHH, using the right outer cord as the knot-bearer. *Rows 28-37:* Double ASK; do two rows of SK before alternating the position of the knots. *Rows 38-41:* HDHH, using the left outer cord as the knot-bearer. *Rows 42-51:* Square knot sinnets of eight cords knotted over four center filler cords. *Rows 52-55:* HDHH, using the right outer cord as the knot-bearer. *Rows 56-70:* Triple ASK (three rows of SK tied in a pattern before alternating the position of the cords). *Rows 71-74:* HDHH, using the left outer cord as the knot-bearer. *Rows 75-79:* ASK. *Rows 80-83:* HDHH, using the right outer cord as the knot-bearer. *Rows 84-89:* Square knot sinnets in groups of four. *Rows 90-95:* HDHH, using the left outer cord as the knot-bearer. *Rows 96-99:* Square knot sinnets of eight cords knotted over four center filler cords. *Row 100:* Horizontal half hitches tied over the ⅜-inch dowel rod, which now acts as the holding-cord or rod. (Instructions for tieing the horizontal half hitch appear in the box at the right.) *Rows 101-102:* HDHH, using the left outer cord as the knot-bearer. *Row 103:* Horizontal half hitches tied over 1¼-inch dowel rod. *Row 104:* Tie off the fringe in groups of four with OK, or, if you wish, make tassels.

For each tassel, cut eight cords 27 inches long. Fasten a 12-inch holding-cord with pins to a pillow or similar backing, and tie on the cords (folding in half) with a LHK. Knot those 16 cords (in groups of four) in SK. Next, take the holding-cord and tie the ends together. Now, work three rows of ASK (four rows altogether) in a circle. Release the top of the bow, and thread one end of the holding-cord through the opposite side of the top row of knots.

Then, slip four cords of the matching color group on the wall hanging through the center of the tassel, and knot the holding-cord in a square knot over the cords of the hanging. Run the ends of the holding-cords through the tassel center, and knot a SK up high on the cords of the hanging so that it will not show in the tassel. Cut off the ends of the holding-cords, and paint the knot with a drop of white glue. Finally, cut all of the cords to the same length and tie the ends of the cords.

To make the hanging cord, make a square knot sinnet 21 inches long, tied with four cords. The outer two cords are 161 inches long and the inner two cords are 80 inches long. Begin knotting 28 inches below the ends.

To attach to the dowel, place the ends behind the dowel, and bring the first pair of cords over the front of the dowel and behind themselves, crossing each other and returning again to the front of hanging. Continue knotting in square knots until desired length is reached.

Make the two top tassels as previously described. Cut six pieces of cord, each 20 inches long. Then, tie the pieces at the center with a cord six to eight inches in length. Run the ends up through the tassel and out of the top. To attach the tassels to the sinnets, run the ends of the tassel-holding-cords and the filler-holding-cord into the sinnet.

If you are forever trying to solve the problem of what to give the person who has everything under the sun, don't overlook the possibility of giving a handcrafted macrame wall hanging. One of these beauties will impress anyone. These also will be greatly appreciated as wedding, house-warming, and graduation gifts. However, unlike the smaller macrame projects that have been presented throughout this chapter, you'll have to think ahead and allow yourself plenty of time to complete the work, as this is a large-scale project.

The horizontal half hitch

To make this particular knot, you can begin at either the right edge or the left edge. This cord will serve as the knot-bearer — you will knot all other cords over it. While you are knotting, keep this cord taut and held horizontally over the other cords. Loop the adjacent cord in a clockwise direction over the knot-bearing cord if it is the far right cord; if the knot-bearing cord is the far left cord, loop the adjacent cord in a counterclockwise direction.

So far, this is exactly like you would make the horizontal double half hitch. The only difference between the two knots is that in the horizontal half hitch you loop the knotting cord over the knot-bearing cord only once, instead of twice as is required when tieing the horizontal double half hitch. If a visual aid will help you understand this better, refer to the horizontal double half hitch diagram on page 74, but do only the first loop and stop.

A custom-made dollhouse for the doll at your house.

chapter 5

DECOUPAGE AND PAINT

Through the years, the art of painting has played many roles. The cave man painted his walls as a form of recordkeeping. The 'Old Masters' painted as a means of self expression as well as for a livelihood. And, the nineteenth-century woman painted both to exercise her artistic talents and because it was simply the ladylike thing to do. Today, men, women, and children enjoy all sorts of painting projects—painting on wood, metal, plastic, paper, and fabric, even sand painting— because these are stimulating, challenging, and rewarding.

From the day you did your first finger painting, you were initiated into the drip and dabble craft of painting. From finger painting your fascination probably introduced you to the paint books that held page after page of magic— paint the drawings with water and color magically appeared. Then, you gradually progressed through your first paint box of water colors, your own jars of poster paints, and possibly a number painting set of oils. Today, you may be experiencing the thrills of acrylics, spray-paints, and even house painting!

No matter how advanced your painting expertise may be, on the following pages you will find something you'll enjoy doing. These gift ideas require a minimum amount of talent and skill, plus a little patience. But, they will challenge you to drip and dabble up a few ideas of your own. Given as a gift, these projects will be long cherished as a work of art. And, you'll be just as proud of your masterpiece!

Delight the doll in your house by giving her a custom-made dollhouse. The task isn't as arduous as it sounds; in fact, you'll be surprised by the amount of fun you have playing architect, builder, and interior decorator.

But, as any young miss will tell you, dolls today have a very definite preference about where they live. Very few dote on the McKinley mansions of yesterday. Today's dolls are mad for the mod dwellings like the one opposite.

This contemporary classic sports walls made of transparent plastic. The rest of the frame is composed of balsa wood strips, laminated plastic, and cardboard sheets, which can be purchased at hobby shops. (All of these materials are light and sturdy, and they can be cut easily with an art knife.)

The streamlined furnishings complement the architecture. All of the sofas, chairs, and tables are quickly and easily made from prepainted children's building blocks. Glue round blocks to square- and rectangular-shaped blocks to create contemporary chairs, sofas, and beds. Even the far-out fireplace is a snap to make. An ice cream carton lid serves as the fire pit, and a spray can lid attached to a wooden dowel makes the hood. The carpet and the tabletop are cut from gift wrap paper and then are glued to heavier paper. Accessorize the walls with pictures—these are made by gluing small pieces of gift wrap paper to very lightweight cardboard. Or, cover one wall with a wild supergraphic painted with bright poster paints. Of course, dolls always insist on swimming pools these days. This particular one is cut from laminated plastic. Blue paper was glued to the bottom of the pool, and a balsa wood diving board was added. Dolls really have it made.

DECOUPAGE

Decoupage, a variation of cut and paste, evolved from a method of ornamenting furniture in Venice during the sixteenth and seventeenth centuries. In the eighteenth century, French ladies trimmed prints from hand-painted wallpaper, glued them to trays, screens, and boxes, and applied up to 60 coats of lacquer.

This craft was brought to America during the nineteenth century, but it didn't catch on with the busy post-Revolutionary women because of the coatings and sandings required. During the Victorian period, however, a simplified form of decoupage took hold. This involved pasting a picture on a wooden box top, outlining it with metallic braid, and giving the box top six to ten coats of clear varnish. This was a far cry from the 60-coat French process, and it became popular with American women.

Today, cut-and-paste decoupage is enjoying a strong revival. Even more popular is transfer decoupage, a simplified technique. And don't forget about the rubber stamp method, the easiest of them all. New timesaving products, such as thin decoupage prints and fast-drying varnishes, are partly responsible for this interest.

Decoupage projects can be done with materials you have lying around your house. You can make stunning decoupage plaques from boards and varnish from the workshop and pictures taken from old magazines. But, if you need help with decoupage ideas, take a trip to your local craft shop. There you'll find thin prints specially made for decoupage, and numerous varnishes, brushes, and scissors to help give your project a professional look. If you have questions about a project, ask the shop's proprietor.

★ **These ingenious decoupage lunch boxes are unusual, to say the least.**

Remember that decoupage is versatile. The craft works easily on many surfaces—wood, glass, pottery, porcelain, stone, silver, lead, iron, steel, and tin. You can also use the transfer method on plastic, but the cut-and-paste technique should not be used, as the paste may have an adverse effect on the plastic. Consider decorating wooden boxes for many people on your gift list. Decoupage playing cards to the top of one and fill the box with bridge equipment. Or, stock one box with sewing materials for a pretty sewing box. Or, decoupage the top of one with foreign stamps and fill the box with stationery, stamps, and a pen. This should give you a few ideas, so now it's time to get started.

CUT-AND-PASTE DECOUPAGE

As has been stated before, you can use the cut-and-paste decoupage technique on almost any material. But since the steps are the same no matter which material is used, only wood and metal will be discussed in detail. **CAUTION:** For all materials except new wood, you must clean surface with paint or varnish remover.

If you want to decoupage the top of a wooden box, first give the entire box three coats of flat enamel, any color you choose. Take the design motif from a single print or from a composite of several prints. (All papers should be similar in thickness and texture.) Keep in mind the shape and size of the surface to be decorated when planning the design, as scale is important to the success of decoupage.

Cut the print or prints and trim the edges very carefully, using decoupage scissors or very sharp manicure, embroidery, or buttonhole scissors. Hold the paper horizontal, in the left hand. Move the paper slowly, feeding the edges into the blades of the scissors. The right hand does not move except to operate the blades.

When all the elements have been cut out, arrange them on top of the box. The elements of the design should be butted but not overlapped. Each overlap is an extra layer of paper, which will require several more coats of varnish to remove. With a small artist's brush, apply a thin layer of white glue to the back of the paper, coating the edges well. Press the print onto the box with a roller. This will remove wrinkles and the air bubbles from under the print. With a damp sponge, wipe away any glue that may seep from under the edges of the paper, and dry the box with a soft cloth.

When the glue is thoroughly dry, pour a small pool of fast-drying clear varnish in the center of the box top. Immediately brush it out to the edges of the box with smooth, even strokes. Now, cover the box with an inverted cardboard box to keep off the dust and allow the varnish to dry for 24 hours. Then, lightly sand the box top with fine sandpaper (#400). Wipe away the dust with a damp sponge and dry. Repeat the coating and sanding process until the painted background and the pasted print are perfectly blended. This will take 10 to 20 coats of varnish, depending on the thickness of the paper. With the last three coats of varnish, cover the sides as well as the top of the box. Finish the box with an application of white wax furniture polish, lightly buffed.

Decoupage lunch boxes are unusual, to say the least. Decorate a workman's lunch box with a theme that fits its owner. Cut out prints from anything—newspapers, magazines, posters, maps, wallpaper, wrapping paper, and greeting cards, just to name a few sources.

Paint the lunch box with three coats of flat enamel. Then, place the cutouts in an attractive arrangement on the sides and top of the lunch box. Paste your design on the lunch box, using white glue applied with an artist's brush. Press out all air bubbles and wrinkles. Using a damp sponge, wipe away any glue that may have seeped from under the print. When the paste is completely dry, cover the lunch box (except for the bottom) with a coat of fast-drying clear varnish. Place an inverted cardboard box over the lunch box to keep dust from settling on the varnish, and let dry for 24 hours. When the varnish is dry, sand the finish lightly with fine sandpaper (#400). Repeat coating and sanding process until design and background are completely blended. This should take 10 to 20 coats.

If you wish, trim the edges of the lunch box with ribbon braid. Line the inside of the lunch box with fabric or adhesive-backed plastic.

Decoupage the vacuum bottle inside the lunch box, too, or you can leave it out and give the lunch box as a casual summer handbag.

★ **The transfer method of decoupage is really quite easy, even for beginners.**

1. Applying the transfer medium to the print. 2. Removing the paper. 3. Laying print on board. 4. Applying finish.

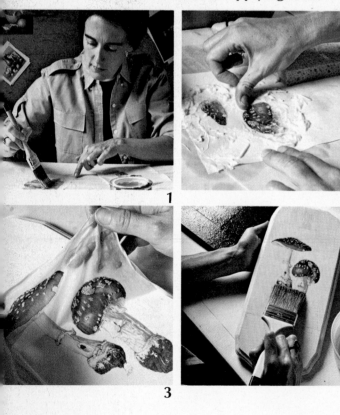

1

2

3

4

TRANSFER DECOUPAGE

If you've always wanted to decoupage, but are 'all thumbs' with scissors, then try transfer decoupage. This version of the popular art of decorating with cutout paper prints substitutes another step for the cutting. You transfer the print to the intended surface with a special medium that picks up the printed design but not the paper backing on the print.

The transfer process is one of the newest decoupage methods. It allows you to apply almost any kind of printed picture to a great variety of surfaces—wood, glass, china, plastic, and metal. Depending on your skill and patience, you can decorate anything from a minuscule pillbox to a full-size room divider.

Those sixteenth-century Venetians who introduced decoupage would hardly believe how easy it is today. Almost anyone can do it.

Decorator boxes and wall plaques are easy to do with transfer decoupage method. First, purchase the transfer medium from a hobby or craft supply store. Then, brush four coats of the special transfer medium onto the front of the picture you have chosen to use. Brush coats 1 and 3 vertically and coats 2 and 4 horizontally. Allow 15 minutes between coats or until the film created is clear. Clean the brush in soap and water after each use.

When the final coat is transparent, allow the print to dry for at least two hours. Then, with a single-edged razor blade, trim 1/16 inch off all four edges of the picture.

Now, soak picture, face down, in sudsy water (1 tablespoon soap to 1 gallon water). Soak the picture for at least one hour. Rinse picture in clear water. Place wet print, face down, on a smooth, hard surface and rub it firmly to peel the paper from film. If necessary, add water or resoak picture. The picture will show through the film when the paper is removed.

Next, apply a coat of the transfer medium to the back of the picture and to the board or top of the box. The surface should be already painted or stained for a colored background. Make certain the surface is clean and dust-free.

Position the picture on the board or box top. Use your fingers or a rubber roller to press the picture to remove air bubbles and any excess transfer medium. If air bubbles persist, puncture the bubble with a pin and press it smooth. Wipe off excess water and transfer medium.

Allow the picture to dry until it is completely transparent. Now, apply a fast-drying clear varnish with a brush, brushing in one direction with long, flowing strokes. If the brush leaves any hairs on the surface, remove them at once. Allow the finish to dry completely before applying the next coat of varnish. When dry, sand each coat with very fine steel wool. Apply as many coats of varnish as necessary to create a smooth surface.

RUBBER STAMP DECOUPAGE

'Where there's a will, there's a way,' and some crafty hobbyists have developed a quicker and easier way to decoupage—with a rubber stamp. Yes, it's even easier than transfer decoupage.

To make these hornbook facsimiles, reminiscent of the earliest type of primer used by the colonists, draw a paper pattern. Then, transfer the pattern to ¾-inch plywood and cut it out with a jigsaw. Or, make them from cutting boards, cheese boards, or wooden hand mirrors (with the looking glass removed).

Stain or paint the boards with flat enamel. Allow this to dry thoroughly. When the background finish is dry, rubber stamp numbers, letters, or old sayings on to the front of the hornbooks. Allow the ink to dry and then apply at least six coats of fast-drying clear varnish or decoupage medium. Allow each coat to dry completely, and then sand lightly with fine sandpaper or fine steel wool. Wipe away the sanding dust with a damp sponge and repeat the coating and sanding process until the hornbooks have a satiny smooth finish. Then, give them a final coat of wax furniture polish and buff lightly.

These hornbook facsimiles make charming gifts for collectors of Early American accessories. They make lovely wall decorations, or, by using the back side, they make practical cheese boards and cutting boards. Keep this unusual gift idea in mind. It is appropriate for almost any gift-giving occasion—thank-you, birthday, housewarming, or bridal shower. Make them assembly-line fashion, and you'll soon have a library of Early American hornbooks.

★ **From the past—hornbook facsimiles.**

The previous four pages have given you three different decoupage techniques, each easier than the one before. Study them and try all three, or choose the one that best suits you.

If you choose the first decoupage method, start with an easy design motif. The simpler the motif, the easier the cutting task. With practice, you may then easily graduate to very delicate, complex design motifs.

For beginners using any of the three techniques, it is wise to start with a small project—a wooden box or tray. Once you've mastered the craft, think larger and perhaps try a piece of furniture or a room divider.

GIFTS FOR PAINT DABBLERS

On the following few pages, you'll find some unique gift ideas specially geared to the paint and palette people. Many of the gifts are made from odds and ends you probably have around your house. Give them a face-lift with a fresh coat of paint, and they will be ready to be put to a new use. Try a couple of these projects.

HAND-PAINTED GIFTS FOR ADULTS
Everyone knows people for whom gift selection is difficult. If you have one of these people on your gift list, give a hand-painted gift.

These painted driftwood wall plaques make a unique gift. Search lakes, shores, and river banks for variety of aged wood. Take your trea-sures home and allow them to dry. Then, brush them smooth and clean with a stiff brush. Draw your design on to the wood, or, if you are an experienced tole painter, paint the design directly on the wood, using acrylic paints. When the paint is completely dry, spray the entire surface with a clear lacquer to seal the design. Attach glue-on picture hangers to the back.

Colorful key chains are made by cutting various shapes from balsa wood or plywood. Drill a hole in each shape for the chain and sand with fine sandpaper. Cut cross sections from various shapes of molding and dowel rods, and arrange them in a desired pattern on the balsa wood and glue in place, using a white glue.

Hand-painted driftwood wall plaques.

Coat the entire surface with gesso and let dry. Paint the background surface with bright acrylics and the trims in contrasting colors.

Owl memo boards make a handy, inexpensive gift. Cut the owl shapes from a 12x18-inch sheet of cork. With a coping saw or knife, cut a piece of beaver board the same size as the cork and sand the edges. Glue the cork to the beaver board. Draw on the details and paint them with acrylics. Attach a picture hanger.

To make these bright cutting boards, cut shapes from 1x12-inch hardwood. The sun and flower are 10 inches in diameter, the watermelon is 8½; the butterfly is 8¼x9½; the turnip is 8x11; and the fish is 8x9. Drill a hole an inch from the edge for a hanger. Sand with wood and coat one side and the edges with gesso. When the gesso is dry, sketch the design and paint with bright acrylics. Now, apply two coats of flat

★ **Wood or fiberboard key-keepers.**

★ **1. Key chains. 2. Owl memo boards. 3. Cutting boards. 4. Wig stands.**

1

2

3

4

varnish, drying between coats. On the unpainted cutting side, sand off any paint spots and rub with mineral oil. Run a foot of plastic lacing through the hole and knot.

These boutique wig stands, at left, will delight every lady on your list. Begin by gluing heavy string to a foam wig stand for the hairline or hat. Make a nose from instant papier-mache. Let dry. Seal entire head with two coats of gesso. Let dry. Brush glue on face and neck.

Sketch in the facial features and paint with enamel. Paint on hair or a hat and brush with an antiquing glaze. Let dry and then seal the entire head with clear plastic spray.

These bold key-keepers, above, are big enough to find quickly in a handbag, a pocket, or even when hanging on the wall. There's a design to fit almost any reason for carrying a key.

Sizes vary from 3½ inches to 5 inches. The vine-covered cottage key chain measures 5 inches square. The others are smaller. Draw the pattern on ⅛- to ¼-inch-thick wood or fiberboard. Cut along the outline, using a saber saw or jigsaw. Sand the wood and then paint on your design with acrylics. Coat with varnish and drill a hole for a hanger or chain.

1. Paint flat white areas with white acrylic paint to screen out the emery cloth background.
2. For the sand areas, outline the design with white glue. Fill the outline in with white glue and sprinkle with sand.
3. Turn the block on edge to remove excess sand. Let dry and repeat gluing and sanding to build up the area. When each block is finished and dry, vacuum and spray with matte finish.

The sand painting, opposite, makes a beautiful wall hanging. With contact cement, glue coarse black emery cloth to stiff cardboard backings. Cut the backed emery cloth into desired shapes and trace your designs onto emery cloth.

Decide which areas to paint and which to sand. (See the opposite page for instructions on how to paint the various areas of your design, using white acrylic paint and sand.)

When each block has been sand-painted and is dry, vacuum and spray with matte finish. Now, arrange all the blocks on a framed ¼-inch hardboard panel. Cut strips of mounted emery cloth to fit the spaces and glue them in place. Coat the strips with white glue and sand. Let dry and repeat the gluing and sanding.

TOYS AND GAMES FOR CHILDREN

If you're tired of spending large amounts of money for toys and games, try making some of your own. The children will love them.

To make this tumbling clown, you'll have to revive the old craft of whittling. Cut an 8x4-inch base from pine, two 8-inch rails from balsa wood, and four 5½-inch lengths of dowel rods. Drill holes in the base and rails and glue them in place. Cut the clown shape from medium-weight cardboard. Glue a ½-inch dowel through the hands. Paint the cardboard with poster paints and spray with varnish. To weight the clown, glue metal washers to the head and feet.

This whittled pull-toy horse is made by first constructing a 4x6-inch platform from scrap lumber. Then, carve axles from scrap wood, making sure that the ends are round. Nail and glue the axles in place. Carve a 1-inch wheel from soft wood. Mount the wheels on the axles and hold them in place by gluing on smaller carved wheels. Carve a 6-inch-tall horse from soft pine or balsa wood, then paint and glue in place on the platform.

Tumbling clown and pull horse—fun whittling gifts to make and give.

★ **Personalized catchall toy can.**

★ **Colorful toys for girls and boys.**

This catchall toy can started out as an ordinary garbage can. The transformation was simple. First, prepare the metal for painting with one or two coats of white gesso on both the inside and outside. Also apply the gesso to a length of heavy chain. Using acrylic paints, paint the inside with two coats of white and the outside with three coats of red. When the paint is dry, cut felt strips to circle the top and bottom of the can and cut strips to make vertical stripes on the sides of the can. Cover lid with pie-shaped segments of the felt.

Cut two circular shapes of felt to fit the inside of the can, and stitch a padding of another material between the felt layers. Glue felt strips to the inside rim of the can.

Paint the chain with a variety of colors of acrylic paints, and weave felt strips in the links to help muffle the sound. Wrap the can's handles with yarn and glue in place.

Try making one for each of your children or grandchildren. Personalize each can with the child's name cut from contrasting-colored felt.

To make the train chalkboard, cut shape from insulation board. Sand edges and coat board with gesso. When dry, gouge out ($1/16$ inch deep) the shape of the chalkboard. Then, gouge out a space for the chalk holder. Paint board with acrylics; glue in the chalkboard. Cut a molding strip ½x1½x16 inches; stain and glue in place. Spray chalk holder with clear enamel.

For suction dart board, cut a circle from insulation board. Sand, coat with gesso. Paint board; let dry, then spray with clear enamel.

Make the llama tack board from insulation board. Sand and paint board with gesso, then with acrylics. Finish with clear enamel.

To make the clown toss game, cut two triangles from wood or insulation board; glue these to the back side of the clown shape, which is also cut from insulation board. Paint with gesso, acrylics, and clear enamel. Make bean-filled felt bags, using the food patterns, at right.

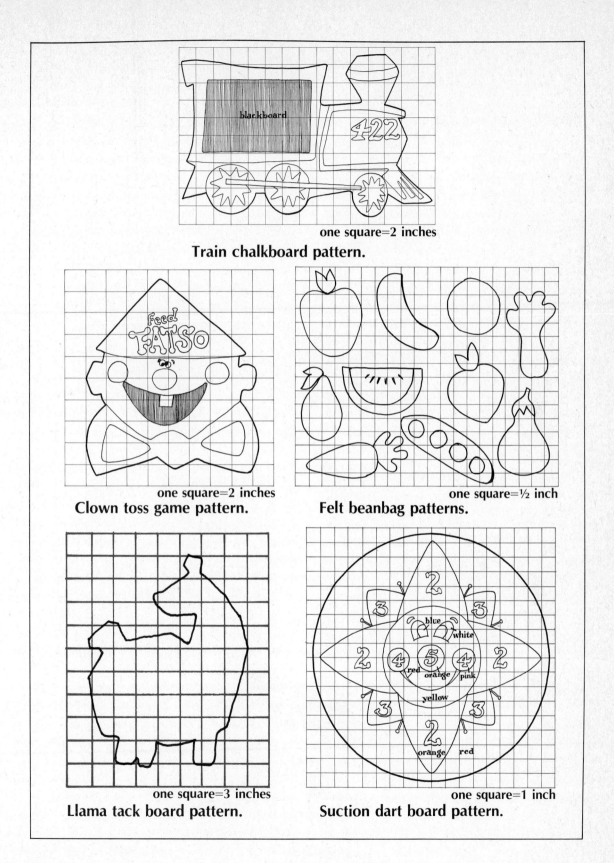

one square=2 inches
Train chalkboard pattern.

one square=2 inches
Clown toss game pattern.

one square=½ inch
Felt beanbag patterns.

one square=3 inches
Llama tack board pattern.

one square=1 inch
Suction dart board pattern.

Easy-to-assemble puzzles that will delight youngsters on your gift list.

These easy-to-assemble puzzles prove that good things come in both large and small packages. The patchwork pony can be used as a big floor puzzle or can be glued to a heavy backing for a child's bedside rug. Make one from durable indoor-outdoor carpet remnants. Below the pony is a perky piglet from Winnie the Pooh stories; the puzzle is cut from a single pine board. The owl puzzle is also cut from a pine board and slips into a wooden frame. The cookie cutter puzzle, lower left, has a heavy cardboard base with surprise pictures painted under the five cookie cutter puzzle pieces.

To make these highly unusual puzzles, use the patterns that are pictured on the opposite page. The patterns are drawn to a scale of 1 square equals 1 inch. To use the patterns to the best advantage, redraw them onto a piece of paper that has been marked off in 1-inch squares.

To make the pony puzzle, gather up some 9x9-inch indoor-outdoor carpet squares in complementary colors. (Purchase sample pieces from a carpet store.) You'll need a total of 29 pieces; eight gold (A), ten blue (B), and eleven red (C). Following the sketch on the opposite page, draw the pieces on the back side of the carpet with chalk. Cut the top part of the carpet with a mat knife; use sharp scissors for cutting the rubber section. (The rubber backing shreds if it is cut with a knife.) For a younger child, make a paper tracing of the outline on a large sheet of brown wrapping paper to help him in putting the puzzle together. Once the puzzle is put together, number the pieces on the back side, and key the numbers on the large-sized tracing you made from wrapping paper.

The piglet puzzle takes a piece of ¾-inch pine that measures 16½x11½ inches. Sand the board lightly and draw the piglet shape onto the board, following the sketch on the opposite page. Cut out the puzzle pieces with a saber saw, using a metal-cutting blade. Begin cutting at a junction of lines. Hold the blade almost flat to the surface to begin, then gradually turn it in to start. (The neck is a good place to start cutting.) Cut the large shapes, such as the body, first; then, cut the smaller ones, as they are less apt to break. Sand the pieces until they are smooth and will easily release from the puzzle form. Using acrylic paints, paint the sections pink, blue, and red according to the sketch. While the paint is drying on the puzzle pieces, rub burnt umber on the frame with your fingers.

Cut a fiberboard backing the same size as the top piece to fit, and glue it onto the frame. Nail the fiberboard to the frame at the corners. Arrange the puzzle pieces in place, then coat the entire puzzle with a matte varnish.

For the intriguing owl puzzle, cut a plaque 14x17½ inches from ¾-inch pine and a backing piece 15½x19 inches from ¼-inch plywood. Now, following the sketch, draw motifs to be cut out with a saber saw, onto the pine piece. Begin cutting at the top and work downward. Clamp the board when you get close to the bottom to hold it together. Sand all the pieces, then paint the motifs according to the sketch on the opposite page. Use numerous colors of acrylic paint. The decorative part of the owls should vary; use individual motifs—dots, lines, etc. Now, cut ¼-inch pine to fit around the edges to frame and hold the puzzle pieces in place. (You will need two pieces that measure 15½ inches for the top and bottom and two pieces that measure 17½ inches for the sides.) Nail these pieces onto the plywood backing. Coat all the puzzle pieces and the frame with polymer medium finish for longer wear.

To make the cookie cutter puzzle, select five cookie cutters and trace each shape on to a piece of heavy cardboard. For ease in cutting, choose simple shapes or simplify them while you are drawing them onto the cardboard. Cut out the designs with an artist's knife. Leave a ¹⁄₁₆-inch margin around each shape so that the cookie cutters will release easily. Sand the edges of the cardboard and coat the entire surface with gesso. Cut a piece of cardboard the same size as the first piece. Glue this backing to the top piece. Now, in the recessed areas, paint figures that depict the cutters used. (See the snowman and the chicken in the photograph at the left.) Use fluorescent paints. Be certain that you touch up the recessed edges with the fluorescent paint. To finish the project, give the puzzle a coat of clear enamel.

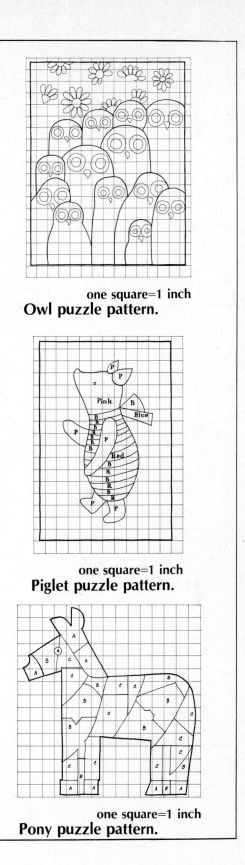

one square=1 inch
Owl puzzle pattern.

one square=1 inch
Piglet puzzle pattern.

one square=1 inch
Pony puzzle pattern.

chapter 6

CANDLES & CANDLEHOLDERS

In the seventeenth and eighteenth centuries, tallow candles were the best means of illumination in both the Old World and the New World. These forerunners of the light bulb were made from beef, pork, goose, deer, opossum, and bear grease. At best, they were inefficient and smoky.

Today, wax candles are made and used for pleasure rather than necessity. Improved materials and techniques have freed candlemakers from hoarding animal fats, and today the craft of candlemaking grows more popular with every year.

We've come a long way since candles were made and used out of necessity for illumination. Today, nearly every home has one or more decorative candles that are used to help create an atmosphere of warmth and charm. You can make many of these yourself.

The wide variety of new candle styles and simplified techniques are responsible for the soaring interest in do-it-yourself candlemaking. As a hobby, this craft affords great pleasure, stimulation, and challenge. With a little practice, you will be able to give beautiful hand-crafted candles and candleholders to your friends at a fraction of the retail price.

The fascinating craft of candlemaking is inexpensive and really quite simple. Only two materials are needed—a suitable wax and the proper-sized wick. And the only essential equipment is a heat source, a melting pot, a mold, and a thermometer.

With very little work and cost, you can set up a candlemaking corner in your own kitchen, using materials from the local hobby shop and paraphernalia from your kitchen cupboards.

The collection of candles at the left illustrates that it is not necessary to invest in candle molds if you use your imagination. Any container that will hold hot wax can be used to shape a candle. The wide variety of styles shown here were molded in tart, gelatin, aspic, and ravioli molds, cone-shaped pastry tubes, paper and foil candy and cupcake liners, plastic measuring spoons, soup ladles, and cookie cutters.

To employ some of these utensils as candle molds, you must use a little plastic clay. When using a cookie cutter or pastry tube, lay tube on a cookie sheet and seal it around the base with clay to prevent wax seepage. When using a soup ladle or any other utensil with a rounded base, use the plastic clay to keep the mold level while the wax hardens.

The wick is important in that it makes the candle burn properly. When you are using tall molds, set the wick in place before you pour the melted wax. Cut the wick longer than the candle. Thread it through the mold and tie the wick around a pencil across the top of the mold. This keeps the wick in position.

For short or stacked candles, insert the wick after the candle is made. Using a hot ice pick, make a hole down through the center of the candle. Make sure to cut the wick long enough for the entire candle. Thread the wick through the hole and fill the hole with melted wax. If stacking more sections, as with the stacked stars in the foreground of the picture, make a hole in the second shape, thread it onto the first shape, and add the melted wax. Let the wax harden before adding another layer.

A collection of candles molded in kitchen utensils.

HOW TO MOLD CANDLES

First, purchase materials at a hobby or craft shop. If you need help or have questions, discuss your project with the shop's proprietor.

MATERIALS NEEDED

When making candles, nothing is more important than working with the right materials. So, in order to start out right, heed the following.

Wax — There are several kinds of wax, each with separate qualities and characteristics. The best is a petroleum wax, 143/145 A.M.P. This wax is

hard and can be used for most candle projects. Another wax, 128/130 A.M.P., is good for short candles but not for tall ones. Do not use paraffin (a canning wax that can be bought in supermarkets), as it is too soft.

Save your old candles. These can be melted and remolded into small candles. Or, melt them and use them to decorate other candles.

Wicking — There are two types of wicks to choose from — woven cotton wicking and wire-core wicking. Woven cotton wicking is added

These are the things you'll need to make molded candles.

before the wax is poured. Use this type for all pillar candles when the wick can be held erect inside the mold. Wire-core wicking gives more consistent results because the wick burns more uniformly. After the candle has been unmolded, push a heated ice pick down through the center of the candle. Then, thread the wicking through the candle and secure it with melted wax.

The size of wick you need depends on the size of the candle and on the type of wax used. In most instances, use a medium-sized wire-core wick such as #44-24-18. If the flame goes out, try a larger size. If the flame smokes, use a smaller size. If you decide to use a woven cotton wick, try a #10 bleached woven wick in candles with a diameter of two inches or less, a 30-ply wick in 2- to 4-inch diameter candles, and at least a 40-ply wick in candles with over a 4-inch diameter.

Additives—There are many commercial products you can add to wax to alter its appearance, texture, and fragrance. These are coloring, wax scent, stearine, Crystalsheen, and mottling oil.

Coloring—Add color to melted wax with crayons, fabric dye, or candle wax color chips. A ¼-inch piece of crayon melted in hot wax will color 3½ ounces of melted wax. To use fabric dye, simply sprinkle the powdered dye evenly over completely melted wax in the melting pot. When using candle wax color chips, shave off small pieces and melt in wax that has been heated to 210 degrees.

Wax Scent—Use only commercial wax scents. Perfumes have water or alcohol bases and will not work. Both liquid and solid wax scents are available in a wide variety of fragrances.

Stearine (stearic acid)—This chemical will make wax harder and give it an opaque quality. It will also intensify the candle's color.

Crystalsheen—This plastic additive will give a gloss to the candle's surface.

Mottling Oil—The addition of oil causes tiny internal cracks in the wax, giving a colored candle a soft mottled appearance.

The second step in candlemaking is to assemble all your materials and equipment in one area before you start to work. You will need the following equipment: a double boiler with lid, a candy thermometer registering to 375 degrees,

a metal mold, a large container to hold water, a clean, soft cloth, and a knife or cheese cutter. Also, as wax spillage is common, cover work area with several layers of newspaper.

Next, use 143/145 A.M.P. petroleum wax. This is available in 11-pound slabs. Using a hammer and screwdriver, break up the wax so that it will fit in the melting pot. Put the wax in the top section of the double boiler with water in the bottom section, making sure that no water gets mixed in with the melting wax. Remember that wax is highly flammable, and as such, it should never come in contact with direct heat.

As the wax melts, prepare a clean, dry metal mold. Spray the inside of the mold with mold release so the candle will release easily. Then, wipe it with a soft, clean cloth.

Next, thread the wick through the hole in the bottom of the mold and bring it up through the mold. Tie the wick to a pencil and pull the wick so that the pencil is held firmly across the top of the mold. Holding the wick tightly, press plastic clay over the small hole and wick. Cut the wick one inch above the clay. Now, tape over the wick and the clay with masking tape.

When the wax is heated to 210 degrees, add any additives such as coloring or scent. (If you are using fluorescent colors, do not heat the wax to over 175 degrees.) Test the color by placing some hot colored wax in a cup of cool water. When cool, this is the true color.

Transfer the hot wax into a container with a spout if your double boiler does not have one. Then, using a hot pad, hold the mold at a slant and slowly pour the wax down the side of the mold. Pouring the wax in this manner prevents bubbles from being trapped in the liquid wax.

Place the wax-filled mold into a water bath—a container filled with cool water—and weight down the mold. Make certain that the water level is lower than the height of the mold, but higher than the wax level. The water bath will eliminate many of the candle's surface imperfections.

After about 45 minutes, the wax will have cooled enough to have shrunk. Break through the crust close to the wick and refill the well with wax heated to 210 degrees.

When the wax has cooled for eight hours, squeeze the mold to release the candle. It may be necessary to tap the end of the mold on a padded surface. If the candle still does not release, place it in the refrigerator for about 45 minutes and try it again.

When the candle is released, scrape off the ridge left by the mold, using a cheese cutter or knife. Polish the candle with a soft, dry cloth and then with a wet paper towel.

SURFACE DECORATIONS

Once the candle is polished, take it one step further by applying a surface decoration. You can do this by decoupage, dribble waxing, wax painting, antiquing, or sculpturing.

Decoupage—This involves applying a design or motif cut from paper to the candle. First, cut out the design with decoupage scissors. Then, heat an electric skillet to 230 degrees and place several layers of paper toweling in the skillet. Lay the cutout design, face down, on the toweling. When the design is heated, brush it with uncolored wax that has been heated to 210 degrees. Use tweezers to pick up the design. Then, transfer the waxed design onto a smooth candle. Now, glaze the candle by holding the wick and dipping it in 210-degree wax. Finally, immerse the candle in a cold water bath.

Dribble Waxing—Decorate your candle by dribbling several colors of melted wax down the sides of the candle. Purchase several colors of dribble wax at your hobby shop. Heat each color separately to 175 degrees in a small pot with a spout. Slowly pour the wax around the top edge of a smooth candle. The wax will dribble down the side. Repeat with other colors.

Wax Painting—Paint embossed candles with melted wax. Heat beeswax to 200 degrees and separate into small juice cans. Place cans in a large pan of boiling water and dye the wax. Using a cotton swab or sable brush, paint details of an embossed candle with an oil wood stain. After a few minutes, wipe off the stain.

Sculptured Candles—This is the most challenging type of surface decoration because it requires you to shape thin layers of wax into flowers. The flowers are then secured to the sides of a smoothly polished candle.

First, prepare sculpturing wax by mixing equal parts by weight of low-temperature and medium-temperature petroleum wax and beeswax. Heat wax to 170 degrees. Divide wax into two pots and dye one for petals and one for leaves. Wipe a cookie sheet sparingly with cooking oil. Then, pour a ⅛-inch thick sheet of wax onto the cookie sheet.

When wax is cool, lift it out and place it on several layers of paper toweling in an electric skillet that has been set at its lowest setting.

Petals and leaves are easily cut when the wax is warm. Use a craft knife to cut around cardboard patterns. For each flower, cut a 2-inch circle out of the petal wax. This will be the backing. Warm the petals and press edges between fingers to thin the edges and shape them.

Adhere the petals to each other and to the backing with melted wax. Overlap each petal. Warm the leaves, thin the edges, shape, and add the veins. Secure leaves to flowers. Pour a small amount of 170-degree wax on the backing of each flower and press onto the candle.

Safety precautions

Candlemaking is not dangerous if you take precautions. Heed this advice:
1. Keep hot wax out of children's reach.
2. Turn pot handle to back of stove.
3. Always use a thermometer.
4. Never heat wax to over 300 degrees.
5. Use hotpads when handling hot wax.
6. Never leave melting wax unattended.
7. Keep baking soda and a lid handy.

IN CASE OF FIRE: If wax catches fire in melting pot, smother fire with lid and remove pot from stove. If fire is caused by spilling wax on burner, turn off burner and sprinkle with baking soda. Never use water to extinguish a wax fire.

IN CASE OF BURNS: If hot wax spills on the skin, hold burned area in cool water. If skin is badly burned, do not peel off the wax. Contact a doctor.

HOW TO MAKE BEESWAX CANDLES

Beeswax candles are the easiest of all candles to make. There's no mess because the wax is not melted, dyed, or molded. You can make these candles by hand-rolling either smooth or honey-combed, predyed 8x16-inch sheets of beeswax around a piece of woven cotton wicking.

Beeswax usually rolls easily at room temperature, but if you have difficulty, hold the beeswax sheet under warm water for a few minutes. Then, place the sheet on a smooth, clean working surface. Cut the wick one inch longer than the size of the sheet you are using. Lay the wicking along the edge of the beeswax and press the wax firmly over the wicking so it will be held securely in place. The wax may crack a little, but this is not important. Roll the wax once more over the wicking and gently pull the wick at the top of the candle to make certain that it is held tightly in place. (The candle will burn longer if the wick is tightly covered.) Now, continue rolling the beeswax candle evenly and snugly until you reach the end of the sheet. If you want to make a thicker candle, continue rolling up more sheets.

Should you wish to decorate your candles with glitter or sequins, just pinch them or push them in place. They will adhere without glue because beeswax is naturally sticky.

8-inch beeswax candles are made by bending the 8-inch side of the sheet over and around a 9-inch wick. Use as many sheets as necessary for the desired thickness. Each sheet adds ½ inch. If you wish to make a 3-inch-diameter candle, you'll need 6 sheets of beeswax.

16-inch beeswax candles are made in the same way as the 8-inch candles, except this time bend the 16-inch side over and around a 17-inch piece of woven cotton wicking.

14-inch beeswax candles or candles of any height under 16 inches are made by carefully scoring a straight line across the wax sheet with scissors. Cut along this line, using scissors, a razor blade, or a craft knife.

Two 16-inch spiral candles can be made from one 8x16-inch sheet of beeswax. Score, then cut the beeswax diagonally from one corner to the other, making two triangles. Place a 17-inch wick along the 16-inch side and roll over the wicking as before.

Two-toned spiral candles can be made from two contrasting-colored sheets of beeswax. Score and cut each sheet of beeswax diagonally from corner to corner. This will make two candles. Place an 18-inch piece of wicking along the 16-inch side. Place the contrasting-colored triangle on top of the first triangle with the bottom edges even. Roll the candle. Pinch the top of the candle tightly around the wick. If you wish, use your finger to gently flare out the edges of the candles.

Alternating two-toned spiral candles are made by cutting the beeswax and wicking the same as for the two-toned spiral candle, above, except the second triangle should be cut one inch shorter and narrower than the first. Place the smaller triangle under the larger one, set the wick in place on the 16-inch side, and roll snugly. (Make a triple-toned candle by adding a third and smaller triangle.)

The designs of sculptured beeswax candles are limited only by your imagination. Experiment with various sizes and shapes of beeswax to see what different shapes or design motifs you can come up with. This is not only challenging, it is fun to do, too.

With very little effort, you can make candles in the shape of Christmas trees, flowers, mushrooms, snowmen, birthday cakes, animals, and anything else your imagination conjures up. Just remember that one or more layers of beeswax can be kneaded easily into shapes other than those of ordinary candles. The only requirement is to secure the wick snugly in the center portion of your creation. And, because beeswax burns slowly and is dripless, your designs will last a long time.

CUSTOM-MADE CANDLEHOLDERS

Improve on perfection by complementing your handcrafted candle with a custom-made holder. Together, they make a totally unique and personalized gift idea.

Once again, use your imagination, this time to visualize a novel candleholder idea. If you're a hoarder, you'll find you already have all or most of the materials you will need. Explore the exciting possibilities offered by plastic, glass, and cardboard food containers. Stack the containers with lids and blocks of wood to see the different designs you can create. Then, decorate the would-be candleholders by experimenting with string, yarn, paper, tape, foil, beads, pasta, paint, white glue, and ink. The results are sure to please and surprise you.

These delightful pierced-tin candlesticks are yours for the making.

These pierced-tin candlesticks were made from two 3½x4-inch funnels. With a wax crayon, draw a design, either freehand or by using a pattern, on the inside of each funnel. Place the funnel on a wood block, letting the spout hang over the edge. From the inside, hammer small holes ⅛ inch apart, using a 2-inch finishing nail. Carefully follow your pattern, making certain the holes are uniformly spaced.

To make the candlestick tops, use tin snips to cut the funnel top down ¾ inch in six sections. Curl each of these six sections forward with a pair of needle-nosed pliers.

Using two screw-in candleholders, glue the holders to the funnel tops with silicone glue. Allow them to dry and then spray-paint them silver. The tree in the same picture was made much the same way, using graduated funnels. To assemble, simply stack the funnels.

These fancy-fringed candleholders are a very unusual gift. The secret is in the stiffening—a mixture of ½ starch and ½ glue—which allows you to shape one-of-a-kind designs from ordinary fabric-trim fringe.

The containers are cans cut to various heights, with diameters slightly larger than the candles. Select fringe close to the height of the can. The mixture of starch and glue stiffens and adheres the fringe to the can. Dip the fringe in the mixture. Remove and squeeze out the excess water, mold, and then let dry overnight. To form loops and rays, work on a plastic-covered cardboard sheet with a cylinder the same size as the holder. Place the saturated braid against the cylinder and work the fringe into a pattern. When it dries, glue this design to the fringe-covered can and paint it with spray enamel.

Hurricane candles are natural people-pleasers. You can either make the candles yourself or purchase them. Then, purchase a wide assortment of clear glass containers. Decorate the containers or leave them plain.

All of these glass globes were collected from secondhand stores for less than $1.25. Keep your eyes open for unusual-shaped bowls, rose bowls, fishbowls, and drinking glasses. Place a candle inside and you'll have an instant gift that anyone will enjoy.

Unique, fancy-fringed candleholders.

Hurricane candles are people-pleasers.

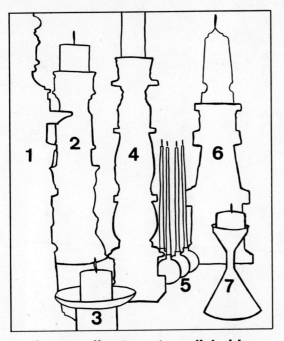

A classic collection of candleholders.

This classic collection of candleholders illustrates how you can make candleholders to reflect the life-style of everyone on your list.

Byzantine candleholders—These tall candleholders (1,2,4, and 6) are made from containers, slips of cardboard, and papier-mâché.

You'll need newspapers, a water jar, white glue, a 1-inch paintbrush, a razor blade, scissors, marking pen, masking tape, lightweight cardboard, corrugated cardboard, string, lace or braid trims, rickrack, paint, and containers such as cottage cheese cartons, jars, plastic containers with lids, and tin cans.

Select several containers and arrange them into a design you like, placing one or more strips of cardboard underneath each container. Then glue and tape all the pieces together.

Once you have the candleholder glued together, cover it with papier-mâché. Tear newspaper into 1½x1½-inch squares and 1½x1-inch strips, and apply them to the candleholder, which has been brushed with glue. Apply several layers, brushing with glue each time. Use long, narrow paper strips to go over the round surfaces and thin areas; use square strips to fill in the flat surfaces. After the final layer of papier-mâché is dry, coat it with gesso and let dry.

Now, apply your special finishing design. Using a marking pen, draw freehand designs where you want them. Brush these designs with glue, and place string, lace, braid, and edgings in place. Repeat until the design is completed. Then, brush over the trim with glue, and allow it to dry thoroughly before painting.

A dry-brush method of painting is used on some of these candlesticks. To accomplish this effect, use black acrylic paint for an undercoat. Cover the entire surface with the black paint; let it dry before adding the next coat of paint. Dry-brush the second coat of paint by using a brush with only a little paint on it. The second coat or dry-brush coat should be a lighter, complementary, or contrasting shade. Lightly brush across the surface of the holder. This technique allows newspaper shapes and the recesses in the trims to show through. (Experiment on scraps of paper first. Acrylic, enamel, or poster paints can be used for this method.) When the paint is completely dry, finish with one or two coats of clear glaze.

For the rub method of antiquing, paint various design areas with different colors of acrylic artist paints. Let the paint dry, then cover the entire surface with raw umber artist's pigment. Work into small area. When the pigment is barely dry, rub it off with a clean cloth. (Dampen the cloth, if necessary.) Let some of the dark color stay in the recesses and around the trim. Spray on several coats of clear liquid plastic, clear lacquer, or varnish for gloss, allowing each coat to dry before applying the next coat. Enamel paints also may be used for this method, but allow a much longer drying time between each of the coats.

Danish-style candleholder — Candleholder number 5 is a multiple taper holder made from Christmas tree ornaments. Remove the hooks and collars from four ornaments. Weight the balls with fine sand or liquid plaster of Paris and insert the four taper candles.

Kitchenware candleholders — Candleholders 3 and 7 can be turned out in assembly-line fashion. Use funnels, saucers, egg cups, and tumblers. Glue them together and give them a coat or two of spray paint. Candleholder 3 is a saucer glued on a spray can lid. Make candleholder 7 by gluing two funnels together.

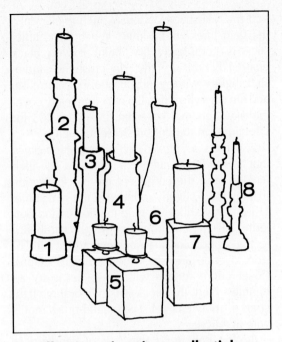

A collection of crafty candlesticks.

This collection of crafty candlesticks is a perfect example of how you can create first-rate originals from second-rate materials. Gayly colored paints and papers, all-purpose glue and gesso, ordinary glass bottles and jars of every description, wooden beads or blocks, and paper cups and plates—plus lots of imagination—are but a few of the principal ingredients necessary for making these one-of-a-kind candlesticks and candleholders.

The techniques used in making most of these novel candlesticks are simple versions of papier-mâché. The pair of dice in the foreground are made of precut, pressure-sensitive circle dots pressed onto wood blocks. The taper holders that you see on the right side are fashioned from beads, knobs, spools, and other wood scraps.

The selection is certainly varied, but you can expand it by employing your imagination. Choose a variety of shapes and colors—as large or small as you wish. Make some of the candlesticks short or slender and some tapered or tall. As you are designing and making the candlestick, keep in mind the person for whom you are making it. Consider his or her favorite colors, interests or hobbies, and tastes, whether they are contemporary or traditional. By doing this,

your handcrafted candlestick will be one of the most personalized gifts he or she will ever receive. It will long be a cherished, much admired gift that will glow and reflect a special friendship between the two of you.

1. Make this chubby candlestick by using any half-pint cardboard or plastic container. Tear newspaper into 2-inch squares. Dip the newspaper squares in white glue, and cover the container completely, including the bottom. Overlap the squares of newspaper. Next, dip heavy string or cord into glue, and shape it into a butterfly motif on the side of the container. Let the glue dry thoroughly, and then cover the entire container with crafter's gesso to seal the newspaper and string. When the gesso is dry, paint the container with any color of spray enamel. Hand-paint the butterfly and the string with an artist's brush and acrylic paint. After the paint dries, spray it with two or three coats of clear glaze—lacquer, varnish, or plastic. Let the candlestick dry for 24 hours, then antique it lightly, using an antiquing foam glaze.

2. This antique silver candlestick can be imported from your own kitchen. Leaving the lids on, stack, glue, and tape various-sized containers together. (This candlestick is comprised of three jelly jars, a spray can lid inverted to hold the candle, and a low plastic food container.) You may use glass, tin, plastic, or paper containers. Cut two circles from corrugated cardboard about ½ inch larger than the base of the jars. Cut another circle from lightweight cardboard to fit the base of the holder. Tape and glue the circles to the stack. Cut flowers and leaves from lightweight cardboard, bending the cardboard to conform to the curve of the jars. Glue some of the smaller flowers on the larger ones. Glue the flowers all over the surface of the candlestick. Use rubber bands to hold them in place while the glue is drying. Now, glue heavy string or cord around the bases of the containers and the tops of the jars. When the glue dries, crumple household aluminum foil that has been cut a little larger than the length and width of the holder into a loose ball. Open the foil and cut it into pieces, slightly larger than the shapes you are covering. Glue the pieces of foil individually until the entire surface has been covered.

Smooth the foil with your fingers or a cotton swab as you glue each piece. Don't, however, smooth out the foil completely. Leave some of the wrinkles in for the antiquing. When the glued foil dries, spray the holder with black enamel. Let it dry for a few minutes, then rub it with a cloth. This will give it an antique look.

3. *This catsup bottle lady* utilizes the same finishing technique as that given in the directions for candlestick No. 1. Use a bottle of any shape for the base, and for the top, a spray can lid inverted to hold the candle. Hand-paint the design with brush-on acrylic paint. Draw all the detail lines with India ink. Then, give the candlestick two coats of clear glaze.

4. *Make this stunning candlestick* by stacking an assortment of jars in an interesting arrangement and then by gluing them together. Invert a jar lid or plastic saucer on top to hold the candle. Using the papier-mâché technique, glue dampened colored or white paper towels to the jars. For color, glue pieces of torn tissue paper all over the layer of paper toweling. Allow this to dry overnight, then glue on decorative paper towel motifs of any design.

5. *Lady luck* will smile on you when you make and give these candleholders. Cut two 4-inch lengths from 4x4-inch wood. Sand the cubes and then paint them with several coats of shiny black enamel. When the paint dries, glue circles cut from adhesive-backed paper or vinyl, or buy precut pressure-sensitive labels, which are packaged in colors. Follow a die for placement of dots. Apply three or four coats of clear varnish, sanding between coats. Purchase inexpensive brass candle cups and attach them to the tops of the dice with epoxy.

6. *This sculptured candlestick* uses a slightly different technique. For the base, glue and tape stacked jars or bottles together, or use a Styrofoam pedestal-shaped base, glass lantern, and a spray can lid. Mix powdered papier-mâché (found in most craft supply stores) with a little water in a small, deep bowl. Keep the mixture tacky, but add more water if necessary. (It sometimes helps to add a little white glue.) Spread the mixture onto the candlestick, smoothing with your fingers as you go. Allow the candlestick to dry until the papier-mâché coating turns a gray color. With the papier-mâché mixture,

add the leaf shapes, about ¼ inch thick. Make the vein lines with a knife. When the candlestick is completely dry, paint it with black enamel. Let this dry, then dry-brush the candlestick lightly with green, turquoise, chartreuse, and olive acrylic paint. Do not completely cover the black enamel basecoat. (See page 105 for directions on the dry-brush technique.)

7. *Here's a simple, yet striking candlestick* that is made by cutting a 4x4 to a 6½-inch length. Sand the corners of the block smooth, making them slightly rounded at the same time. Using spray adhesive, glue the flower and butterfly designs cut from lightweight cardboard to the wood block. To achieve added dimension, overlap and stack the cardboard shapes. Cover entire surface with gesso; let it dry 20 minutes. Paint the block with two or three light coats of spray enamel. Then, hand-brush motifs with acrylics.

8. *You can build this pair of candlesticks* from an assemblage of objects that, under ordinary circumstances, you would throw away. Look around to see how many similar-sized items you can come up with, then start stacking an accumulation of beads and knobs, wood drapery rings and coasters, spools, slices cut from wood dowels, or what have you. Drill holes into the center of the pieces when necessary, then thread all the objects onto a metal rod. Fasten all of this together with a nut at the top and at the bottom of the rod. Or, if you wish, glue all of the pieces together with epoxy glue or white glue. Using high-gloss enamel, paint them in vivid colors. When the paint is dry, spray them with two or three coats of clear glaze.

After having read the directions for making the collection of crafty candlesticks, you should have the basics down pat. The result of your project, however, will depend on and vary according to the containers that you stack, the colors that you choose, and the design motifs that you use. Set your busy fingers to work, and begin creating vast numbers of expensive-looking candleholders from very inexpensive materials. Paint each of the items that you stack a different color, or paint the entire candleholder one color. But be certain that you give each of them a one-of-a-kind distinction.

The easy-to-make candlesticks shown at the right hold tall or short candles and will please the hostess of any party. They are all fashioned from such basic materials as wood knobs, several sizes of cardboard cylinders, and cores from rolls of tape, toilet tissue, and shelf paper. You might find all of these things hidden away on a seldom-used shelf or in a rarely opened drawer. You can easily vary the heights to suit your desires by gluing together two or more of the units. Paint the candleholders with enamel, acrylic, or poster paint.

Wood-stack candleholders like the crafty ones shown here can be made from any kind or combination of wooden items. Try stacking drawer knobs, large beads, empty spools of thread, blocks, scraps of lumber and wood turnings, drapery rings, and coasters. Paint holders with high-gloss enamel, either all one color or alternate the sections with contrasting colors.

The knobby candleholder, at left in the photo, is made by drilling holes in the center of eight 1-inch-square wood knobs. Spray-paint four of the knobs and the candle cup one color and the other four knobs another color. Assemble on a threaded rod, alternating colors. Fasten them together at the top and bottom with a nut.

To make the matching compote, center of the photo, use a 6-inch length of wood turning. Paint the turning in vivid stripes. Attach a large, round metal lid to the top of the turning with epoxy glue, and the project is completed.

The unusual candlesticks, far right in the photo, are made by gluing wood beads together. Varying the height of each candlestick makes for a most interesting arrangement. After the glue has dried, spray-paint the candlesticks. If the tapers won't fit into the holes, simply drill the holes a little larger.

The circle-and-cylinder candleholders, at right, are made of throw-away materials. The base for the candle cup, right, is three cores from large tape rolls glued together and painted. The other two holders are cylinders cut to different heights. Undercoat them with gesso, let them dry, and paint. Apply a finishing coat of glaze. To finish, glue on circles sliced from cylinders or pieces of dowel rods.

Wood-stack candlesticks.

Circle-and-cylinder candlesticks.

1.

2.

3.

4.

5.

6.

The glittering glow candles pictured here illustrate what you can do to dress up something that is plain and ordinary. By applying some glue, pieces of tissue paper, and cardboard egg cartons, and some paint, these once-unpainted candle cups have been transformed into jeweled candleholders flashing with brilliant color. Each cup will delight any of your friends.

Start by buying several clear glass candle cups, available at most variety stores. Set them in front of you on a covered work surface, and, throwing caution to the wind, dream up fanciful decorations. Don't limit yourself to the examples pictured here. Study the directions listed on this page and on the next, and with this information, create patterns of texture and brilliance that will bedazzle your friends. Whatever the design, your friends will enjoy the functional candle holders.

The jeweled candle chimneys are made from ordinary clear glass cups, refinished with a white glue solution, bits of colored tissue paper, and nail polish. The flower- and star-shaped holders are made from reworked cardboard egg cartons, tempera or poster paint, India ink, felt-tip pens, and nail polish.

With scented candles placed inside, candle cups make lovely gifts, especially for people who are hospitalized or otherwise confined at home. One of these delicate-looking gems will brighten up anyone's day.

And, they're so easy to make, even a child can make them without much supervision. Keep this clever idea in mind in case you ever need a craft project for a youth group. Think of how much fun your Scout troop could have making these for Christmas or Mother's Day gifts. Or, perhaps a church youth group would enjoy making these candle cups for the shut-in members of the congregation. The materials needed for making glittering glow candles are inexpensive and quick to collect. The project could be finished easily in three working sessions—one to cut and shape, one to paint, and one to assemble. In fact, even your women's club might be interested in these as a service project. They could be mass-produced to make enough to decorate individual food trays for special occasions at small hospitals, a particular ward in a large hospital, or nursing homes. The uses for these delightful candle cups are almost as endless as their design potential.

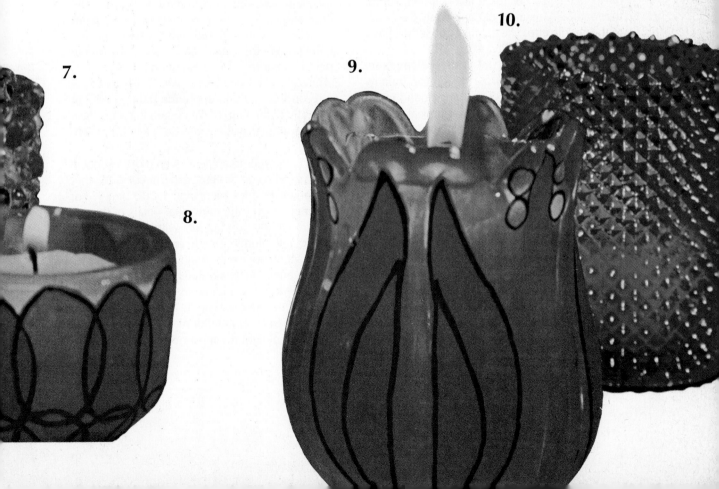

7.

8.

9.

10.

1. and 7. Jewel-glass chimneys—The decoration on these two candle cups is applied by using a tissue paper technique that is fully explained on page 113. Tiny many-colored dots of tissue paper are glued to a pebble-glass candle cup. If you're quite good with an artist's brush, forgo the more time-consuming tissue paper technique and use stained glass paints, which are available at most craft shops. Paint each pebble of the pebble-glass cup. This type of paint is translucent, so the candle's light will shine through even the heaviest painted areas.

2. Scalloped candle cup holder—Dress up a frosted candle cup with an egg carton holder. (See detailed explanation for egg carton construction on page 113.) Accurately cut your design from the egg carton. Form, assemble, and glue your holder. Using tempera or poster paint, paint the candleholder any color or colors. When the paint on the egg carton is dry, paint on any design motif you choose, or cut motifs from gift wrap paper and glue them to the candleholder. For the final finish, coat the entire candleholder with clear nail polish, clear glaze, or clear varnish.

3. Water lily candle cup—With a bit of imagination, you can transform several egg carton sections into a water lily candle cup. Stagger the petals in two or three layers. Then, repeat the motif with tissue paper and apply the petals to the candle cup. The gemlike cup is the center portion of the water lily.

4. Abstract candle cup—This contemporary beauty illustrates how your design can be anything you wish. Either copy things found in nature or just arrange shapes that appeal to you. Make this design from tissue paper or hand-paint the candle cup with two shades of nail polish. In order to effect overall unity, use the same design on the candle cup as you use on the candle cup holder.

5. Flame candle cup and candleholder—You can duplicate this candle cup and candleholder easily by combining an egg carton candle cup holder, complete with handle, and a tissue paper-decorated candle cup. Cut the flame motif from orange and yellow tissue paper and glue on the pieces, overlapping one another. Then, outline each motif with black tempera paint to create a stronger contrast. Repeat the flame motif when you shape the egg carton candle cup holder so as to achieve a coordinated effect. This duet is a sight to behold.

6. Perky posy candle cup—This candle cup is as easy to make as it is appealing. Simply cut little flowers from blue tissue paper and glue them at random around the cup. Then, complete the candle cup project by using black tempera paint to outline the flowers and red to color the center of each flower.

7. See explanation given for number 1.

8. Stained glass candle cup—Make this elegant candle cup with oval-shaped pieces of tissue paper. Glue the ovals on the candle cup in an overlapping pattern. Then, in order to highlight the design, outline each oval shape with black tempera or poster paint. If you wish, make a matching candle cup holder.

9. Tulip candle cup—The design of this candle cup carries the original design of the cup one step further. The cup's design is that of a tulip, but without the color and the detail. Apply abstract petal shapes cut from tissue paper to the cup, and outline these shapes with black tempera paint, a felt-tip pen, or poster paint.

10. Solid color candle cup—Pebble cups generally are easy to find, but not necessarily in the color that you are looking for. Don't let this stop you, though. Purchase a clear pebble cup, and either paint it with stained glass paint or cover it with colored tissue paper, making certain that the paper adheres tightly to the pebble texture. Use a solution of two parts white glue and one part water. Brush this mixture on the cup and apply the paper, pressing it tightly to the cup. Make certain that the edges are flat and that there are no air bubbles left.

NOTE. In order to achieve even more variety in your candle cup designs, experiment with other materials besides paint and tissue paper. For example, cover the individual petals of the egg carton candle cup holders with printed cotton fabric, felt, aluminum foil, or vinyl-coated tape. Also, don't forget the highlighting possibilities of materials such as glitter, sequins, and tiny glass beads. Try adding an element of surprise to the glittering glow candle—a rhinestone dewdrop on an inner petal or maybe a tiny ladybug—just to delight the most observant people.

These directions for decorating candle cups are not complicated. In fact, the following paragraphs will explain how easy it is to decorate candle cups and to make candle cup holders. Remember that this step-by-step instruction is only a guideline. After successfully making one of the illustrated designs, experiment with your own ideas and designs.

Jewel-glass chimneys—First, cut a variety of designs from colored tissue paper (Fig. 1). Next, lightly brush a glass cup with a solution of two parts white glue and one part water. Press the tissue designs to the cup (Fig. 2). Be sure that you have all the edges of the tissue paper pressed flat against the glass with no air bubbles underneath the paper. Then, brush the cup with more of the glue and water solution.

When the cup dries, coat it with clear nail polish, clear glaze, or clear varnish. If you like, accent the designs by outlining them with black tempera paint, using a very fine artist's brush or a felt-tip pen (Fig. 3).

Instead of using the tissue paper technique, try painting your design directly onto the candle cup, using stained glass paint, colored nail polish, tempera, or poster paint. When dry, always apply a finish coat of clear nail polish, glaze, lacquer, or varnish.

Flowerlike chimney holders—Start by cutting one cup from an egg carton. Trim it to equal height on all sides (Fig. 5). Next, fill the cup completely with sand. Cut a piece of cardboard to fit the top of the cup (Fig. 6); glue this lid to the opening of the cup (Fig. 7), and trim the lid so that it is flush with the sides of the cup. Now you have a solid, weighted base for the candle cup holder.

For the decorative top of the holder, cut a large flower shape from egg-carton cardboard (Fig. 8). After soaking the cut pieces in water for about four minutes, place them over the bottom of a plain drinking glass or a candle cup (Fig. 9). Hold the cardboard to the glass with string or rubber bands. When the cardboard dries, remove it from the glass and glue it to the inverted sand-filled base (Fig. 10). (Figs. 11, 12, and 13 show other interesting designs.) Then, paint the holder with tempera or poster paint and finish it with two or more coats of clear nail polish, glaze, or varnish.

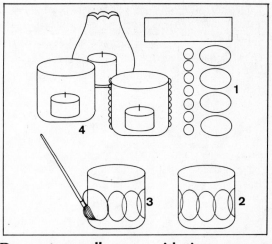

Decorate candle cups with tissue paper.

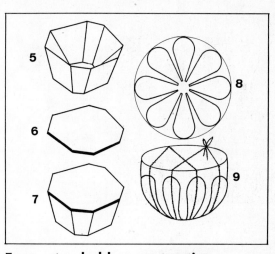

Egg carton holder construction.

Flowerlike chimney holder ideas.

Baker's clay modeling projects offer unlimited gift possibilities.

chapter 7

GIFTS CHILDREN CAN MAKE

If you are a youth group leader or a mother, you know how much fun children have making things with their hands. You also know how proud a child is of his finished project. On the following pages you'll find lots of unusual, inexpensive gift ideas, specially geared for children from the ages of six to twelve. Select one of the easy ideas, then help your child get started on a gift for Grandmother, Dad, or Brother and Sister. With the little hands happily occupied, you may even have a little extra time to undertake a gift project, too.

BY NIMBLE FINGERS

When your children are bored on a rainy day, set them to work making gifts for friends or family. Contained in the next twelve pages are gifts that most children with nimble fingers can make without the help of Dad or Mom—gifts using toy balloons, mosaics of tiny pieces of colored paper, toys using simple wood construction or papier-mâché, or simple rubbings. Nimble-finger techniques will blow away boredom on any cold, rainy day.

Baker's clay modeling projects are fun to make, the materials are kitchen staples, and the cost is minimal. You'll need the following:
  4 cups of unsifted flour
  1 cup salt
  1½ cups water
  cookie sheet
  aluminum foil
  cookie cutters
  watercolor brush
  water-base acrylic paints *or*
    permanent felt-tip ink pens
  clear fixative/lacquer/or varnish
The variety of projects pictured on the opposite page are good examples of the different creations a child can make easily.

If the children are very young, let them experiment with the dough before starting out on any projects. And warn them not to nibble at the dough. It isn't edible.

Make the dough by mixing the flour, salt, and water. Do not halve or double the recipe. Make a separate batch for each child or project. Then, set the dough on a large piece of aluminum foil, and let your child create all sorts of figures, jewelry, and wall plaques by molding the dough like ordinary clay.

Mold the dough with your hands or pat it down and cut it with cookie cutters, depending on the shape and design desired.

After the children have made the design, place the project on a cookie sheet and bake in an oven, preheated to 350°, for one hour or until the dough-clay is hard.

Allow the clay to cool, and then give each child a watercolor brush and let him weave a pattern on the hardened clay with water-base acrylic paints (these paints will wash off with soap and water, making cleanup easy), or use a permanent felt-tip ink pen for his creations. As a final loving touch to the gift, give each project a shiny finish with a coat or two of clear fixative, lacquer, or shellac (varnish). When the finish is completely dry, string the hanging gifts with a length of ribbon or some gold cord and gift wrap them appropriately.

Five handcrafted gifts that children will have a lot of fun making.

If you have children, you already know how much a child enjoys giving something that he has made himself. Teachers are aware of this fact, and they usually have their students make a special art project for Mom or Dad before special holidays. Remember the plaster of Paris handprint, or the family portrait in finger paints that you received for Christmas when your child was only a first or second grader?

Your child's teacher didn't just dream up these projects to give the children something to do. She was teaching them a valuable lesson. The children were exploring the crafts, working with their hands to improve their coordination, exercising their unfolding imaginations, learning a new form of self-expression, and learning to share things with others.

As a parent, you can continue this teaching process at home. The next time your child asks 'What can I do now?', let him make a special handcrafted gift for someone.

The five handcrafted gifts above are made by utilizing unusual crafts that will intrigue your child, and so, keep him happily occupied for many hours. Each process is quite simple, and the necessary materials are inexpensive and readily available. In fact, you probably have most of them around the house. Think of all the fun your child will have making a sand cast wall plaque, a mosaic place mat, a set of wooden bookends, or a papier-mâché sheep bank or doll.

All of these projects belong to the children, but you help them a great deal by organizing the activity. Assemble all the materials that will be needed ahead of time, guide the use of the equipment, and direct cleanup after completion of the project. Once the projects are under way, avoid laying down a multitude of rules for the children to follow. A lengthy verbal list of dos and don'ts will only spoil the fun and hinder creativity. And remember that your child's work is an expression of himself and is highly vulnerable to attack. So, praise his efforts rather than criticize. Who cares if the sheep's tail looks like a fifth leg or if your child's flowers don't look at all similar to those in Mother Nature's garden? Encourage your child to paint, draw, or mold things as he sees them, not as you think they should be.

Each of the crafts is explained in detail on the following pages. For the maiden voyage, you'll probably be involved in the project, but once your child has mastered the technique, he should be given free rein. From then on, he's on his way to a rewarding experience with crafts.

SAND CASTING

Materials:

1. bag of sand
2. plaster of Paris
3. flexible container
4. old tools and utensils
5. scoop
6. plastic pail or pitcher
7. large brush
8. gummed picture hanger
9. food coloring (optional)
10. spray shellac (optional)
11. Lots of newspapers

Sand casting can be messy, so work in the backyard, basement, or garage.

Start by pouring sand into a dishpan or similar flexible container. Don't fill it to the brim—leave a few inches for the plaster. Then, pour in enough water to wet the sand. Help the water penetrate the sand by using a scoop or your hand. Pat the sand down with your hands. Brush away excess sand from edges of pan.

Draw a design in the sand with your fingers, an old tool, or utensil. Each depression you make allows room for plaster. If you don't like a design, just 'erase' it and start over.

Mix the plaster with water in a pail or pitcher. Instructions are on the package. Dissolve any lumps with your fingers. If you want colored plaster, add a little food coloring. Mix it thoroughly, or let it streak in swirls.

Pour plaster slowly onto design, letting it spread into all the depressions. Cover the sand surface with about ½ inch of plaster. When you're finished, pour out any plaster left in the pail. It will be hard to pry loose if you let it set. Never pour wet plaster down a sink!

When the plaster has set, carefully lift out the plaque with your hands. Lightly brush away excess sand until you can see the design. Don't try to brush it all off—it can't be done. When the plaque is completely dry, you can spray it with clear shellac. Apply a gummed picture hanger to the back and it is all finished.

Dampen sand.   **Mix plaster of Paris.**

Make depressions.   **Pour plaster.**   **Lift out plaque.**

Cut tiny bits of paper.

Glue onto poster board.

Glue on plastic ribbon.

Seal with clear plastic.

MOSAIC PLACE MAT

Materials:

1. poster board
2. paste
3. scissors
4. scraps of paper
5. transparent plastic
6. pencil
7. perforated plastic ribbon

Cut the poster board to a 14x18-inch rectangle. Draw the basic outline of the design on the poster board. The poster board may be any color you choose—white, black, red metallic, or any other color. Cut out bits of paper for the design—construction paper, gift wrap paper, wallpaper, foil, magazines, or any other type of paper you have around the house.

For a special gift, make a set of four place mats. They can be all the same design or different designs. The choice is yours.

This same paper mosaic technique may also be used to make coasters. The principle is the same, you just work on a smaller scale. Cut six 4-inch squares of cardboard or poster board. Draw your design on the cardboard, cut bits of paper, glue them in place, and seal the design with transparent adhesive plastic.

It takes patience! But, all those little pieces of paper must be glued to the poster board one by one. Use paste or glue and finish one area before pasting further. Try not to paste too many different colors in a small area. Let the pieces vary in size and shape. As you glue the pieces of paper to the poster board, let some of the poster board peek through a little so you can maintain the appearance of an authentic mosaic craft technique.

For a finishing touch, highlight the design with some unusual material, such as perforated ribbon (available in hobby and display stores).

To protect your work and to allow the place mat to be cleaned with a damp sponge, seal it with transparent, adhesive plastic. Cut the plastic to size, allowing a little extra to tuck under the edges. The place mat is now ready to be given to someone.

Tape legs to balloon.

Cover with papier-mâché.

Glue yarn on balloon.

Paint face and legs.

PAPIER-MÂCHÉ SHEEP BANK

Materials:
1. balloons
2. white glue
3. small skein of yarn
4. masking tape
5. tempera paint and brush
6. newspaper
7. wheat paste
8. scissors
9. empty egg carton
10. pie tin or plastic dish
11. paper drinking cups

To make the sheep bank, first inflate and knot a long balloon. Now, make the sheep's legs from paper cuts. Cut a piece from the side of the paper cut to 1x2 inches, with the top half flat. Roll up and tape the rest of leg section. Then, tape legs to the balloon. To make the nose, snip off one of the raised dividers from an egg carton. If it's not already slit down the middle, cut a small opening. Then, tape the nose to the front end of the balloon.

Cover the sheep (except for the tip of the nose) with two coats of papier-mâché, and let the surface dry. Cut two slits near the nose for inserting ears and a bigger slit on the back of the bank for coins.

Now, cut yarn into small pieces of equal length. Wind each piece into a small curlicue. With white glue, attach the yarn curlicues to the sheep's body (except the face and legs). When the glue is completely dry, paint the yarn. For a tail, braid together nine short strands of yarn and glue them in place.

It is now almost finished. Cut two cardboard ovals for ears and glue them in place. Then, paint the face and legs. Don't forget to add some dots for eyes. Now the bank is ready to give, but first drop in a penny for luck!

Other animal banks may be fashioned in much the same manner. For example, try taping two balloons together to make a giraffe. Or, use round balloons to make a piggy bank. Regardless of what balloon you use, always apply two coats of papier-mâché.

120

SPRAY-CAN DOLL

Materials:
1. balloons
2. wheat paste
3. small skein of yarn
4. felt scraps
5. old nylon stocking
6. newspaper
7. tempera paint and brush
8. adhesive tape
9. paper napkin
10. scraps of cardboard
11. spray can

This project is fun from the very beginning. Blow up a balloon, and tie a knot in the bottom of the balloon to keep the air in. Then, twist the top end to form a head. Apply adhesive tape to the twisted section to hold it. Next comes the papier-mâché body. To make the paste solution, read the directions on the wheat paste sack. It's a messy process, so protect yourself. Dip strips of torn newspaper through the mix-ture and wind them around the balloon. Continue dipping and winding the newspaper strips until the balloon has been covered at least twice. Cover all but the bottom one-fourth.

While the papier-mâché is still wet, pull a nylon stocking tightly over the figure and knot it at the top of the head. To tighten the stocking, also tie a knot around the neck and the bottom. Let the papier-mâché dry.

To make arms, glue on double-thick scraps of paper napkins below the head. Insert oval-shaped scraps of cardboard and glue them to the napkin arms to make hands. Paint the head one color and the body another. When dry, glue on felt eyes and a mouth.

Cut off the tails of nylon at the top and bottom. Trim an edge off the bottom so that the doll will stand straight over a spray can.

To make the hair, wind yarn around an 8-inch piece of cardboard 25 times. Knot the yarn in the middle. Snip the folded ends, glue the hair in place, and you're done.

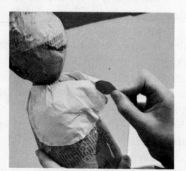  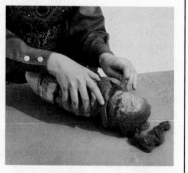

Twist and tape balloon. **Cover with papier-mâché.** **Slip on nylon stocking.**

Attach arms and hands. **Wind yarn around card.** **Tie yarn in the middle.**

BOOKENDS

Materials:

1. metal bookends
2. ⅛-inch balsa wood
3. two pieces of 1x6 pine (6 inches long)
4. coping saw
5. screen molding
6. sandpaper
7. glue
8. tempera paint and brush
9. vise
10. felt
11. model knife
12. shellac (optional)
13. a piece of scrap lumber
14. rubber bands
15. wood grater or rasp

Pencil a few guidelines on each pine block. The 1x6s may need to be trimmed to match the width of the bookends. Then, secure the block in a wood vise, and saw along the guidelines with a coping saw. Sand the edges smooth and straight. If the edges turn out jagged, use a wood grater or rasp to file them down quickly. Then, sand the rest of the block, working with the grain, not across it.

Apply glue to the outside of the metal bookend, and press the wooden block to it. Holding the block firmly to the bookend, wrap a few rubber bands tightly around the two. Let the glue dry completely before removing the rubber bands. Next, cut a strip of sculptured screen molding to fit the bottom of the bookend, and glue it in place. Paint the entire bookend, using tempera, acrylic, or enamel paint.

Draw a daisy design on the ⅛-inch balsa wood. Cut out the design, using a model knife. Use smooth, even knife strokes so as to achieve a more professional look. Paint the pieces of balsa wood with tempera paint, and, when dry, glue them to the bookends. If you like, brush on clear shellac to protect the paint. The final step is to glue a piece of felt on the inside of the bookends and on the bottom.

Cut 1x6s to size.

Sand edges smooth.

Glue board to bookend.

Paint the bookends.

Cut balsa wood motif.

Glue on the design.

Rubbings allow the unartistic to produce artistic wall hangings.

A hobby showcase for collections.

Sleepy owl wall decoration.

Children of all ages will love to make rubbings once you introduce them to this ancient craft. A fantastic picture, suitable for framing, can be rubbed from practically any hard surface with an interesting texture. Look around for likely items—tire treads, vegetable graters, playing cards, plastic straws or straw, or cut paper. These are just a few items you can use.

First, select the items you want to rub. Arrange flat items on a board and lay newsprint, rice paper, or shelf paper over them. Tape the paper to the board at the corners.

Rub the paper with wax crayons, graphite sticks, or conté crayons. Use the whole length of the crayon, being careful not to smudge the paper. Rub lightly and evenly first, working from the middle to the outside edges.

When finished, remove the paper, spray with fixative, and frame the picture.

Children will enjoy making a hobby showcase for Dad's arrowhead collection display or for an older brother's fossil collection.

Use ⅛-inch hardboard to make the showcase backing; cut the board to suit the size of the collection (this board is 12x18 inches). For the border, use ¼x½-inch balsa wood; use ¼x¼-inch balsa wood for the dividers.

Arrange dividers in the order that best suits the collection's various categories. White glue will hold the collection and the balsa wood in place. If you like, enamel the backing before gluing the dividers or the collection.

This sleepy owl wall hanging, above, is a delightful gift for Grandmother. Your children will have great fun making it from pinecones, camellia pods, acorns, and a tree branch. Or, use other natural materials such as seeds, nuts, shells, driftwood, pebbles, or fossils.

On paper, draw a simple outline of the design you choose. Cut out the main parts of the drawing for use as a pattern. Trace around the pattern on heavy cardboard and cut out.

Glue dried material securely to the cardboard pattern. If using pebbles, use an epoxy cement. The main body of the owl is made by overlapping pieces of pinecones. Start gluing these pieces from the outside edges and then work toward the middle. Add acorns for eyes and a seedpod beak. When all the pieces are glued on the cardboard and have been allowed to dry, carefully brush the design with shellac.

Make a background for your design from heavy cardboard or light plywood. Cut a piece of fabric, such as burlap, one inch larger than the board. Glue the fabric to the board, lapping the raw edges over the back. Place the design on the covered background and glue on the main pieces. Attach a picture hanger to the back.

Making nature pictures is an educational experience for a child. Encourage your child to collect an assortment of leaves, shells, feathers, seeds, rocks, or butterflies. Then, help him arrange them on a matte board or a poster board. Glue the collection in place with white glue, then let your child decide whether he wants to keep and display the collection or give it away to one of his friends.

'Thing keepers,' decorated tin boxes that hold everything from buttons to paper clips, are great gifts for adults that children will have a lot of fun designing and decorating.

These, top right, are made from metal movie cans, but they also can be made from round tin cookie, candy, or fruitcake boxes.

Line the inside of the cans with felt, and begin to decorate the outside. Paint the outside with enamel, or glue fabric all over the surface. Decorate the lids with felt cutouts, enamel paint, or hobby shop decals.

For the spin paint abstract design on the two boxes at the right of the picture, place the painted lids on an old or covered phonograph turntable. As the turntable revolves, drop plastic paint onto the lids from squeeze bottles, a few drops at a time.

Nature pictures—an educational experience as well as a delightful gift.

These owl and pussycat decorative potholders are easy enough for children to make. Cut an owl outline from two pieces of 7x8-inch brown felt. Cut circles from brown and yellow felt for eyes and cut tan felt for wings and beak sections. Glue the eyes, wings, and beak to one piece of the dark brown felt, using rubber cement. Then, glue the two brown pieces together. Make the pussycat the same way. Cut the outline from two 7x8-inch pieces of brown felt. Cut out the inner tan sections and the eyes. Glue the inner sections to the brown felt and then glue the two felt pieces together. With a felt-tip marking pen draw on features.

Children will have fun making wastebaskets from 2-gallon ice cream cartons and glossy paper. With vinyl adhesive, glue 2x9-inch red and white strips to the midsection of the carton. Glue a 2-inch strip of blue paper to the top and bottom, overlapping the red and white strips. To finish, glue on white stars.

Rock paperweights can be a personalized gift. Have the children search the creek beds for smooth water-tumbled rocks. Then let them create their own designs with enamel paint and decals. Paint one design on the rock, leaving the rest of the rock its natural color, or paint the entire rock one color, with a design on top. For instant results, use decals instead of hand-painted designs. After the paint is dry, spray the rock with lacquer or fixative. To personalize the paperweight, paint the receiver's name on the back of the rock.

These lacy napkin rings get their shape from an unlikely source—plaster bandages that have been molded around a glass.

Fold a 4-inch-wide plaster bandage in half and wrap it twice around a 2-inch-diameter glass jar. Slide the bandage off the jar and dip it in water. Then, rewrap it around the jar. Smooth the bandage surface with your fingers and let it set for a few minutes. Gently slide the ring off the bottle and let it dry thoroughly. When dry, spray the hardened bandage with white paint. Decorate the edges and center of the bandage by gluing lace, seam binding, ribbon, or rickrack in place with some white glue.

Decorated tin 'thing keepers'.

Decorative potholders.

Wastebasket magic.

Rock paperweights.

Easy napkin rings.

MORE GIFTS...WITH DAD'S HELP

On the following pages you'll find a selection of old-time favorites. With a little help from Dad, children can make these gifts for their brothers, sisters, and classmates.

Children won't have any difficulty getting Dad in the workshop to help—after all, these are the toys he played with a few years ago. In fact, the only trouble they will have is in getting Dad to continue working after the first toy is made. He'll be very busy playing with the finished woodworking project.

Besides the fun aspects of making these toys, there are some important things that can be taught and learned. All of the toys involve the use of power tools, which must be operated safely. Also, the children can benefit from Dad's skill and supervision during this step.

With the park-pond sailboat, any child will dream of putting out to sea. The 23½-inch-high model is made from ½-inch solid pine, ⅜-inch dowel rods, tin, and a fabric sail.

Use ½-inch pine to cut out the three hull sections and the two cabin sections. Then, cut a centerboard from tin. With pliers, wrap the bottom tip of the tin around a bolt. Bend the top of the centerboard at a right angle ¾ inch from the top. Saw a slot 7¾ inches, beginning at the

Park-pond solid pine model sailboat.

Sailboat pattern drawn to scale.

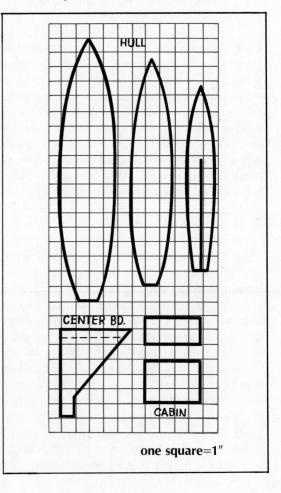

one square=1"

squared end of the boat's bottom section. Slide the centerboard through the slot and glue the five sections together with waterproof glue.

For the sail, connect 10 inches of a ⅜-inch dowel to a 17½-inch length of ⅜-inch dowel with two screw eyes and string. Make a sail of lightweight fabric. Insert mast in a ⅜-inch hole on deck. Tie free end of boom to stern with a 6½-inch string plus two screw eyes.

Give a child a spool racer, and he'll soon forget about all of his model cars. This spool racer, with its rubber-band motor, will really go on a smooth surface. To make it, use an empty thread spool, a ¼-inch dowel three inches long, a bead, a rubber band, and two small nails. Wrap most of a 4-inch rubber band around the nails, and thread the remainder through the spool and bead. Slip the dowel through rubber loop protruding from the bead, and it's ready.

This old-time paddle-wheeler will conjure up dreams of the old riverboat days and Huckleberry Finn. Cut the hull and wheelhouse from ½-inch pine. The hull is 8x4 inches with a pointed bow and U-shaped stern. Cut a 2¾x1½-inch hole in the stern to accept the 2½x1½-inch paddle wheel (see diagram below). Glue the wood block wheelhouse sections to the hull with waterproof glue. Place a rubber band on either side of the lap-jointed paddle wheel, and slip washers over the ends of the rubber bands. Insert the paddle wheel, looping the rubber band ends over notches in the stern 'legs'. Finish with two coats of waterproof varnish.

Spool racer with rubber band motor.

Old-time paddle-wheel boat.

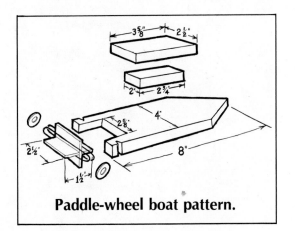

Paddle-wheel boat pattern.

Hummer buttons are easy to make and will provide a child with many hours of fun. This hardboard model will long outlast the plastic version of today. Cut ⅛-inch hardboard discs with a saw in 3-, 2½-, and 2-inch diameters. Drill two holes ½ to 1 inch apart in each of the three discs. Next, drill two holes in each of the two ⅜-inch dowel rod handles. Thread the string through the discs and handles.

The shepherd's flute requires some bamboo and pine to make. The flute has a hole for each finger, a notch, and a pine plug. Begin by mak-

ing two cuts in a length of bamboo. Cut through a solid nodule and just before the next one, so you have a tube with a bottom. Sandpaper the ends smooth. Next, drill four ¼-inch holes. Cut a notch as shown in the line drawing on opposite page. Carve a round pine plug to fit the hole, then square off the top of the plug ⅛ inch. Insert plug and cut both the bamboo and the plug at an angle. (See sketch on page 129.)

To make quoits, a ring toss game, cut six circles from ⅛-inch hardboard, using a jigsaw. The circles are 5½ inches in diameter with a

Hardboard-hummer buttons.

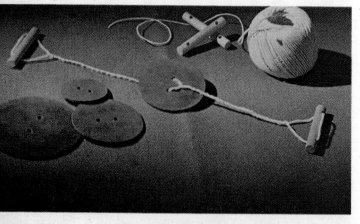

Bamboo and pine shepherd's flute.

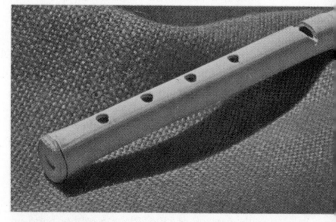

Hardboard quoits and ring post.

Pill-in-the-bottle.

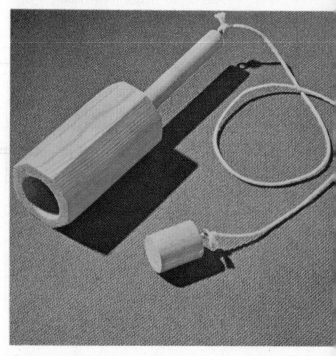

3¼-inch center hole. For the ring post, use a 5x5x¾-inch pine board. Drill a ½-inch hole in the center of the base and insert a 6x½-inch dowel. Paint the rings and post.

To make the pill-in-a-bottle toy, drill a 1-inch hole 2 inches deep on one end and a ½-inch hole 1 inch deep on the opposite end of a 3-inch piece of 2x2 lumber. Plane off the sides of the 2x2 to an octagonal shape. Insert a ½-inch dowel, 4 inches long, for the handle. The 'pill' is a 1-inch length of ¾-inch dowel. Connect it to handle with screw eyes and 20 inches of string.

The monkey-on-a-swing toy will fascinate children of all ages as they squeeze the handles and watch the monkey do his tricks. This 10½-inch-high toy is made of screen molding, pine, 20-gauge wire, and string. The two upright handles are ¾-inch screen molding 10½ inches long. Drill two string holes ½ inch apart, starting ¼ inch from the top of each handle. Slightly round the ends of the 2½-inch pine, which connects the handles, by sanding down the edges. Connect the pine to the handles with two nails driven in 4¾ inches from the top. Cut the monkey from screen molding, making the arms 1¼ inches long, the legs ⅞ inch long, and the body 1⅜ inches long. Drill small holes in the arms, body, and legs to connect them with soft 20-gauge iron wire. Drill holes ½ inch apart in the monkey's hands. Put the monkey upside down to simplify threading the string through the arms and handles.

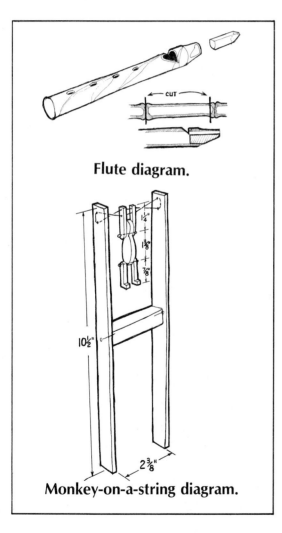

Flute diagram.

Monkey-on-a-string diagram.

Monkey-on-a-string.

★ Imaginative gifts that are quick and easy to make with felt and glue.

chapter 8

EVEN MORE GIFT IDEAS

This chapter proves that when you think you've come up with your last creative idea, half a hundred more spring up from the most unexpected places—a cardboard mailing tube, a plastic food container, even the last rose of summer.

The gift ideas in this chapter range from low-cost or no-cost gift items made from leftover odds and ends to elegant gifts made from materials found in nature, such as flowers preserved by drying, green growing plants, and stunning leather projects adorned with stamped nature designs.

ODDS AND ENDS

Each item in this gift collection is made from scraps of leftover felt. They can be given for any occasion or no special occasion at all!

To make these gift items, follow the directions, and use the patterns on pages 132-133.

1. The 'Four Aces' beanbags are as easy to make as they are appealing. The materials needed for each bag include white felt 7½x4 inches, red and black felt 6x9 inches, scraps of other felt, beans, thread, and fabric cement. Pin the body pattern A (see page 133) on both fabrics and cut them out at one time, with a ⅛-inch outside seam allowance. Next, cut out the limbs, features, and markings. With the machine threaded with white on top and black or red in the bobbin, sew around bodies, catching arms in the seams. Leave bottoms open. Sew front of piece B to body front, catching legs. Glue on all markings and features, using fabric cement. Fill bag with beans and stitch closed.

2. To make this light switch cover-up, cut a 7½-inch circle from light pink felt. Place a switch plate in the center, trace around the openings, and cut them out. Cut features from scraps of felt and glue them in place, using fabric cement. Thread a needle with yarn and use a running stitch for the eyebrows and mous-

tache. Spray the switch plate cover-up with starch and press flat. Cut four lengths of No. 30 wire, each 7½ inches long; bend each at the center and position them on the back of the circle like spokes of a wheel; glue them in place and cover the wires with pink felt in the same circle shape. For the beard, wind yarn around the switch plate 10 times, cut, and tie. Do this three times. Glue the knotted area of each under the mouth. Use the same method for the hair by winding the yarn around two fingers 10 times. Cut, tie, and glue the yarn in place.

3. To make this book cover and marker for a 4x7-inch paperback book, use a 9x16-inch piece of felt, transparent thread, and spray starch.

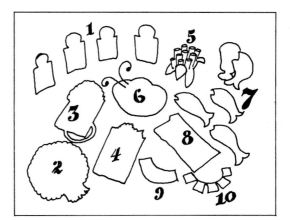

Spray the felt with starch, then press it with a warm iron. Fold over the top and bottom edges about ½ inch and press. Fold in the sides 3¼ inches and press. Test-fit the cover to the book and make any necessary adjustments; stitch along the top and bottom edges of the cover.

Cut the lion body parts and features from other scraps of felt. Position these on the front of the book cover and glue them in place, using fabric cement. Cut a 1x17-inch strip of felt for the tail bookmark. Make a tassel by winding yarn around two fingers six times. Cover the tail strip with glue; place three No. 30 wires along the center lengthwise, with the tassel at one end. Sandwich the wires and the tassel by folding the tail in half lengthwise. Trim the tassel evenly, and stitch the tail to the cover so that it centers in the proper position.

4. *For the 'Men Only' book cover,* make the cover according to the directions given for No. 3. Then, cut the body, clothing, and features from felt, using the pattern given on the opposite page. Position these on the front of the cover and glue them in place. For the hair, wrap yarn around three fingers 20 times, and glue or sew the yarn to the head after the bookmark is attached. For the bookmark, cut a bright pink felt strip 2x13 inches and another strip 2x11 inches. Cover the shorter strip with glue and place two sets of three No. 30 wires about ¼ inch from the edges. Cover the shorter strip with the longer strip and let dry. Cut the center of the end of the unglued strip up five inches to form the legs. Cut toes on each leg two inches long, making each toe ⅛ inch shorter than the preceding toe, starting from the center. Roll each toe up to sandwich the felt, and glue in place. Sew the bookmark to the edge of the front cover, locating it so the feet extend at the proper place. Glue on hair.

5. *Make this porcupine pencil holder* with green felt. Cut 12 pieces 2½x4 inches (A), 10 pieces 3½x4 inches (B), and 7 pieces 4½x4 inches (C). Roll the strips around a ⅜-inch dowel, gluing at the overlap. Place the dowel on the 2½-, 3½-, and 4½-inch edges. String the tallest 'quills' with florist wire to form a circle, using a darning needle to punch the holes. Repeat with the 3½-inch size, making a circle around the first circle. Glue this circle to the

first circle. Repeat the same procedure with the smallest size. Cut eight legs, using pattern piece D. Glue No. 30 wire down the center of four of the legs, then glue on the other set of legs to sandwich the wire. Glue two heads (E) together, sandwiching the wire from ear to ear. Form the nose by overlapping the bottom notched area and gluing. Cut a ¾x4-inch strip (F), overlap, and glue the ends together. Glue this strip to the inside of the head. Add eyes and legs, skipping a quill between each leg. Cut a band ¾x12 inches (G); glue the band around the bottom to hold the quills and legs in place. Slip the head over the front quill and glue securely. Insert several pencils, ball-point or felt-tip pens in the holder and your gift is ready.

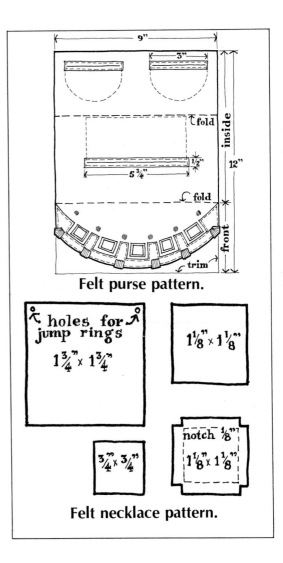

Felt purse pattern.

Felt necklace pattern.

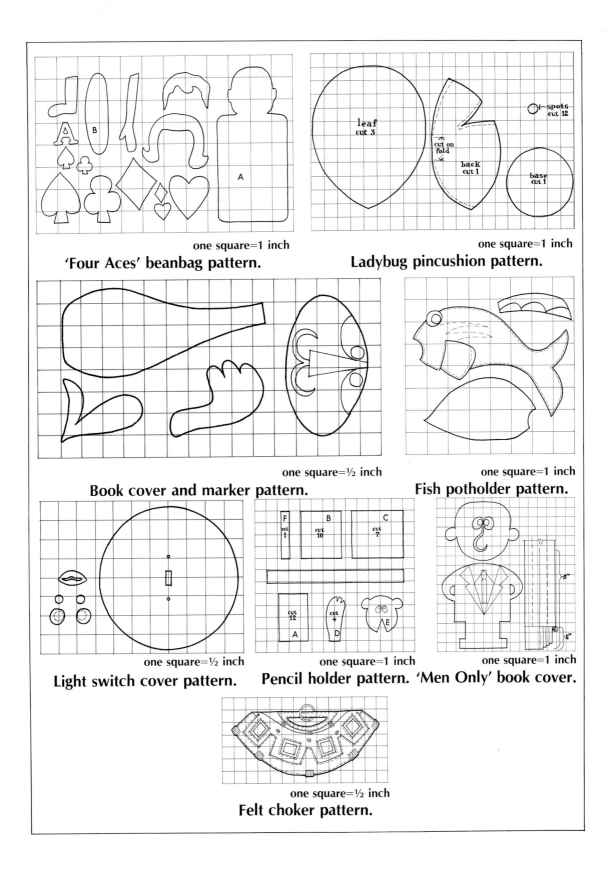

one square=1 inch
'Four Aces' beanbag pattern.

one square=1 inch
Ladybug pincushion pattern.

leaf cut 3

cut on fold

back cut 1

spots cut 12

base cut 1

one square=½ inch
Book cover and marker pattern.

one square=1 inch
Fish potholder pattern.

one square=½ inch
Light switch cover pattern.

one square=1 inch
Pencil holder pattern.

one square=1 inch
'Men Only' book cover.

one square=½ inch
Felt choker pattern.

A china doll, wooden toy soldiers, and a miniature drum.

6. *To make the ladybug pincushion* (see sketch page 133), cut body from felt and sew the darts. Put ½ of a 5-inch foam ball in the cover; sew on base covering by hand. Cut velvet tubing into four 9-inch pieces; slip-stitch two pieces on body. Cut 12 dots from black felt; stitch or glue to body. Slide chenille stems into remaining tubing; sew ends closed. At center front about one inch from bottom, punch two holes. Force ends of chenille stems into the holes and stitch the tubing. Curl the antennae. Cut the leaf and sew the ladybug to the leaf base.

7. *For these fish potholders,* cut two front pieces and two back pieces in contrasting colors according to pattern. Cut open gill line and position fin. Stitch. Sew the fronts together and the backs together. Cut upper fins free form; catch in top stitching as you sew back and front together. Leave bottom open. Glue on eyes.

8. *The felt purse* is made by cutting three pieces of felt—yellow, pink, and orange—according to the sketch, following the outside line to form a 9x12-inch rectangle. Hand-stitch mirror tiles face down on yellow, cross-stitching at corners. Cover with pink on the right side. Machine-stitch around tiles. Cut away pink and yellow to expose tiles. Add orange to the top side; sew around tiles, and cut away orange.

Stitch orange strips at the pocket top to the yellow felt only. Slit between the stitching lines. Next, stitch around the pocket shapes through all felt layers. Stitch three pieces around the outside; trim the front to a crescent shape. Embroider trim as shown.

9. *To make the felt necklace,* cut four pieces of felt—one yellow, one pink, and two orange—like the sketch on page 133. Position the mirror tiles on the yellow, mirror side down; hand-

sew across the corners. Place pink on the right side of yellow; machine-sew around the tiles. Cut the felt away to expose the tiles, leaving a yellow border. Position orange on the right side of the pin; stitch around base and tiles. Cut away to leave a border. Position orange on backing layer behind the yellow; stitch around the edge and cut out. Cut away the pink close to the stitching. Add decorative embroidery and a ring; hang by a twisted wool cord.

10. For this felt choker, cut twenty 1¾-inch felt squares—five each of red, gray, lavender, and orange. Glue the lavender to the gray, cutting away the edges to reveal the gray. Repeat with orange on lavender, notching corners to reveal lavender. Cut a cardboard square slightly smaller than the gray square. Sandwich cardboard between gray and red, backing the square. Glue a small tile to orange. Let this dry for at least 24 hours.

Bore small holes in the upper corners of each unit with scissors or an awl. Join with rings and attach a small chain.

This lovely china doll can be yours for the making. For the clay parts, use ½ pound of clay that can be oven-baked. Form clay hair around a wooden darning egg and slip off gently. Model lower arms and legs from clay; bake in an oven until dry. Paint with poster paints, then spray with clear lacquer. Paint a wooden darning egg

and add features. Spray with clear lacquer. Glue clay hair to the doll's head.

Make a pattern for the fabric body parts. Cut the body parts from good-quality muslin. Sew the arm and leg side seams. Glue the clay parts securely into the ends of the cloth parts, and stuff the cloth sections with cotton. Glue trim around the raw edges. Stitch the seams of body pieces, inserting the arms and legs in place. Leave neck open. Stuff body tightly and insert darning egg head. Glue around neck and cover raw edges with trim. Dress doll in any style.

This regiment of toy soldiers will delight the boys in your family. To make them, glue wooden spools together for the body. Glue a wooden drawer pull on top for a hat. Cover with gesso, and then paint with acrylics.

For the drum, cut and decorate a mailing tube. Glue gold foil to toothpicks, and insert the toothpicks into wooden beads for sticks.

A game of ninepins can be created from lumberyard turnings, knobs, and a croquet ball. To make the game, purchase wooden turnings from a lumberyard. Stain the turnings, and then spray them with varnish. Stamp each turning with a number on all four sides of the top. Paint and varnish nine wooden knobs. When dry, glue the wooden knobs to the tops of the turnings. Paint and lacquer a croquet ball to complete the set.

Ninepins, a great indoor game for both young and old.

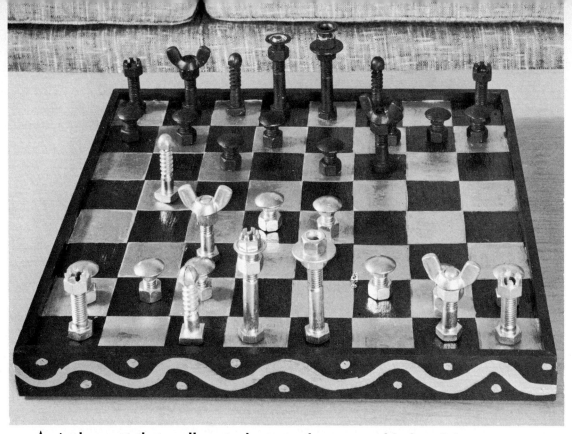

★ **A chess set that really gets down to the nuts and bolts of the game.**

This imaginative and functional chess set can be put together in just a few hours. Men and women alike will have fun giving or receiving this gift. Men in particular will enjoy making this chess set because they're working with things they know, but this shouldn't discourage women from trying the project. In fact, if you don't know what nut or bolt to ask for, take the picture along with you to the hardware store and ask the clerk to help you select all the materials you'll need. Then, just assemble the various pieces, give the gift to your unsuspecting husband, and never divulge the fact that you still don't know a nut from a bolt!

To make the chess pieces, gather a supply of nuts and bolts and experiment by threading various shapes together. Add washers and fancy crown bolts to identify the figures. When the pieces are threaded in finished shapes, secure them with glue. Then, paint them with acrylic paints, spray-paint, dip them in paint, or leave them unpainted if you have made the set with two different kinds of metal.

To make the chess board, cut a ½-inch-thick piece of plywood into a 16-inch square. Then, using two colors of vinyl, cloth, or metallic

tape, cut the 2-inch-wide tape into 2-inch squares. Alternating colors, stick the tape to the board. Or, if you prefer, paint the board one color and use the 2-inch squares of tape to form the checked pattern. When the board is completed, lay a 16-inch-square piece of clear plastic or glass on top of the chess board.

Shade pulls are a unique and welcome gift for any occasion that calls for a small, inexpensive gift. But, don't settle for run-of-the-mill shade pulls. Concoct your own designs by combining odds and ends with your own ingenuity. Here are some thought-starters, using everything from spools and spoons to tees and toys. Start with any small object you have around the house, and build your design from that.

1. Glue two matching spools together; serrate the raised rims with a sharp kitchen knife. Drill a small hole in a wooden knob, then thread a cord through the hole and pull the knot inside. Glue this to the end of one spool and attach a matching knob to the other end. Paint the spools and knobs with acrylics and trim with ribbon.

2. Drill a small hole in an unpainted wooden mustard spoon. Saturate a knot on the end of a hanging cord with white glue; wedge the saturated knot firmly in the hole of the spoon. Paint the spoon in bright colors.

3. Twist a small hole in the end of an unpainted wooden construction toy. Paint, then secure toy in a vise, and hammer a row of small nails through the wooden beads placed around edge. Nail tacks around the holes on each flat side. Cover the holes with buttons. Attach a screw eye to the outside of the shade pull and attach a cord.

4. Stain an unpainted wooden napkin ring dark brown or spray-paint the napkin ring a bright color. Take a spring from an old clock and glue it inside the ring. Attach a screw eye to the napkin ring and attach a cord.

5. Paint a cork fishing float any color. Push colored thumbtacks and copper carpet tacks into the cork in a random pattern. String the float between colored wooden beads.

6. Carve out shallow depressions in a piece of bark or driftwood to hold pretty pebbles or shells. Paint the driftwood, then rub it with dark pigment for an antique effect. Attach the 'gems' to the driftwood with white glue. Attach a screw eye for hanging it on a cord.

7. Paint a construction toy wheel with oil paint. After the paint dries, apply a thin layer of white glue around the rim. Wrap yarn around the edge, pressing it in place as you go. Fasten a small screw eye in the top of the wheel, then glue several rows of yarn around the center holes on each flat side. Hammer silver-headed nails through flat wooden beads around the yarn. Glue silver buttons over the holes.

8. Paint pieces of a Chinese puzzle, then glue these pieces to two MahJongg counters. (Dominoes can be substituted, if desired.) Twist a screw eye in the top for the string.

9. Drill a hole through a wooden knob, then thread a cord through the hole and pull the knot inside. Attach the knob with glue to the bowl of a wooden stirring spoon. Pencil in features, then paint with acrylic paints.

10. Use children's beads that are already painted in bright, cheery colors. Trim a cylindrical bead with several narrow pieces of decorative tape. String the cylindrical bead between the round beads and the buttons. Tie a knot after the last bead.

11. For a thick tassel, drill holes through the tips of colored golf tees. Then, string the tees. Next, string various sizes of wooden beads. Tie a knot after the last bead.

In addition to being a great gift idea, these unusual shade pulls are always a best seller at bazaars. With a little planning and organization, you can turn out vast numbers of them.

Handcrafted shade pulls for any gift-giving occasion.

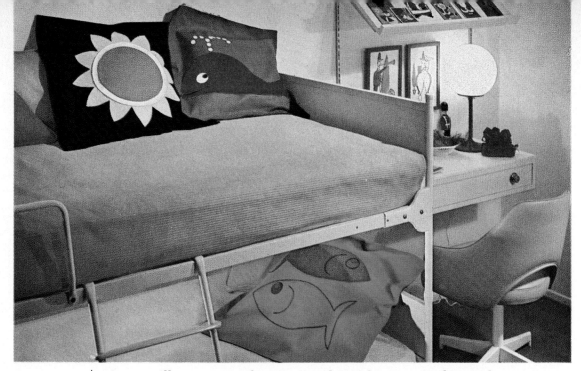

★ Throw-pillow covers that are made without a single stitch.

This assortment of throw-pillow covers, above, is easy to make and provides several clever gift ideas. To make them, lightly sketch a pattern on one 24x24-inch piece of felt. The sun, whale, and two fish are good patterns to start with. Be sure to look for other patterns. You'll find lots of pattern possibilities throughout this book. Trace the patterns onto felt pieces, cut them out, and glue them on with white glue. Use a dark marking pen to outline the shapes and to add any detail lines. On a second 24x24-inch piece of felt, cut a slit across the back large enough to insert a sofa pillow. Glue the two squares together, wrong sides together, to form the face and back of the pillow cover. Larger or smaller pillows can be made by cutting the felt to fit any ready-made cushion you may have.

This collection of gifts, opposite page, top, is sure to hit the nail on the head for any occasion. These items are made from scrap lumber and tin cans decorated with tacks, nails, handles, hooks, and hinges. Use these items as ideas, and then see what attractive things you can design.

The cap rack can be made to fit any space. This one is made from a 1x3x12-inch piece of redwood. Screw in three enameled hooks, and then, using tacks and nails, design a decorative pattern around the hooks and the front edges of the redwood strip.

Design a carrier to tote napkins and flatware to the picnic table for a great gift for any of your friends who enjoy outdoor eating. To make the carrier, join two 1x10x15-inch pieces of redwood. Attach three soup cans, already painted, to an 8¼x3½-inch base for holding all the gear. Nail a cake tin onto the front side and a handle to the top. Then, stud the cake tin and the corners of the front with decorative tacks.

For a decorative wall plaque or paperweight, pound carpet tacks into a 6-inch board at different heights to form the medallion pattern.

For other patio people, fashion hurricane lamps. Paint a tuna can, add a glass chimney, and place on a redwood base. Decorate the base with ornamental tacks and nails.

A decorative planter to hold not-so-pretty pots can be quickly and easily built from five pieces of redwood. Adorn the corners with decorative hinges, and then add a design fashioned from decorative tacks.

Redwood bookends make a useful as well as an attractive gift for people of all ages. Cut two equal lengths of redwood. Glue the wood to metal bookends with epoxy glue. When the glue has dried, decorate the bookends. Arrange upholstery tacks around the edges and in each corner, making certain that they are evenly spaced. In the center of each bookend place a piece of diamond shape tin. Trim with tacks.

These handy hang-ups, below, will delight every hobbyist on your gift list. If you tailor each one to a specific hobby, you will have made an attractive wall hanging as well as a place to keep often-used tools within easy reach.

The needle-and-thread hang-up is a must for every mother and seamstress. Paint a picture frame a bright color, then insert felt-covered hardboard in the frame. Glue bright felt patches onto the felt backing. Next, screw in place brass cup hooks or shoulder hooks. Using gummed decorator tapes, make tabs for the see-through boxes. Fill the see-through boxes with iron-on mending tape, pins, thread, and buttons. In the other patches, place a measuring tape, pin cushion, and scissors. Attach a hanger on the back of the picture frame.

The scissor hang-up will be helpful to nearly everyone. To give scissors a permanent home, arrange shapes cut from felt (using real scissors as a guide) on felt-covered hardboard. Drill holes in the hardboard for golf tee hangers. Glue the tees in place. Insert the hardboard in a brightly painted frame, and attach a hanger on the back of the frame.

For your flower-arranging friends, let them know that good tools are their best helpers. This felt tree blossoms with basic ones—flower shears, picks, flower holder, and florist tape. Cover a piece of hardboard with felt. Then, cut the tree and colorful blossoms from bright colors of felt. Hang all the flower-arranging tools on brass shoulder hooks. Then, glue the hardboard into the frame and attach a hanger.

★ Tack-trimmed redwood gifts.

With a little extra thought and effort, you probably will be able to come up with many other handy hang-ups to help some of the hobbyists you know. For someone who spends a considerable amount of time knitting, arrange a pair of scissors, cable holders, a crochet hook, a large needle, and needle tips. Using a larger picture frame, collect and hang a small box of wax crayons, a pad of paper, a pencil, and a pair of blunt scissors for an unusual gift for a small child. Or, make a desk organizer for a home office. This item will be appreciated by many men. Hang a pad of paper, a pen or pencil, a small calendar, and a roll of cellophane tape. Keep thinking, and chances are that you'll come up with many other ideas.

★ These handy hang-ups will delight every home hobbyist.

Shown on this page and on the following three are a myriad of great gift ideas. These gifts are just right for giving or for selling at a bazaar. Complete how-to instructions begin below and continue on page 144. Patterns for the more difficult projects are included as an aid to you.

1. This hearth broom cover is both pretty and practical. Draw around a broom and cut a paper pattern, allowing for side seams. Cut felt, using the paper pattern; seam the sides of the cover. Scallop the bottom edges. Slide the cover over the handle onto the broom. Cut a 2-inch felt strip long enough to fit around the broom; glue it to the cover. Add straw flowers and a felt bow.

2. and 3. For wood-block candleholders, use 4x4-inch blocks of wood. Paint the block white; when dry, glue on tissue paper designs. If desired, use a combination of foil and tissue. If foil is used, glue it directly to the raw wood. Then, spray the tissue and foil with a finish coat of clear lacquer or acrylic.

10

11

12

13

14

15

16

17

18

19

20

21

22

23

24

25

28

27

29

26

30

31

32

33

144

Drill a small hole in the top center; sink an inverted finishing nail to hold the candle, or use commercially made candle cups. Wood tape, balsa, and linoleum cutouts may also be used to trim the wood blocks.

4. and 6. These clever pencil holders are cut from ¾-inch-thick plastic foam. Paint the foam with gesso. Then, paint with acrylic paint. Apply two coats. Attach a painted tin can to the back of the foam to hold the pencils.

5. To make this papier-mâché treasure chest, cover a purchased chest with 1x4-inch strips of newspaper dipped in a ⅔ glue and ⅓ water solution, overlapping as you go. Let dry.

Glue designs (cut them from shirt cardboard or use heavy cord) to the chest. Apply gesso to the papered areas, then cover with acrylic paints after the gesso has dried thoroughly.

To antique: Paint with watered-down black acrylic paint. Let dry a little, then rub off with a damp cloth until you have desired color. Coat with clear varnish. Line drawers with felt.

7. and 8. These balsa tree ornaments are easy to make. Cut the shapes from 1-inch-thick balsa. Give them a sealer coat of gesso, then paint with acrylic paints.

9. This stand-up doll would make a nice playmate for any little girl. Cut the doll any size you wish from ½-inch plywood (see pattern at right). Cut out the feet and glue them to the bottom of the legs. Undercoat the doll with water-base paint, then paint with acrylic paint. Paint on features. Glue lace trims on the doll as indicated by the broken lines on the sketch. Cut out a dress from any fabric; bind the edges with bias tape. Add decorative trims to the hem.

10. These hand trivets are made from corrugated paper. Cut the paper into ½-inch strips. Spread white glue on the smooth side and roll the paper into the desired shapes. Butt the ends to add a new strip when needed. Spray-paint colored parts separately from both sides before assembling. Glue separate parts together.

11. This lady hat stand holds hats, wigs, or headbands. Cut two corrugated cardboard pieces in simple head-neck-shoulder shapes. Cut a narrow vertical slot (⅛ inch wide) halfway up the center of one piece and halfway down the center of the other piece. Slip one over the other to make the stand. Paint the stand

white; cut features and headdress from adhesive-backed vinyl. Glue yarn along the edges; spiral the ends as shown in the photo.

12. These yarn flowers are probably a little different from any you've seen before. (The sketch below will aid you in making the flowers.) To make a leaf or petal: Wind a 36-inch length of No. 22 wire tightly onto a No. 1 knitting needle, leaving 1½ inches straight at each end. (This is done by hand or by placing a knitting needle in an electric drill.) Grasp the ends with pliers; stretch until the spiral portion measures about 16 inches. Twist the straight ends together for a stem. Make the spiral section pointed at the stem end. Hold the stem in one hand; press at points A and B until the spiral is a circle for a leaf or petal.

Tie the yarn at point A (leave a 4-inch end). Now, tie the short end to point E at the base of the stem. This leaves a loose end about three inches long. Gently wind yarn from A to B, then under to C, over to D, etc., until the yarn is in every coil. (Make the leaves about an inch longer than the width.)

At the top, wrap the yarn around the top loop; pull it to the back of the leaf or petal. Cut the yarn, leaving a 7-inch end. With embroidery

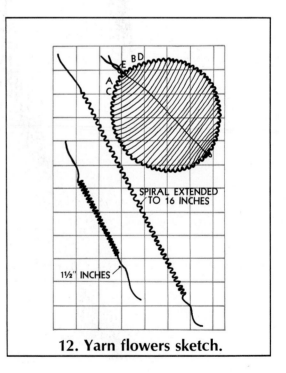

12. Yarn flowers sketch.

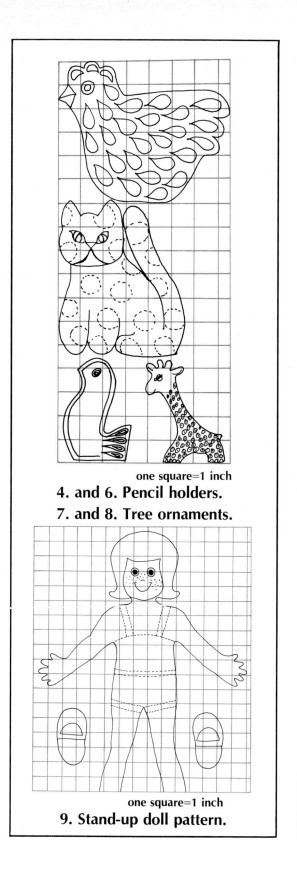

one square=1 inch

4. and 6. Pencil holders.
7. and 8. Tree ornaments.

one square=1 inch
9. Stand-up doll pattern.

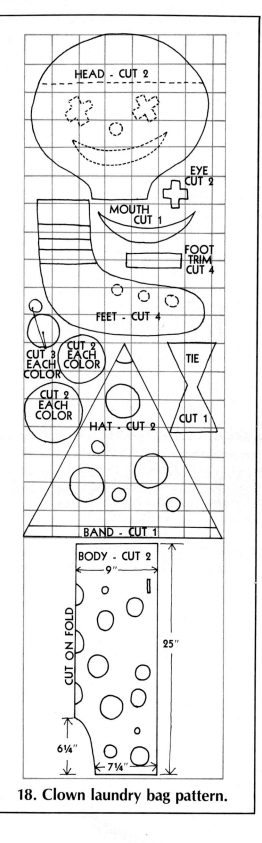

HEAD - CUT 2

EYE
CUT 2

MOUTH
CUT 1

FOOT
TRIM
CUT 4

FEET - CUT 4

CUT 3
EACH
COLOR

CUT 2
EACH
COLOR

TIE

CUT 2
EACH
COLOR

CUT 1

HAT - CUT 2

BAND - CUT 1

BODY - CUT 2
9"
CUT ON FOLD
25"
6¼"
7¼"

18. Clown laundry bag pattern.

needle draw the end back through the loop (under wire and over yarn). This anchors the yarn at the top so you can pull it tightly to make the center vein. Wrap the yarn three times around the stem at point E; tie to the 3-inch piece of yarn you left at the start.

To attach the petals to the stem: With pliers, bend a small circle in the end of No. 14 covered wire. Have six petals ready. With No. 22 bare wire, attach the petals one at a time to the end of the No. 14 wire. Put in a center. Trim loose yarn ends. Cover the wire and the yarn ends with some floral tape.

13. Try a yarn-covered candleholder. Saw a section 7½-inches long from a cardboard rug tube. Cover two 5-inch corrugated circles with felt. Glue these circles to the top and bottom of the tube. Wind yarn on the tube, gluing where necessary. Add fringe trim.

14. To make this string holder, crochet a cover with rug yarn to fit the size funnel you are using. Push a ball of string into the cover then pull the string end through the funnel. Slide the funnel into the cover. Add paper or felt features and round button or wooden bead feet.

15. This colorful orange candleholder is made by stacking and gluing tall and short molds together. Cover the edges with white cord dipped in glue. Let dry. Spray with orange enamel. When dry, brush the candleholder with antique glaze. When the glaze is about dry, wipe the candleholder with a soft cloth. Wipe the outer areas only, allowing the glaze to remain in the grooves and depressions.

16. Make this black candleholder by stacking and gluing tin cans together. This one is made from three tuna cans, one soup can, one juice can, and one olive can. Apply two coats of black enamel until the cans are completely covered. Trim the candleholder with hand-painted flowers, using several colors of enamel.

17. To make a versatile planter, give a papier-mâché treatment to a large throwaway container, a paint bucket, or a potato chip can. Cover the container with 1x4-inch newspaper strips dipped in a ⅔ glue and ⅓ water solution, overlapping as you go. Let dry thoroughly.

Glue designs (cut from shirt cardboard and heavy cord) to the planter. Apply gesso to the papered areas, then cover with acrylic paints.

To antique the planter: Paint it with watered-down black acrylic paint. Let dry a little, then rub with a damp cloth until you have the desired color. Coat with clear varnish.

18. This clown laundry bag makes a great gift for children. (See pattern on page 145.) Cut the clown body from a 36x25-inch piece of gold burlap. Make two 1-inch buttonholes on the front piece, 3½ inches from the top and ¾ of an inch from the edges. Cut two or three circles each from red and white felt. Make three red pompons and one white pompon from yarn. Glue the circles and pompons to the burlap. Cut feet from black felt. Sew two pieces together ¼ inch from the edge and turn. Glue two hot pink felt strips and three buttons to each foot. Stuff with cotton ¾ inch from the top.

Cut the head from flesh-colored felt; stitch together ¼ inch from the edge. Turn. Glue on features. Stuff with cotton to ½ inch of the neck. Cut a hat from hot pink felt; sew together ½ inch from the edge. Tie the ends of 12-inch cable cord together; glue the cord to the back side of the peak. Glue large red pompons to the front side at the peak. For the hat band, cut a piece of white felt ¾x8 inches. Pink edges; glue in place. Glue on felt circles. To assemble: Sew body pieces, right sides together. Leave the top and bottom of the legs open. Turn. Gather legs to fit feet; place toes to the outside. Sew the legs securely. Turn down ½ inch of the top edge; make a 3-inch hem. Stitch the head at the top center of the back section. Glue an orange tie over the stitching. Run two lengths of cable cord 80 inches long through the hem for the drawstring.

19. Hanger covers always make lovely gifts. To make these, cut pieces of felt to fit a hanger. Cut the front and back pieces for each section. Sew the back pieces together. Repeat for the front. Cut appliqués from the felt; stitch or glue in place. With the right sides together, sew the back to the front. Turn. Clip at the curved corners. Turn and press the cover flat. Slip the cover over the hanger; seam the bottom edges together. If the edges don't meet exactly, trim them wherever necessary.

20. Make a Santa beanbag from felt. Cut the face from a half circle of white felt. Cut the hat and the entire back piece from red felt.

Stitch the hat to the face front. Stitch three rows of white fringe in place for the beard. Sew or glue on a red pompon nose.

For eyes, use two balls from blue fringe. Sew eyebrows, cut from tape, in place; add 1-inch eyelashes. Sew the back and front pieces together; leave opening and add beans. Sew the opening closed, and add a tassel to the hat.

21. To make the tree beanbag, cut the front and back triangles from moss green felt. Stitch on fringe trims. With the right sides together, stitch the pieces together. Leave a small opening and add the beans. Sew the opening closed.

22. This chicken pillow will be a welcome addition to any teen-ager's collection. To make it, cut two 14-inch circles for the front and back from yellow felt. Appliqué the wing and head to the front piece. Then appliqué the comb, beak, and eye to the pillow front. Cut pieces for the tail and feet, doubling and stitching each. Insert the tail and feet to catch them in the seam when joining the front and back pieces. Stuff the pillow with batting or a round pillow form. Hand-stitch the last section closed.

23. Make this bunting doll by cutting two pieces of fabric in proportion to the doll for the bunting; sew the right sides together. Leave an opening to turn the fabric. Slip-stitch the opening closed after turning the fabric.

Stuff a cotton stocking for the doll with Dacron batting. Tie off a portion for head. Stuff further; tie off below heel portion of sock. Sew on buttons for eyes. Add a mouth and freckles with embroidery floss. Use a piece of lace to wrap the doll. Sew on yarn hair.

24. These adorable stuffed animals are made from gloves. Use nylon gloves and Dacron stuffing so the animals will be washable.

For the bird, sew across the thumb portion of the glove; cut. Stuff the fingers first, then the palm. Cut the top portion of the glove after stuffing. Fold down the top edge; slip-stitch closed. Add felt wings and a beak.

For the horse, sew across bottom of glove fingers to make the short legs. Do the same on thumb for the nose. Stuff fingers first, then the palm and the thumb. Cut top part of glove after stuffing. Fold down top edge; slip-stitch. Add a yarn tail and other features cut from felt. Sew legs back to make the animal stand.

25. This pretty tote bag is a genuine people pleaser. Try some fancy stitches on a sisal place mat that measures 13x19 inches. Then, cut two 10½x12¾-inch pieces of felt for the lining. Convert a 12-inch zipper to 11½ inches by tacking across the zipper ½ inch from the base. Trim off the tabs. Lay the felt flat, place the zipper face side down ½ inch from the edge of the zipper. Open the zipper. Place the other side of the zipper face down on the second piece of felt ½ inch from the edge; stitch along the outer edge of the zipper.

Fold both sides 1½ inches to the inside so the zipper will close to seal them. Stitch with a zipper foot through the zipper and the two thicknesses of the felt.

Close the zipper; stitch the felt together with ¼-inch seam on the other three sides, beginning and ending at the zipper junction. Fold the place mat over the lining; hand-stitch the two together along the top, ⅞ inch from the top on both sides. Overcast the side edges together. For the handle, attach two ⅞-inch curtain rings to a 36-inch length of chain.

26. To make this cute elephant pillow, cut two 17-inch squares of green fabric for the pillow background. Cut the canopy from striped fabric. For the cage bars, cut and hem eight 1½x6-inch strips. Turn and press. For the cage floor, cut a 3½x17-inch gold strip. Fold in half. Seam, turn, and press. Cut four 2½-inch circles for wheels; four 1-inch circles for wheels, and four 1-inch circles for center of the wheels. Appliqué the pieces on the front of the pillow, using the picture for placement.

For the elephant, cut two pieces for the body from gold fabric; cut four ears and four saddles. Cut two ovals for eyes or embroider with a satin stitch. Seam around the ears and the saddle. Seam the elephant on the wrong side. Leave an opening to allow for stuffing. Turn and press. Add the stuffing. Turn the opening in at the top; slip-stitch shut. Add ears, saddle, and fringe tail. Slip the elephant into the cage.

27. Any cook will like a butterfly potholder. From ¼ yard of plain fabric, cut two pieces, using pattern A. (See pattern on page 149.) Cut one piece of A from quilted fabric for the body. Cut all the other pieces as indicated on the pattern. Appliqué the pieces on the right and

148

left sides of the butterfly front. Slip the filling into each side. Lay two sections of the butterfly together, back to back, making a narrow seam down the middle (this leaves raw edges on the front side, but these edges will be covered).

Seam around the body G on the wrong side. Clip the seams at the curves. Make a small cut in the center back of one piece. Turn to the right side; fill with cotton. Sew up the slit with overcast stitches. Stitch the body over the seam made in the butterfly proper.

28. This hen-on-a-nest will keep eggs warm. Cut a bias strip 1½x3½ yards long. Make 1⅓ yards of piping; use the rest for cording.

Cut the cover according to the pattern at right from 11x22-inch printed fabric. Stitch the beak on each side. Stitch the center back seam between the marks, and stitch the forehead to the breast between the marks. Sew the piping on the lower edge of the chicken, starting at the breast to the tail. Run a basting thread on the neck and stuff the head and beak. Insert 13 inches of cording, formed into three loops, in the top of the head; stitch closed. Sew wattles, leaving the top open. Trim, turn, and stitch the wattles to the head.

For the tail feathers, form loops of covered cord 7½ inches, 8½ inches, and 9½ inches, with the smallest loop placed at the top. Arrange piping at the tail, then sew the tail closed at the edge. Form wings in the same way.

Cut lining from a plain-color fabric (9x12-inch piece). Baste lining and padding together down the seam allowance to the back of the padding. Sew to the inside of the chicken.

To line basket, draw around bottom of basket on paper. Carefully roll the side edge of basket on the paper, marking each side, top, and bottom halfway around basket. Cut two of these paper patterns; fit them into the inside of basket.

The inner measurements of the basket are enough smaller than the outer measurements that a seam allowance is provided. Stitch the parts of the side lining together. Check for fit; stitch in the bottom of the lining. Trim. Turn the seam allowance under; stitch to basket top.

29. To make this handy reminder board, cut a 12x24-inch piece from burlap and one from percale for the lining. Sew a 5-inch seam at the center six inches from the top. Sew two leaves

on one side of the stem; one leaf on the other side. Assemble the eight-petal flower that is six inches across. Sew the centers from contrasting felt colors. Place the flower on the burlap, with the tip two inches from the top. Sew or glue the petals in place. The petal overlaps the top of the stem ¾ of an inch. Sew or glue a dot between the petals. Make three flowerpots. Sew the rims to the pots, with a ¼-inch seam. Sew the top pot in the center of the burlap eight inches from the bottom. To make the pocket for the pencil, stitch from the top to the bottom of the pot. Center the second pot over the top one about five inches from the bottom. Stitch sides and the bottom. Center the largest pot over the second pot two inches from the bottom. Stitch the sides and the bottom in the same manner as the first two flowerpots.

With the right sides together, stitch the burlap and the lining. Leave a 5-inch space on one side to allow for turning. Turn and press the fabric. Stitch rickrack and ball fringe trims. Fold and stitch a ½-inch hem at the top for a dowel. Add a cable cord or several strands of yarn to each end of the dowel.

30. These perky felt flowers are made by cutting 3- or 4-inch circles of felt. Cut several circles, triangles, petals, and thin strips about

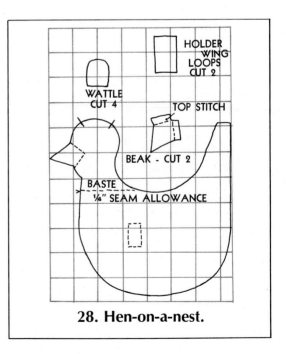

28. Hen-on-a-nest.

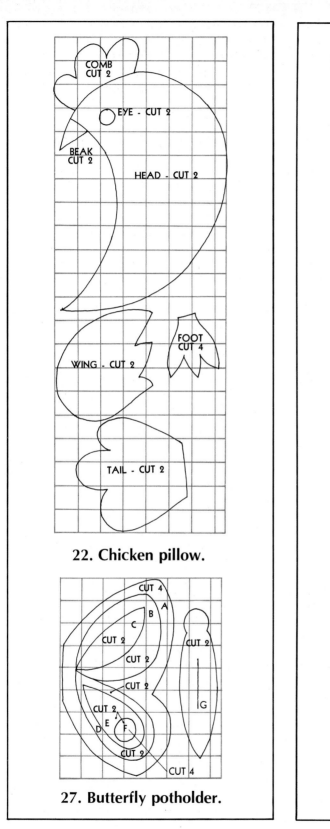

22. Chicken pillow.

27. Butterfly potholder.

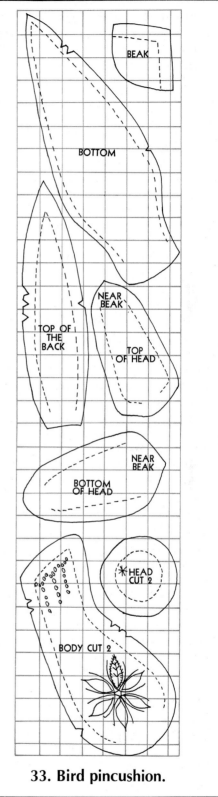

33. Bird pincushion.

one inch long. Glue these onto the circles to form flowers. Cut interlining for each flower about ⅛ inch smaller than the felt. Sandwich between felt circles to give the flowers more body.

Glue circles together, leaving an opening on the edge to insert a dowel or wire stem. Glue the stems in place.

Cut leaf shapes from green felt. Line with interlining as for the flowers. Sew or glue the leaves together and add the stems.

31. To make these stocking dolls, use small-size socks with fold-down cuffs. Stuff the toe with Dacron batting to form a ball; tie with yarn or cord. Continue stuffing past the heel. Stuff this part very full so the doll will sit. Cut off the cuff. Slit the lower part of the body to form legs. Stuff lightly; slip-stitch closed. Cut off the cuff for the cap. Then, cut the remaining part in two for arms. Stitch the side and the end of the tube to make an arm. Turn, stuff, and whip-stitch to the body; make the arms reach forward or up. Add features and other details. Pull the stocking top over head.

32. This flapper food container is very easy to make, and it can serve many purposes. To make it, first cover a 2-pound coffee can with some white felt. Then, add felt hair below the plastic lid to ensure that the lid fits the can properly. Cut out curls from felt, and glue them to the can. Follow the same procedure with the facial features, and add a hat cut from felt or paper.

If paper is used, glue at the top of hat and the side seam. Slash the bottom seam allowance, and glue to the brim. With fabric, stitch.

33. For this colorful bird pincushion, cut pattern pieces from purple and pink velvet. (See pattern on page 149.) Cut on the solid lines; stitch on the dotted lines. Assemble the body; leave openings where head will cover. Stuff. Sew the head. Cut and sew the beak; stuff. Sew the head together; leave an opening at the base where it will be hidden; stuff. Blind stitch openings; attach to the head and body. Simulate wings with embroidery stitches or fabric appliqués that are sewed on.

Making gifts from clay is easy, inexpensive, and fun. And best of all, there are no limits as to the kinds of gifts you can create. Start with simple items, and then go on to more complex ones.

Although there are different brands and grades of clay available, generally don't bother selecting a special one. Just make sure that it has a water base. On the other hand, you can purchase Model-Light, a clay that is self-hardening. This type of clay will save you much work, as it need not be baked.

The examples across the page use the inexpensive ceramic mix that needs to be baked. Whichever type of clay you use, you can be sure of rewarding your friends with fun gifts.

Work the clay in your hands until it becomes soft. For beads, pick off small bits and roll them between your palms into pellets of the desired sizes. Pierce beads with a round toothpick. Arrange the beads on a foil-lined cookie sheet and bake in a 300° oven for 18 to 20 minutes.

To paint the jewelry, after baking and cooling, coat with gesso first, then brush with acrylics. Slip the shapes over a toothpick and place the pick into a block of white foam until the paint dries. To dye the jewelry, mix 2 to 3 teaspoons liquid dye to ½ to 1 teaspoon powdered dye, 1 cup water, and ½ teaspoon salt into a saucepan; bring to a boil. Stir until the dye dissolves, then drop in the plastic pieces and simmer about 15 minutes. Stir frequently.

The jewelry, opposite, is made by rolling the plastic clay on a board and then by cutting the shapes with a craft knife. Make loops from wire and insert them into the clay. Incise or imprint details on the jewelry with shells, buttons, or other objects, and paint with a brush. String the jewelry on wire, cord, or yarn. For the five-fish necklace, attach the shapes to a yarn-wrapped dowel. Use lark's head knots (see page 76) to hold the fish in place on the 6-inch dowel.

For the yarn-trimmed jewelry, bottom photograph, make large holes in the beads before baking. Wrap the various pieces with different colors of yarn. For cords, twist eight strands of fine yarn together, using knots as spacers. Suspend small yarn-covered beads from the tips of tassels on some. For earrings, thread the yarn through the holes, through small wooden beads, and then tie the beads to earring backs.

Once you have learned how to make these gifts, turn your attention to other ideas. You'll find that there are many clay gifts that you can model with ease in your leisure time.

★ Rolled and cut plastic clay jewelry.

★ Yarn-trimmed plastic clay jewelry.

GIFTS FROM NATURE

With the present emphasis on ecology, people are becoming more aware of nature and the beauty that it holds. On the following 18 pages, you will find some fantastic gift ideas using materials found in nature—flowers that can be preserved by drying, green plants that can be arranged in miniature gardens, and leather projects that can be stamped and tooled.

HOW TO DRY FLOWERS

If you've ever said to yourself or a friend, "Aren't these flowers beautiful? If only they would stay like that," now is the time to do something about it. You can preserve your best roses, azaleas, carnations, or any other flowers in your garden by drying them.

For something that is so easy to do, it's hard to believe the spectacular results that can be achieved by drying flowers. The centerpiece pictured below illustrates the lasting beauty that can be had. You can get equally beautiful results by drying a single stem or a group of the simplest blooms. Regardless of the arrangement you decide on, rest assured that seeing garden-fresh-looking flowers during the dead of winter will raise anyone's spirits.

You can dry flowers in one of two ways: by hanging them in a dark place—an attic or a room that is dark and dry—or by dipping them in a solution of silica gel.

If you hang the flowers, pick them just before they reach full bloom. The flowers will shatter if picked too late. Strip them of foliage and hang them in bunches in a dark, dry room for two to three weeks. Once dried, steam the stems when you want to bend the flowers.

A more permanent drying process involves using silica gel. First, gather an assortment of flowers in various stages of growth, from buds to mature blooms. Be sure to pick the flowers on a warm, sunny day—never just after rain. Trim the stems of excessive foliage and ensure that the blooms are free of dust or spray residue. Clean the flowers in cold water.

Cover the blooms with silica gel and seal them in an airtight container.

Use a solution of glycerin and water to preserve the beauty of fall foliage.

Pour a 2-inch layer of silica gel (found in most garden and hobby shops) into a cake tin or other sealable container. Then, cut the flower stems to a 2-inch length, and place the flowers into the silica bed, making sure that the flowers do not touch each other. Gently add more crystals until the whole bloom head is covered. Then, replace the lid, and tape around the edges to ensure that no air gets to the flowers. The presence of air will ruin the flowers.

The flowers will dry in anywhere from two to eight days, depending on the texture and the maturity of the flower. When the flowers feel crisp, lift them out of the crystals. Blow away any particles that may adhere to them. Then, lay the flowers on top of the mixture, seal the container, and leave them in the container for two or three days.

When the flowers have dried and you are ready to make your arrangement, wire on additional stems with mediumweight florist's wire (readily available), and wrap the stem and the wire with green florist's tape.

HOW TO DRY FALL FOLIAGE

The colorful fall foliage above was preserved with a glycerin process. In a quart jar mix one-fourth to one-third glycerin with two-thirds or three-fourths warm water. Remove two inches of the bark and cut slits in the stems. Then, insert the foliage in an upright position and leave it for one or two weeks. At least once a day, rub a glycerin-saturated cloth over both sides of the leaves. When the liquid level stops decreasing, the branches are ready to combine with other materials in a long-lasting arrangement. The arrangement above contains fall leaves, eucalyptus, cattails, and zinnias.

Once you have mastered the above techniques, you'll be able to tackle any dried arrangement. Don't confine yourself to working out intricate flower arrangements like those on these two pages; dry single blooms during the season and store them for later use. A dried flower arrangement—single or group—that you have made says much more to a hospital patient than a purchased one.

A terrarium in an apothecary jar.

A miniature garden in an aquarium.

GREEN AND GROWING GIFTS

Green, growing plants are a versatile and always appreciated gift. To trim the cost of the gift and also make it more personal, purchase plants from a greenhouse or use cuttings from your own plants, then repot them in a gift container. The container possibilities are as endless as the variety of plants available.

Terrariums, tiny gardens growing inside glass containers, make excellent gifts. The recipient needs only to give the plants minimum care to maintain green, healthy plants. In addition, the imitation of nature on a miniature scale will provide a fascinating conversation piece.

The dry, hot air of the house in winter is no handicap to plants in a terrarium, where moist air is trapped. Since the moisture is so well conserved, the garden under glass will hardly ever need watering as most plants do.

To make a terrarium, start with any clear glass container that has a tight-fitting lid. The containers that are shown on these two pages range from a large, widemouthed jar, an apothecary jar, an aquarium, to a globular glass bowl. Wash and polish the container until it sparkles. Then, line the bottom of the container and part of the sides with a layer of sphagnum moss. On top of this, pour a ½-inch layer of dry charcoal flakes to keep the soil sweet. Add a 1-inch layer

of gravel to provide proper drainage. On top of the gravel, place the potting soil. A good mixture for terrariums is two parts loam, two parts coarse sand, and one part leaf mold. Take the plants out of their pots, removing ¼ of the soil. Arrange each plant so it will contrast in size, shape, and color with its neighbor. Set the plants in the soil and fill in around them with more soil until the root system is completely covered.

Not all plants are suited to terrariums. The high humidity would cause some to decay. The best plants are those native to woodlands and marshy places. Listed below are some plants that need humidity, grow slowly, and help to create an interesting terrarium. Most must be ordered from plantsmen specializing in wild flowers: Begonias, baby's tears, miniature and trailing ivy, small-sized ferns, moss of almost every sort, rattlesnake plantain, gloxinia, small palms, African violets, coleus, fittonia, partridge-berry, hepatica, common and striped pipsis-sewa, maranta, wintergreen, goldthread, and small yellow ladyslippers.

Before planting the terrarium, decide where and how it will be displayed. If it is to be viewed from one side, put the larger plants in the back and the smaller ones in the front. If it is to be viewed from all sides, center the larger plants and surround them with smaller ones. The plant placement is very important to the success of your terrarium. Keep in mind that you are imitating a scene in nature.

After planting, place bark or stone chips on top of the soil for added texture. Spray the plants with an atomizer, making sure no soil is left on the leaves. Add only enough water to dampen the soil. This initial watering is the trickiest step in making a terrarium. Moisten the soil, but don't drench it or you will be plagued with mold. If you are doubtful about the right amount of water, stay on the dry side because you can always add more water if the foliage shows signs of wilting and discoloring.

Use the glass lid to control humidity. If moisture condenses in noticeable amounts, remove the cover for a day or leave it partly open until the excess moisture disappears. Place the glass garden in good light, but not in full sun. Full sun will cause too much heat to be trapped in the glass container and will wilt or kill the delicate plants growing within it.

A dish garden or a green planter also makes a nice gift. Once again, purchase the plants from the greenhouse or florist shop, and transplant them into a planter of your own choice.

The way you first pot a plant is vital to its future health. If it is potted incorrectly, the chances of it growing well are very slim. The most important factor is the quality of the potting soil. Most houseplants thrive in a potting soil mixture composed of gravel, peat moss, and soil in equal proportions. You can make up your own potting soil or buy it commercially prepared, but just make sure that when you use it, it must be moist, not dry.

To transplant a plant, first put a layer of broken chunks of clay pots or small rocks in the bottom of the pot. Then, place some of the potting soil on top of this. Now, place the plant on top of the soil and fill the pot with potting soil. Add the potting soil to the sides, top, and bottom of the plant, making certain that the entire root system is completely covered. Press the soil down firmly and water the plant thoroughly. Set the newly repotted plant where it will receive light but not direct sun until after it has become adjusted—usually from two to three days will be sufficient.

A Christmas terrarium in a glass bowl.

A terrarium planted in a glass jar.

Once an old roaster, now a planter.

PLANTERS TO MAKE OR TRIM

Even the simplest, most inexpensive plants can look expensive in a decorative container. The only problem is that plant containers are oftentimes expensive. Why not solve this problem by making your own plant boxes, stands, and cover-ups for clay or plastic pots!

Even some of the most unlikely items can make interesting habitats for plants. If you look around your house, you will probably find many items that can be used for this purpose. Recycle such items as shaving mugs, teakettles, pots and pans, earthenware crocks, coffee grinders, coffee mugs, water glasses, goldfish bowls, brandy snifters, and pitchers for planters.

The planter at left started life as a roasting pan. After it was scrubbed and spray-painted, two lightweight metal chains were fastened to the handles and suspended from ceiling hooks.

A few bright colors of yarn can vibrantly transform a lightweight plastic foam flower pot with 'wild and woolly' color. (See top left drawing on the opposite page.) Paint the lower half of the pot with white glue; wrap several rows of each color of yarn around the pot and press it into the glue. Repeat on the top half.

A clay pot can be covered with fabric. (See bottom left drawing on opposite page.) Start with the top inch of the fabric, and glue it on the side up to the rim. Make vertical cuts every two inches, two-thirds of the way up the sides; press into the glued surface of the pot as you stretch and overlap the fabric. Cover the rims of the pot and saucer. Paint the sides of the saucer.

A pedestal planter is easily made when you use two paper paint buckets separated by a decorative foam pedestal (available at hobby and floral shops). (See top right drawing on opposite page.) A corsage placed at the base of the pedestal adds a decorative touch.

Give a beauty treatment to a miniature bushel basket. (See bottom right drawing on opposite page.) Purchase the basket already painted or spray-paint it yourself. Then, add two strips of velvet ribbon to the basket.

Trim a foam pot with yarn.

A planter made from paint pails.

Floral fabric covers a clay pot.

Paint a basket and add trim.

Here are some other ideas that may be thought-provoking. Try some of them.

For a star-studded pot, trim a paper paint pail with star shapes cut from self-adhesive paper, vinyl, or tape.

To make a drum planter, cover a round carton with foil paper. Encircle the carton, top and bottom, with wide metallic ribbon. Loop double strands of gift cord around heads of corsage pins that are stuck through the carton.

Make a pretty hanging basket by first painting a paper paint bucket. Then, glue narrow strips of felt in vertical lines up the sides of the bucket. Suspend the bucket with lengths of velveteen cording that you string through three holes spaced equidistant under rim of pot.

Spray-paint a clay pot a bright, cheerful color. Glue a strip of heavy yarn fringe just under the rim. Pin a Christmas tree ornament of gift wrap medallion on the fringe.

Cover a clay pot with white glue. Then, press a width of velvet to the bottom section. Then, fit a strip over the rim—notch the fabric so it fits smoothly inside the pot. Glue paper doily cutouts around the pot.

A ribbon basket-weave coat gives a plastic pot a pleasing cover-up. Weave ribbon into a flat panel of fabric twice as wide as the pot is tall. Sew the ribbon ends together at the top and bottom so they won't separate when pressed tight to a pre-glued pot.

A garden tool and gloves with a fancy container make a nice gift for a gardener. A plain plastic pot, a coat of paint, and pre-glued paper stripes give the package stylish flair.

Octagonal boxes, available at import gift shops, gift-wrapping departments, or stationery stores, make ideal planters for small plants.

For a florist-shop touch, wrap a pot in a large sheet of foil giftwrap paper. Gather the paper at the top. Tie a strip of wide ribbon around the pot and make a large bow.

These ideas should get you started and might even inspire you to think of a few new ones. NOTE: Make certain the pot in which your gift plant is growing will fit inside the decorated container. Form a deep saucer of three or four thicknesses of aluminum foil to cover the bottom of the fancy pot. This will catch overflow water, which could damage the top.

LEATHER ARTISTRY

Leather is one of man's oldest natural resources. It played an important part in the settling of this country. Without it, the early settlers might not have survived. Leather provided two basic needs—clothing and shelter. To these people, working with leather was most assuredly a necessity rather than a craft.

Today, working with leather has become a means of expressing creativity and accomplishment. On the next few pages, you'll find some beautiful leather projects that will make handsome gifts—complete with patterns and instructions. Check the yellow pages in your phone directory for a leather supply shop or a craft and hobby shop near you. Here you will be able to purchase all kinds of leather, leather kits, patterns, tools, and accessories—rings, clasps, rivets, buckles, and lacings.

CUTTING INSTRUCTIONS

You can make your own pattern, or use patterns designed for leather projects. Cut out the individual pattern pieces. On all pieces marked 'cut two,' make a duplicate paper pattern.

Leather is a product of nature, and, therefore, is subject to its varying conditions. Climate, the food and care given the animal, and the season of slaughter are a few of the many factors that may produce flaws in the skin. These are natural and in no way mean the skin is inferior. Place pattern pieces on the skin in such a way as to avoid the flaws. All lengthwise grain line markings on the pattern pieces should be placed parallel to the animal's backbone. Keep in mind that the skin's greatest strength is down the center, and parts that will receive the most wear should be cut from this area.

After the pieces have been laid on the skin, trace around the pieces with chalk. Then, with shears or a razor knife, cut out the pattern pieces, using long, even strokes.

GENERAL ASSEMBLY INSTRUCTIONS

Sewing leather by machine usually entails some minor adjustments on your sewing machine. First, change needles—use a size 11 needle for lightweight leathers and a size 14 needle for heavier weights. Adjust the stitch regulator to allow for seven to ten stitches per inch. (For sheer suedes, as many as twelve stitches per inch may be applied.) An extra-strength, more elastic thread (cotton-wrapped polyester thread) is needed for sewing leather projects.

To make seams, follow the sketches at the top of page 159. Hold seams together with paper clips or mending tape (1). Gently position leather under the presser foot and stitch. Tie the threads at the top and bottom of the seam. (Avoid backstitching—this weakens the leather.)

Clip curved seams to reduce bulk (2). Then, apply rubber cement to all seam allowances, including curved seams (3). To flatten seams and lessen tension and pull, pound the seams with a mallet (4), then lightly lift them. Now, place brown paper between the leather and the iron and press the seams with a warm iron—do not steam the leather.

HOW TO LACE

Lacing adds the finishing touch to handmade leather articles. How good the finished project looks depends very much on the lacing. With the following instructions and the illustrations on page 159, plus a little practice, you will soon be doing a neat, smooth job of lacing.

Threading the special leatherworking needle is the first step in lacing. Using a razor knife, cut the end of the lacing to a point. Spring the threading end of the needle open, and insert pointed end of the lacing into needle, smooth side up. Close the needle on the lacing, and tap the needle with a mallet so that the prongs pierce the lace and lock in place.

The backstitch lacing is a lacing used for handbags. Lace with the front or outside of project facing you. (See sketches opposite.)

Begin lacing the front to the gusset at the top hole in the front and gusset. Place the gusset (flesh side up) on the front (flesh side up), aligning the holes and the edges to determine the gusset alignment. Lace as shown in the illustration (1), lacing through the front only in the

The sketches below show you how to seam leather.

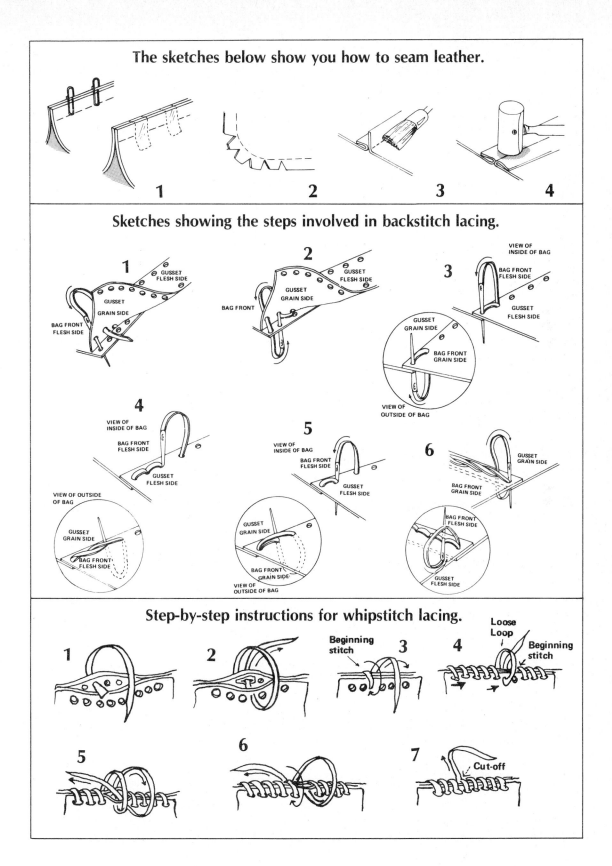

Sketches showing the steps involved in backstitch lacing.

Step-by-step instructions for whipstitch lacing.

first hole, then through the front and the gusset in the second hole. Take the needle through the first hole in the gusset and back through the first hole in the front (2). Pull the stitch tight and proceed to the third hole in the gusset and front, going through both this time (3). Pull the lace up through the third hole, then take it back through the second hole of the gusset and front (4). Continue lacing through the next hole, then back through the preceding hole (5). Using this lacing technique, lace the front and the gusset together. To tie off the lacing, at the last hole in the gusset and front, lace back through the next to last hole in the front and lace between the gusset and front to secure the lacing (6). Trim off excess lacing.

The whipstitch (see sketches on page 159) is used on small leather projects such as billfolds and coin purses. Begin lacing, starting in between the two layers of leather (1). Leave about ¼ inch at the end. Make a ⅛-inch slit in this end of the lace. Put the needle through the second hole, then thread it through the slit in the end of the lace and through the opposite

hole (2). Continue lacing, tightening as you go (3). Lace around the project, leaving a loose loop in the second hole from the beginning stitch (4). There will be one unlaced hole between your first and your last stitch. Spread the two leather layers, and lace through the last hole, up between the leathers and through the first loose loop. Pull the first loop tight, over the end of the lace (6). Pull the end of the lace tight to take the slack out of the last loop (7). Cut off the end of the lace with a knife, and tap the lacing with a mallet.

HOW TO STAMP LEATHER

Stamping designs on leather increases its natural beauty. All of the designs shown on these pages were created with four easy-to-use leather stamps—the pear shader, the seeder, the veiner, and the camouflage tool. You can create hundreds of designs with these tools.

Leather must be moistened with water before you can shape or stamp it. With a damp sponge, rub the leather first on the flesh side and then on the grain side. Apply the water as evenly

Nature designs for your leather projects made from four stamps.

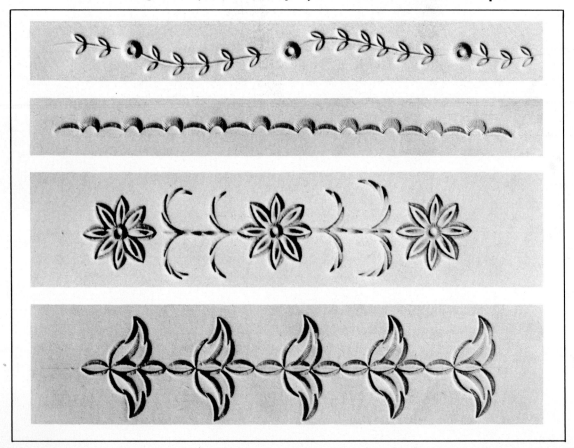

as possible. When the leather begins to return to its natural color, begin stamping the designs.

Hold the leather stamp in an upright position, resting it lightly on top of the leather. Now, strike the stamp with a wooden mallet. By tilting the stamp one way or another, you can produce many other designs.

HOW TO DYE STAMPED LEATHER

To achieve more contrast, dye stamped leather designs, using spirit-solvent leather dyes. To dye the surface and leave the stamped impressions natural, wrap some cloth around a wooden block. Apply dye to the cloth and blot on a paper towel until the cloth has only enough dye to color the surface. With the cloth, rub the surface of the leather. Apply more dye as needed. Dye the edges. After the dye has dried, finish with a coat of leather cream wax.

This charming barrette is made from a 2x5-inch piece of heavy leather and an orange stick. Cut an oval-shaped paper pattern. Place the pattern on the leather and draw around it. Cut out the barrette. Punch two holes in the barrette an inch from each end. Rub the leather with a damp sponge, and stamp the design, using a seeder and a veiner. Curve the barrette.

This wristband and watchband will appeal to any teen-ager on your gift-giving list. Both are cut from heavy leather and may be dyed.

To make the wristband, cut one piece of leather 6⅝ inches long by 2¼ inches wide. Cut off the corners. Then, on each end cut six ¾-inch slits down the center of the band. Begin ⅜ inch from the end, cutting three slits, ⅜ inch apart. Leave a ¾-inch space, then cut three more slits, also ⅜ inch apart. Now, cut a ⅝-inch-wide band to desired length. Attach a buckle at one end and punch holes in the other. Decorate the two bands with a stamped design and metal rings. (This one uses a seeder and a veiner.) Thread narrow band through wide band.

To make the watchband, use a 1¾x9-inch piece of leather. Taper one end, and attach a buckle with rivets on the other end. Make snap closures from two ½x1½-inch pieces of leather. Attach snaps, and rivet closure. Stamp design with a seeder, a pear shader, and a veiner.

A charming stamped leather barrette.

Stamped wristband and watchband.

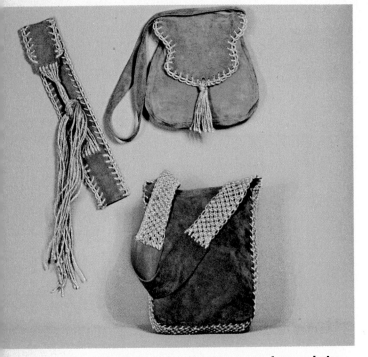

Leather belt, flap bag, and pouch bag.

LEATHER TRIMMED WITH MACRAME

Once you make these macrame-trimmed projects, you'll find them almost too pretty to give away. Each is easy to make. Simply expand pattern pieces below, follow assembly sketches, opposite page, and read the directions.

To make the leather belt, you'll need some heavyweight suede in the color of your choice, one roll of jute cord, one No. 1 drive punch, and some rubber cement.

Cut two pieces of suede 2 inches wide and 5 inches less than your hip or waist measurement. Cement them together, wrong sides together. Stitch around the belt on the seam line. Punch holes for the macrame with a No. 1 drive punch.

For the macrame trim, start on the right side of the belt and use the lark's head knot (see page 74) to attach two 16-foot strands to the top two holes on the belt sides (1). This leaves four strands hanging. Tie a square knot (see page 75). Insert the inside strand through the third hole and tie another square knot (2). Then,

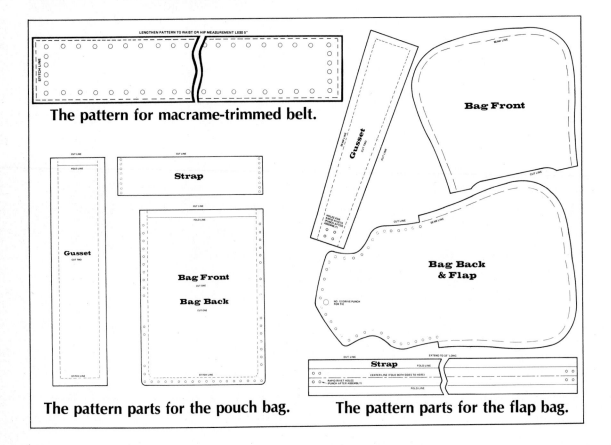

The pattern for macrame-trimmed belt.

The pattern parts for the pouch bag.

The pattern parts for the flap bag.

163

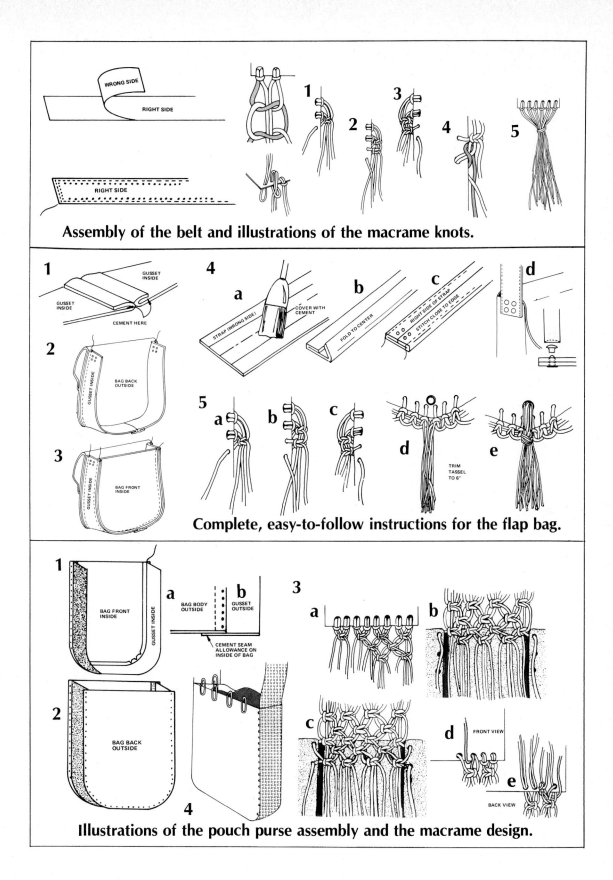

Assembly of the belt and illustrations of the macrame knots.

Complete, easy-to-follow instructions for the flap bag.

Illustrations of the pouch purse assembly and the macrame design.

insert the inside strand through the fourth hole. Tie a square knot. Continue this procedure until you reach the end of the belt. Tie square knots just opposite on the other side of the belt so that the knots will be uniform in appearance.

With 16 feet of cord, begin the left side of the belt at the same end as the right side so the knots will be uniform on both sides (3). When the trim is finished, tie it off by inserting the two inside strands through the hole and by pulling it tightly (4). Take one strand and wrap it around the two top strands, tie a square knot on the back side, cut the excess strand off, and glue. Continue this process until you have tied off the last two strands in the last hole. To attach the ties to the belt, cut jute cord in twelve 40-inch strands (5). Double each strand and attach through the first (of six) holes in the end of the belt, using a lark's head knot. Repeat for each hole in each end of the belt. After the strands are attached, pull two of the twelve strands around the entire amount and tie in an overhand knot. Trim the ties to desired length. Repeat on the other ends of the belt.

For the flap bag, you'll need sturdy buckskin-like suede leather, one roll jute cord, rubber cement, a No. 1 drive punch, a No. 12 drive punch, and 8 small rapid rivets.

Using the pattern on page 162 and the instructions on page 163, cut out the bag pieces. Stitch the gusset pieces together (at the end without the rivet holes). Open the seam, cement, and press flat (1). Stitch the gusset to the bag back with the right sides of the leather together (2). Clip curves, cement the open seam allowance, and tap with a mallet. Stitch the gusset to the bag front in the same manner (3). Clip the curves, open all seams, cement, and tap with a mallet to flatten the seams. Apply cement to the entire wrong side of the strap (4a). Fold on the fold lines to the center line of the strap. Tap with a mallet to flatten (4b). Stitch along both sides to strengthen the strap (4c). Attach the strap to the handbag with four rapid rivets on each side (see rivet hole location on the gusset and strap pattern pieces) (4d). Punch rivet holes with a No. 1 drive punch. To set the rapid rivets, use a rivet setter and a mallet. Place the rivet cap on the post. Place the con-

cave end of the rivet setter on the cap (be certain the rivet setter is centered so the edges of the setter will not mark the rivet cap), and tap sharply with the mallet once or twice. Check to see that the rivet is set tightly in the leather.

To trim the bag, cut two strands of jute cord 10 inches long. Begin at the top right side of the bag flap and attach the two strands to the top holes in the flap, using the lark's head knot. This leaves four strands hanging. Tie a square knot (5a). Insert one strand through the third hole down (5c). Tie another square knot. Then, insert the inside strand through the fourth hole. Tie a square knot (5b). Continue this procedure until you reach the center front of the bag front.

Cut two strands of cord 10 inches long and begin on the left side of the flap at the top of the bag, and tie knots as shown in the illustration so the knots will be uniform (5c). To make the tassel, trim the eight strands to 6 inches (5d). Take the remaining length of cord and pull it through the hole in the bag flap (made by the No. 12 drive punch). Tie the 24 strands in one overhand knot. Trim all of the strands of cording to the same length (5e).

To make the pouch bag, use sturdy buckskin-like suede leather, two balls of jute cord, a No. 1 drive punch, rubber cement, and white glue.

Stitch the gussets together (at the ends not marked for the fold—see pattern, page 162). Press the seam open, cement, and press flat with the fingertips (1b). Tap with a mallet to make the seam lie flat. Following the pattern markings, punch the holes for the macrame trim. Topstitch the bag front to the gusset (1a, page 163). Clip the curves in the gusset. The bag front will overlap the gusset, exposing the holes for the macrame. Cement and press the inside seam allowance flat (1b). Topstitch the bag back to the gusset in the same manner (2). Attach eight strands of jute cord (23 inches each) to the strap, using the lark's head knot. Begin with one row of four square knots. Continue the length of handle with alternating rows of square knots (3a). Tie the macrame to the bag at a row of four square knots (3b). On the next row tie three alternating square knots; the next row, tie four square knots. Repeat, tieing on the row with four square knots. Following this

procedure, continue around the gusset (3c). At the end of the gusset, continue the macrame strap nine inches as before. To tie the macrame into the strap, insert the two outside strands through a single hole in the strap. Wrap one strand around both strands (3d). Using the two strands, tie a square knot (3e). Continue this procedure until you have tied off jute in all eight holes in the strap. Cut the strands close to the square knot, and apply glue to each knot. Allow the glue to dry. Fold the top edge of the gusset, bag front and bag back, on the fold line. Then, cement the hem down, using some paper clips to secure the hem (4). To complete the pouch bag, topstitch the hem.

METAL-TRIMMED LEATHER PROJECTS

These metal-trimmed leather projects are even quicker and easier to make than the macrame-trimmed leather projects we just featured.

Metal-trimmed leather projects.

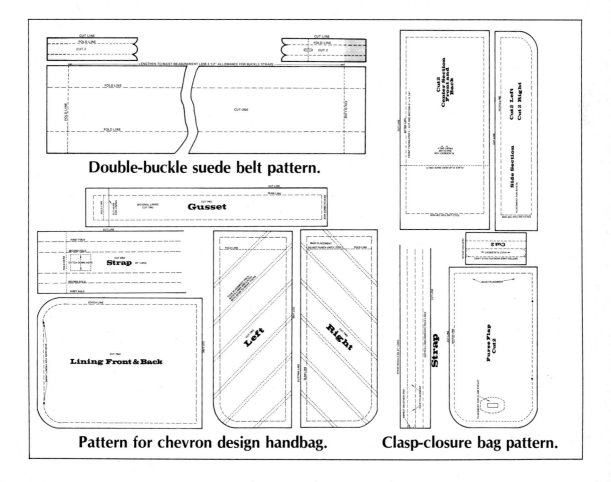

Double-buckle suede belt pattern.

Pattern for chevron design handbag.

Clasp-closure bag pattern.

166

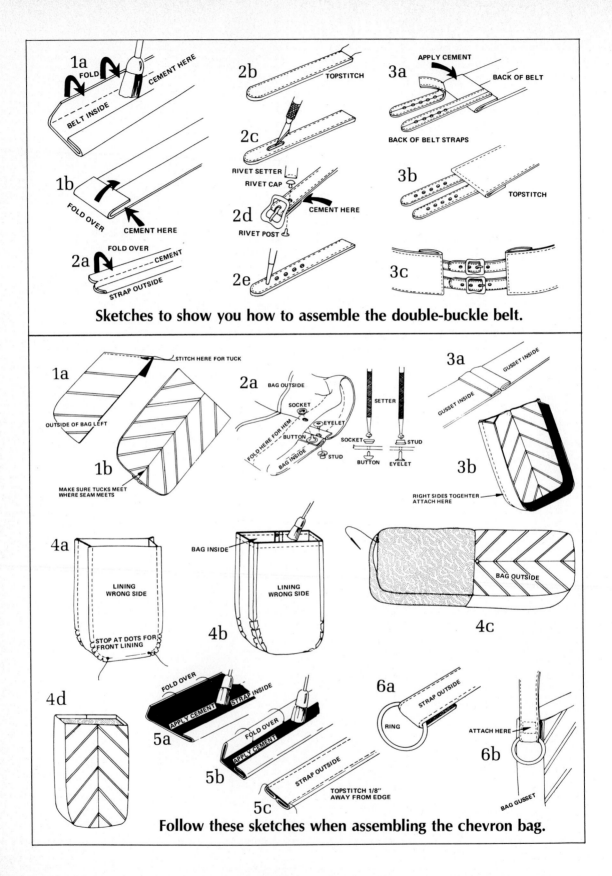

Sketches to show you how to assemble the double-buckle belt.

Follow these sketches when assembling the chevron bag.

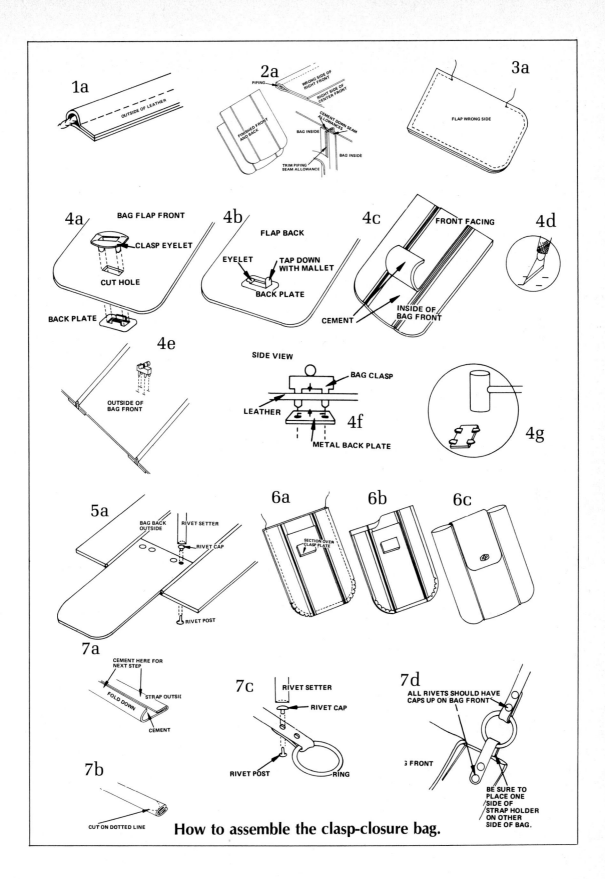

How to assemble the clasp-closure bag.

For the double-buckle belt, use sheer lambskin suede or supple, lightweight garment cabretta; polyester thread; a No. 1 drive punch; two rapid rivets; rivet setter; and two ½-inch buckles.

After expanding the pattern on page 165, cut out the belt. Folding on the fold lines, bring the outer edges into the center (1a, page 166). Tap with a mallet to crease. Coat the end of the belt with cement, fold in on the fold line, and tap this fold with a mallet (1b).

To make the buckle straps, coat the wrong side of all four buckle straps with rubber cement, then fold the outside edges into the center, and tap with a mallet (2a). Starting at the end, topstitch around the straps (2b). Cut a slit approximately ¼ inch long in the two straps to hold buckles to accommodate the buckle tongues (2c). Slip the buckle onto the strap, and insert the tongue in the slit. Cement the loose end to the strap, and punch a hole for the rivet. To set the rivet, insert the cap in the topside of the belt and the post in the underside. Position the rivet setter on the cap, and strike the setter with a mallet (2d). The other two straps need only have holes punched in them. Following the pattern for placement, use a drive punch to punch five holes in them (2e). Attach the straps to the belt with rubber cement. Coat that area of the belt where the straps are to go. Also, apply cement to the topsides of the strap ends to be covered by the belt. Attach the straps (3a), and tap with a mallet. Come in from the edge about ⅛ inch and topstitch around the belt (3b). The belt and buckle should resemble those in the illustration (3c).

To make the chevron bag, use sheer lambskin suede, supple, lightweight garment cabretta, or buckskin-like suede leather; thread; a No. 1 drive punch; a leather needle (size 11); 1 baby dot snap; a No. 5057 setter; two 1¼-inch rings; and ½ yard cotton lining (optional).

Expand the pattern on page 165, lay it on the leather, and cut out the pieces. To make the tucks, fold the bag on the lines indicated on the pattern, and sew about 1/16 inch away from the edge. Do this on all four front and back pieces, making nine tucks on each piece (1a, page 166). Join one right side to one left side, making the purse front. Repeat for the back (1b).

Cement down the seam allowance. Next, set the snap (2a). To assure alignment of the snap holes, punch the hole in the right front panel, then mark and punch the hole in the left back panel (refer to the pattern for placement). Push the button through one hole and place the socket on the bag outside over the button. Hold the setter firmly on the button and strike with the mallet until the button and socket are secure. Push the eyelet through the second hole and put the stud on the bag outside over the eyelet. Hold the setter firmly and strike with the mallet until the eyelet and stud are secure.

Stitch the two pieces of the gusset, right sides together. Cement down the seam allowances (3a). Sew the gusset to the bag front and back (3b). Clip the curves, and cement the seam allowances down. Turn right side out. To make the optional lining (4a), join the gusset linings' right sides together. Join the gusset to the lining back, making sure to keep the right sides together. Join the front lining to the gusset, stopping seams at the dots on the pattern. Clip the curves and press the seams open. Slip the lining, wrong side out, over the bag (right sides together) and sew at the top. Apply a 1½-inch-wide strip of cement to the inside top area of the bag (4b). Pull the bag through the hole in the lining. Stitch the hole together (4c). Push the lining down into the bag and fold the bag top on the fold line (4d). Press together with the fingertips. (If the bag is not to be lined, apply cement to the top inside, fold on the fold lines, and press with the fingertips.)

To make the strap, apply cement to the entire inside area of the strap. Fold the edges on the fold line over to the second fold line (5a). Tap with a mallet. Apply cement to the inside area of the strap again. Fold the strap edges over again, meeting in the middle (5b). Tap with a mallet. Topstitch the strap about ⅛ inch away from the edges of the strap (5c). Loop the strap over a ring (6a). Place the strap on the bag gusset as indicated on the pattern, and sew to the bag as shown (6b).

The clasp-closure bag (pictured on page 165) is easily made with sheer lambskin suede, supple, lightweight garment cabretta, or buckskin-like suede leather; a No. 1504 clasp, 12 medium

rapid rivets; two 1¼-inch rings; 4¼ yards of cord for piping; thread; leather needle (size 11); rivet setter; rubber cement; and a No. 1 drive punch.

Cut out the bag pieces, following the pattern on page 165. To make the piping used between the three sections of the bag front and back, cut four strips 1 inch wide and 13 inches long. The strips should be cut from scraps after the main pattern pieces are cut. The strips may be pieced, if necessary. Center the cord on the inside of the strip, fold over and run a seam as close to the cord as possible (1a, page 167). Attach the front and back sections by lining up the edge of the piping with the edges of the bag right side and back center section, making sure the right sides of the leather are together (2a). Join the left side sections to the center sections, using the same procedure. Repeat for the other side of the bag. Open the seams, and trim the piping seam allowance as close as possible. Cement the seam allowances (2b). To make the flap, sew the flap parts, right sides of the leather together, from dot to dot (3a). Trim the seam allowances and turn right side out. Apply cement to the seam allowance not stitched, turn in, and press together.

To attach the clasp, cut a hole with a sharp knife in the bag flap as shown on the pattern. Place the clasp eyelet into the slot and slip the back plate into position (4a). Fold the prongs over into the depressions and tap (outward) down with a mallet (4b). Apply cement to the entire wrong side of the bag front facing and to the bag front center section. Attach (4c). Cut small slits in the bag front, as indicated on the pattern (4d). Place the prongs of the clasp through the slits from the outside of the bag (4e), and fit the back plate over the prongs (4f). Bend the prongs down over the back plate, and tap with a mallet (4g). Cut a piece of scrap leather 4x2 inches, and cement down over the clasp plate in the bag front inside.

Attach the flap by placing the bottom part of the flap on the bag, as indicated on the pattern, and punch holes for rivets with a No. 2 drive punch. Place rivet caps on the outside of the purse, and push the rivet post through from the back side. Place the rivet setter over the cap and strike with a mallet until secure (5a). Place

right sides of the leather together, and sew the back of the bag to the front (6a). Clip the curves and cement the seam allowances down. Cement down the hem at the top of the bag (6b). Turn the bag right side out (6c).

Next, assemble the strap and strap holders. Apply cement to the entire wrong side of the strap. Fold the edges on the fold line into the center part of the strap (7a). Cement the folded edges and fold again. Tap with a mallet. Trim the edges, as shown in the illustration (7b). Follow this same procedure for the strap holders. Slip the strap over the ring. Punch holes and attach rivets (7c). (Refer back to 5a.) Slip the strap holder over the ring, and punch the rivet holes. Punch rivet holes in the bag. Place the strap holder over the side section of the bag and align the rivet holes. Insert rivet posts from the back side of the bag. Place the cap on the rivet posts from the front and set the rivets (7d). This completes the clasp-closure bag.

None of the projects that have been discussed in this chapter are difficult to do, but practice will make your finished project look more professional. Therefore, if this is your first experience with leathercraft, begin on practice pieces or leather scraps. Then, buy a few more scraps of leather and make very small items such as barrettes, bookmarkers, coin purses, simple belts, and billfolds. This will give you practice in cutting, stamping, dyeing, and lacing leather, and thus, will eliminate many costly mistakes that are often made by beginners, not to mention wasted leather and other materials.

Once you get the feel of the craft, then you might look for a more advanced project in a kit form—such as a handbag, vest, or belt. The kit will provide you with all the materials you'll need and a list of easy-to-follow directions. After you've successfully completed the first kit, you may either stay with the kits because of the convenience, or you may decide to buy your own supplies and design your own pattern. Regardless of which course you decide on, remember that if you ever have any questions regarding the techniques involved in working with leather, the type of materials to use, or how much leather to buy, the proprietor of the hobby shop will be glad to help you.

chapter 9

GIFTS FROM THE KITCHEN

Don't limit yourself to giving kitchen-made gifts only on holidays and special occasions. Anytime is the right time to present some homemade 'goodies,' whether it's a plate of cookies, a box of candy, a loaf of bread, or a jar or two of jam or jelly. When the recipe you are making is completed, it only takes a little extra effort to make the gift look exciting. Clear plastic wrap and a perky, colorful ribbon and bow are sometimes all that is needed. As a bonus, include a copy of the recipe typed on a file card. The recipient will be delighted.

COOKIE CAPERS

As a gift, cookies are favorites that people of all ages enjoy receiving. A plate of cookies handed to new neighbors as they are in the process of getting settled makes an ideal coffee break treat. And, of course, an assortment of cookies at Christmas time is a traditional gift that is enjoyed by both the giver and the receiver. For gift giving, arrange the cookies on a colorful paper plate, or pack a festive container, such as a handcrafted Santa's sleigh, with favorites prepared in your kitchen.

If you are planning to mail your cookie gift, choose soft types of cookies, since they are better travelers than crisp, breakable ones. Use clear plastic wrap to wrap the cookies individually or in pairs, back to back.

Before arranging the cookies snugly in a strong cardboard box or metal container, line the box or container with waxed paper or foil, and put a cushion of crumpled waxed paper or plastic wrap on the bottom. Cover each layer with a cushion of crumpled waxed paper. If you use a metal container, pack it in a heavy cardboard carton and use crushed newspaper or confetti to hold the container in place. Tape the carton closed and tie securely, then wrap in heavy paper. Be sure to print the address on both the carton and the paper wrapping so the package can be delivered safely even if the paper should tear loose.

Pecan Crunch Cookies

    1 cup butter or margarine
    ½ cup sugar
    1 teaspoon vanilla
    ½ cup crushed potato chips
    ½ cup chopped pecans
    2 cups sifted all-purpose flour

Cream together butter, sugar, and vanilla. Add crushed potato chips and pecans. Stir in flour. Form into small balls, using 1 tablespoon dough for each. Place on ungreased cookie sheet. Press balls flat with bottom of a tumbler dipped in sugar. Bake at 350° till cookies are lightly browned, about 16 to 18 minutes. If desired, sprinkle with red or green sugar crystals, or top each cookie with a pecan or candied cherry half. Makes 42.

Black Walnut Brandy Balls

In mixer bowl cream together ½ cup butter, ½ cup sifted powdered sugar, and ⅛ teaspoon salt till fluffy. Stir in 1 tablespoon brandy and ½ teaspoon vanilla. Stir in 1 cup sifted all-purpose flour and ½ cup finely chopped black walnuts; mix well. Shape into ¾-inch balls, using about 2 teaspoons dough for each cookie. Place on ungreased cookie sheet. Bake at 325° till lightly browned, about 20 minutes. Roll in sifted powdered sugar. Makes 3 dozen.

A sleighful of Pecan Crunch Cookies is a fine holiday gift idea.

1. Nosegay Cookies

Prepare a roll of refrigerated sugar cookie dough. Bake following the label directions. Trim the cookies with decorator icing.

2. Fluted Cookie Tarts

1 cup butter or margarine
1 cup sugar
1 egg
1 teaspoon almond extract
3 cups sifted all-purpose flour
1 cup apricot preserves
2 teaspoons lemon juice
¼ cup chopped candied red cherries
¼ cup toasted sliced almonds

Thoroughly cream butter and sugar. Add egg and almond extract; beat well. Stir in flour. Pinch off small ball of dough and place in center of 2½-inch sandbakelser mold; with thumb, press dough evenly and as thinly as possible over bottom and sides. Place molds on cookie sheet. Bake at 350° till lightly browned, about 12 to 14 minutes. Cool. To remove invert molds and tap lightly. (Clean molds with dry cloth only.) Just before serving, combine preserves, lemon juice, and cherries. Place teaspoon of mixture in each cookie tart. Stick in almonds. Makes 3½ dozen.

3. Macaroon Bonbons

2 egg whites
1 teaspoon vanilla
  Dash salt
½ cup sugar
2 tablespoons all-purpose flour
1 cup grated coconut
3 drops red food coloring

Beat egg whites with vanilla and salt till soft peaks form. Gradually add the sugar, beating till stiff peaks form. Fold in flour and coconut. Remove ⅓ of dough to second bowl. With red food coloring, tint remaining ⅔ of dough a delicate pink. Roll pink dough in ½-inch balls. Place on greased cookie sheet. With thumb make small indentation; top with ¼-inch balls of the white dough. Bake at 350° till done, 8 to 10 minutes. Let stand 1 minute; remove to rack. Makes 30 bonbons.

4. Scotch Shortbread Miniatures

1 cup butter or margarine
½ cup sugar
2½ cups sifted all-purpose flour
  Gumdrops

Cream butter; gradually add sugar, creaming till light and fluffy. Stir in flour. Chill several hours. Divide the dough in half. On lightly floured surface roll the dough ¼ inch thick. Cut with floured 2½-inch round cutter. Place rounds on ungreased cookie sheet; slightly crimp edges to scallop. With dinner fork prick each cookie to make 6 pie-shaped wedges. Bake at 300° for 20 to 23 minutes. Cool slightly; remove to rack. Attach gumdrop pieces with light corn syrup. Makes 2 dozen cookies.

5. Brazilian Creams

½ cup butter or margarine
1 cup brown sugar
1 egg
½ teaspoon vanilla
2 cups sifted all-purpose flour
¾ teaspoon baking soda
¾ teaspoon baking powder
½ teaspoon ground cinnamon
¼ teaspoon salt
¼ teaspoon ground nutmeg
⅓ cup dairy sour cream
½ cup chopped Brazil nuts
  Brown Butter Icing
  Brazil Nut Petals

Cream butter and brown sugar. Add egg and vanilla; beat well. Sift together dry ingredients; add to creamed mixture alternately with sour cream. Stir in chopped nuts. Drop from teaspoon, 2 inches apart, onto greased cookie sheet. Bake at 400° till lightly browned, 8 to 10 minutes. Cool cookies on rack.

Frost with **Brown Butter Icing:** Heat and stir 3 tablespoons butter till browned; cool. Slowly beat in 2 cups sifted powdered sugar, 2 tablespoons milk, and 1 teaspoon vanilla. Garnish with **Brazil Nut Petals:** Cover *unshelled* Brazil nuts with cold water; boil 3 minutes, then drain. Cover with cold water; let stand 1 minute, then drain. Crack and shell. Cover nuts with cold water and simmer 2 to 3 minutes; drain. Cut paper-thin lengthwise slices with vegetable parer. Makes 48 cookies.

6. Swedish Ginger Cookies

1 cup butter or margarine
1½ cups sugar
1 egg
1½ tablespoons grated orange peel
2 tablespoons dark corn syrup
1 tablespoon water

• • •

3¼ cups sifted all-purpose flour
2 teaspoons baking soda
2 teaspoons ground cinnamon
1 teaspoon ground ginger
½ teaspoon ground cloves

• • •

Toasted blanched almonds
Pink sugar crystals

Thoroughly cream butter and sugar. Add egg; beat till light and fluffy. Add orange peel, corn syrup, and water; mix well. Sift together next 5 ingredients; stir into creamed mixture. Chill thoroughly. On lightly floured surface, roll out ⅛ inch thick. Sprinkle dough with additional sugar; press in lightly with rolling pin. Cut with floured scalloped, diamond, or round cutter, or other shape. Place, 1 inch apart, on ungreased cookie sheet. Top cookies with almonds. Bake at 375° for 8 to 10 minutes. Cool slightly; remove from pan to rack. Brush center with corn syrup; sprinkle on pink sugar. Makes 8 dozen.

7, 8. Sugar Cookies

⅔ cup butter or margarine
¾ cup sugar
1 teaspoon vanilla
½ teaspoon ground nutmeg
1 egg
4 teaspoons milk
2 cups sifted all-purpose flour
1½ teaspoons baking powder
¼ teaspoon salt

Thoroughly cream butter, sugar, vanilla, and nutmeg. Add egg; beat till light and fluffy. Stir in milk. Sift together dry ingredients; blend into creamed mixture. Divide dough in half. Chill 1 hour. On lightly floured surface, roll half the dough at a time to ⅛-inch thickness. Cut in desired shapes. Place cookies on greased cookie sheet. Bake at 375° for 6 to 8 minutes. Cool slightly; remove to rack. Decorate. Makes about 2 dozen 3-inch cookies.

9, 10, 11. Gingerbread Cookies

½ cup butter or margarine
½ cup shortening
1 cup granulated sugar
½ cup brown sugar
1 egg
¼ cup light molasses
3½ cups sifted all-purpose flour
2 teaspoons baking soda
2 teaspoons ground cinnamon
1 teaspoon ground ginger
½ teaspoon ground cloves
Granulated sugar
Trims

Thoroughly cream first 6 ingredients. Sift together flour, baking soda, and spices; stir into creamed mixture. Chill well. On lightly floured surface, roll dough to ¼-inch thickness. Cut with any shaped cutter. Place, 1 inch apart, on ungreased cookie sheet. Sprinkle lightly with granulated sugar for sparkle. Bake at 375° for 7 to 8 minutes. Remove to rack and cool. Trim with frosting, animal crackers, candies, or gumdrops. Makes about 6 dozen.

12. Toffee Diamonds

1 cup butter or margarine
1 cup brown sugar
1 teaspoon vanilla
2 cups sifted all-purpose flour
1 6-ounce package semisweet chocolate
    pieces (1 cup)
1 cup chopped walnuts
Chocolate Frosting
Walnut halves

Thoroughly cream together the butter, sugar, and vanilla. Add flour; mix well. Reserve ¼ cup chocolate pieces for frosting; stir remaining chocolate pieces and chopped walnuts into dough. Press mixture into ungreased 15½x10½x 1-inch baking pan. Bake at 350° till browned, 15 to 18 minutes. While still warm, cut in 2-inch diamonds. Cool before removing from pan. Trim with dot of Chocolate Frosting; top with walnut half. Makes 5 dozen.

Chocolate Frosting: Melt the reserved chocolate pieces in small saucepan; stir in ½ cup sifted powdered sugar, ¼ teaspoon vanilla, and dash salt. Add just enough milk to make slightly thicker than spreading consistency.

13. Lattice Fruit Bars

1½ cups sifted all-purpose flour
¼ cup granulated sugar
½ teaspoon baking powder
½ teaspoon salt
½ teaspoon ground cinnamon
½ cup brown sugar
½ cup butter or margarine
1 slightly beaten egg
⅓ cup blanched almonds, ground
• • •
½ cup red raspberry jam
1 slightly beaten egg yolk
1 teaspoon water

Sift together flour, sugar, baking powder, salt, and cinnamon; stir in brown sugar. Cut in butter till mixture is crumbly. Add egg and ground almonds; mix well with hands.

Pat half the mixture into an ungreased 9x9x2-inch pan. Spread the raspberry jam evenly over the dough. On floured surface roll remaining dough into a 9x5-inch rectangle. Cut 20 strips, measuring 9 inches long and ¼ inch wide. For lattice top line 10 strips across filling; then arrange the remaining 10 strips of dough diagonally across the top. Combine the egg yolk and water; brush over lattice. Bake at 375° till done, about 25 minutes. Cool. Cut the baked cookies into bars or squares.

14. Swedish Rosettes

2 eggs
1 tablespoon granulated sugar
¼ teaspoon salt
1 cup sifted all-purpose flour
1 cup milk
1 teaspoon vanilla
Powdered sugar

Combine first 3 ingredients; beat well. Add flour, milk, and vanilla; beat smooth. Heat rosette iron in deep, hot fat (375°) for 2 minutes; remove and drain off excess fat. Then, dip hot iron into batter to ¼ inch from top of iron; dip at once into hot fat (375°). Fry rosette till golden, about ½ minute. Lift iron out; tip slightly to drain off excess fat. With fork, push rosette off iron onto paper toweling placed on rack. Reheat iron 1 minute; make next rosette. Repeat with remaining batter. Sift powdered sugar over cooled rosettes. Makes 3½ dozen.

15. Cameo Cutouts

¾ cup butter or margarine
⅔ cup sugar
½ cup dark corn syrup
1 egg
1½ teaspoons vanilla
3 cups sifted all-purpose flour
1 teaspoon baking powder
½ teaspoon salt
1 1-ounce square unsweetened chocolate, melted and cooled

Cream butter or margarine, sugar, and dark corn syrup till fluffy. Beat in egg and vanilla. Sift together dry ingredients; stir into creamed mixture. Divide dough in half. To one half add melted chocolate; blend. Leave other half plain. Chill both doughs thoroughly. On well-floured surface, roll chocolate dough to ⅛-inch thickness. (Keep other dough chilled.) Cut in 2½-inch scalloped rounds. Place on ungreased cookie sheet. Repeat with vanilla dough. With floured tiny fruit cutter (or with thimble), make center cutouts. Switch cutouts to make contrasting centers. Bake at 350° till lightly browned, 8 to 10 minutes. Cool slightly; remove to rack. Makes 6 dozen cookies.

16. Cinnamon Stars

⅔ cup sugar
1 teaspoon ground cinnamon
½ teaspoon grated lemon peel
2 egg whites
1¾ cups ground almonds (7 ounces)
Meringue
Small silver decorative candies

Mix sugar, cinnamon, and lemon peel. Beat egg whites till soft peaks form. Gradually add cinnamon-sugar mixture; continue beating till very stiff peaks form, about 10 minutes. Fold in almonds. Chill dough several hours. On lightly floured surface, roll dough ⅛ inch thick. Cut with 2½-inch star cutter. Place on well-greased cookie sheet. Frost with Meringue, spreading it to the points. Trim with silver candies. Bake at 325° for 12 to 15 minutes. Remove from cookie sheet at once and cool on rack. Makes 36.

Meringue: Beat 1 egg white till soft peaks form. Gradually add 1 cup sifted powdered sugar, beating after each addition; beat till egg white mixture forms stiff peaks.

CANDY FOR A SPECIAL GIFT

Homemade candy is a gift that is appropriate to give regardless of the occasion. When you cook up a batch of your prettiest candy and present it to a friend or a neighbor, you are telling the recipient, 'You are special.'

To make your gift as pretty to give as it will be good to eat, present the candy in a glass container. Apothecary jars are readily available in various sizes and at a very small cost. Or, if desired, wrap the candies individually in brightly colored cellophane paper.

For friends living in other parts of the country, send a box of candy through the mail. The best candy choices for mailing include fudge, taffy, and caramels. Brittles and divinity are not good mailers, since brittles break easily and divinity does not keep well.

To prepare candy for mailing, place each piece in a fluted paper cup, or wrap each piece separately. Arrange the candies in a box or metal container lined with paper doilies. Be sure to include crushed paper on the bottom and top of the candy to hold it securely. Wrap the box and print the destination plainly on the inside and outside of the package.

Pinwheel Taffy Lollipops

  2 cups sugar
  ½ cup light corn syrup
  ¼ teaspoon cream of tartar
  1 teaspoon peppermint extract
    Red or green food coloring
    Wooden skewers

In saucepan combine first 3 ingredients and ½ cup water. Place over heat; stir till sugar dissolves. Cook, stirring occasionally, to soft-crack stage (270°). Remove from heat; add peppermint extract and few drops food coloring. Pour onto large buttered platter.

When candy is just cool enough to handle, divide in half. With lightly buttered hands pull till taffy is porous and light in color. Then, pull and twist into slender ropes—candy should still be warm. Place skewers on greased cookie sheet with pointed ends 3 or more inches apart. Wind strip of taffy over end of each skewer to form circle. Press taffy onto skewers. Let harden. Makes 14 lollipops.

Coconut Peaks

  ¼ cup butter or margarine
  2 cups sifted powdered sugar
  3 cups flaked coconut
  ¼ cup light cream
      • • •
  1 6-ounce package semisweet chocolate
      pieces (1 cup)
  2 teaspoons shortening

In saucepan slowly heat butter or margarine till golden brown; gradually stir in powdered sugar, flaked coconut, and light cream. Drop by teaspoonfuls onto waxed paper. Refrigerate till easy to handle, then shape into peaks. Over hot, not boiling water, melt chocolate pieces and shortening; stir till smooth. Dip bottoms of the peaks into the melted chocolate mixture, then harden on a rack covered with waxed paper. Makes about 3 dozen.

Flower Lollipops

    Wooden skewers
  3 cups sugar
  ¾ cup light corn syrup
  3 tablespoons vinegar
  ⅓ cup boiling water
  ¼ cup butter or margarine
    Dash salt
    Red or yellow food coloring
    Few drops oil of cinnamon or cloves

Prepare molds by cutting flower pattern from cardboard; cover with foil. Cut a strip of foil 2 inches wide; fold in half. Mold into a rim about ½ inch high around foil-covered base, securing as necessary with tape. Punch wooden skewer through rim on one side.

In saucepan combine sugar, corn syrup, vinegar, and water; stir till sugar dissolves. Cook to hard-crack stage (300°). Remove saucepan from heat; add butter, salt, few drops food coloring, and flavoring (add red food coloring to cinnamon flavoring and yellow food coloring to clove flavoring). Pour about ¼ cup candy into each mold. Cool and remove molds. If desired, trim with gumdrops or plastic flowers and leaves. Makes 10 lollipops.

From left: Pinwheel Taffy Lollipops, green and red Crystal-Cut Candies (see page 178), Flower Lollipops, and Coconut Peaks.

178

Crystal-Cut Candies

2 cups sugar
½ cup light corn syrup
½ cup water
  Dash salt
  Few drops red or green food
    coloring
4 to 6 drops oil of cinnamon or
  wintergreen

In saucepan combine sugar, corn syrup, water, and dash salt; bring to boiling. Cook to soft-crack stage (290°). Add food coloring and flavoring (use red food coloring with cinnamon and green food coloring with wintergreen); gently swirl mixture to blend. Pour into 8x8x2-inch metal pan. Let stand a few minutes till slightly cooled and a film forms over the top. Mark candy in little puffs, each about ¾ inch square. Because candy is cooler at edges, start marking from outside and work toward center. Using a broad spatula or pancake turner, press a line across pan ¾ inch from edge, *being careful not to break through the film on surface.* Repeat around other 3 sides of pan, intersecting lines at corners to form squares. (If lines do not hold shape, candy is not cool enough.) Continue marking lines to center. While waiting for center to cool enough, retrace previous lines, pressing the spatula deeper, *but do not break film.* When spatula may be pressed to bottom of pan in all lines, candy will be shaped in square puffs. Cool, then turn out and break into pieces. Makes about 100 pieces.

Caramels

1 cup butter or margarine
1 pound brown sugar (2¼ cups)
1 cup light corn syrup
1 15-ounce can sweetened condensed
  milk
1 teaspoon vanilla

Melt butter in heavy 3-quart saucepan. Add brown sugar and dash salt; stir till thoroughly combined. Stir in light corn syrup; mix well. Gradually add milk, stirring constantly. Cook and stir over medium heat till candy reaches firm-ball stage (245°), about 12 to 15 minutes. Remove from heat; stir in vanilla. Pour into buttered 9x9x2-inch pan. Cool and cut into squares. Makes about 2½ pounds.

Perfect Divinity

2½ cups sugar
½ cup light corn syrup
½ cup water
¼ teaspoon salt
2 egg whites
1 teaspoon vanilla
½ cup chopped candied cherries

In 2-quart saucepan combine sugar, corn syrup, water, and salt. Cook to hard-ball stage (260°), stirring only till sugar dissolves. Meanwhile, as temperature of syrup reaches 250°, beat egg whites till stiff peaks form. When syrup reaches 260°, very gradually add the syrup to egg whites, beating at high speed on electric mixer. Add vanilla and beat till candy holds its shape, 4 to 5 minutes. Stir in the chopped candied cherries. Quickly drop candy from a teaspoon onto waxed paper, swirling the top of each piece. Makes about 40 pieces.

Peanut-Cereal Candy

3 cups crisp rice cereal
1 cup salted peanuts
½ cup sugar
½ cup light corn syrup
½ cup peanut butter
½ teaspoon vanilla

Mix cereal and peanuts; set aside. Combine sugar and corn syrup. Cook, stirring constantly, till mixture comes to a full rolling boil. Remove from heat. Stir in peanut butter and vanilla. Immediately pour syrup over cereal mixture, stirring gently to coat. Pat cereal evenly into buttered 8x8x2-inch pan. Cool; cut the mixture in 2x1-inch bars. Makes 32 bars.

Butterscotch Quickies

2 6-ounce packages butterscotch
  pieces (2 cups)
¼ cup peanut butter
5 cups cornflakes

In large saucepan melt butterscotch pieces and peanut butter over low heat. Remove from heat; add cornflakes and stir till well coated. Drop from teaspoon onto waxed paper. Let stand till firm. Makes about 3½ dozen pieces.

Crystal-Cut Candies, Remarkable Fudge, and Perfect Divinity.

Honey-Sugared Walnuts

2½ cups walnut halves
1½ cups sugar
½ cup water
¼ cup honey
½ teaspoon salt
½ teaspoon ground cinnamon
• • •
½ teaspoon vanilla

Toast walnuts in 375° oven for 10 minutes, stirring once. Butter sides of heavy 2-quart saucepan. In it combine sugar, water, honey, salt, and cinnamon. Heat and stir till sugar dissolves and mixture boils. Cook to soft-ball stage (236°) without stirring. Remove from heat; beat till mixture begins to get creamy. Add vanilla and warm nuts; stir gently till nuts are well coated and mixture becomes thick. Turn out on buttered baking sheet; with two forks, separate nuts at once.

Remarkable Fudge

4 cups sugar
1 14½-ounce can evaporated milk
   (1⅔ cups)
1 cup butter or margarine
1 12-ounce package semisweet chocolate
   pieces (2 cups)
1 7-, 9-, or 10-ounce jar marshmallow
   creme
1 teaspoon vanilla
1 cup chopped walnuts

Butter sides of heavy 3-quart saucepan. In it combine first 3 ingredients. Cook over medium heat to soft-ball stage (236°), stirring frequently. Remove from heat; add chocolate pieces, marshmallow creme, vanilla, and nuts. Beat till chocolate is melted and blended. Pour into buttered 13x9x2-inch pan. Score in squares while warm; top each with a walnut half. Cut when firm. Makes 54 1½-inch pieces.

Top: Crown Coffee Bread and Fruit Bread Trio; Bottom: Apricot Crescent.

GIFT BREADS TO BAKE

Next time you want to give a treat from your kitchen, make a coffee cake or a quick nut bread. A freshly baked coffee cake or pecan rolls presented on a tray or cutting board makes a welcome gift for any busy homemaker. The tray or basket also can be part of the gift. If possible, deliver the coffee cake while it is warm from the oven and at its best. Decorate the home-baked coffee cake or bread gift with a perky, colorful napkin, then wrap it with clear plastic wrap. Add a bow for a simple trim.

Fruit and nut breads also make delightful, easy-to-prepare gifts. Most nut breads are best when wrapped and stored for one day. This allows the flavors to mellow. The loaf will slice more easily, too. For gift giving, wrap the loaf in foil or clear plastic wrap, and decorate the package with a fluffy bow.

Basic Fruit Dough

    2 packages active dry yeast
    2 cups sifted all-purpose flour
    ¾ cup unsweetened pineapple juice
    ½ cup shortening
    ⅓ cup sugar
    2 eggs
    2 teaspoons grated lemon peel
    ¾ cup light raisins
    ½ cup chopped candied pineapple
    2½ to 3 cups sifted all-purpose flour

In large mixer bowl combine yeast and 2 cups sifted flour. In saucepan combine pineapple juice, ½ cup water, shortening, sugar, and 1½ teaspoons salt. Heat just till warm, stirring occasionally to melt the shortening. Add to dry mixture in mixing bowl. Add eggs and lemon peel. Beat at low speed with electric mixer for ½ minute, scraping sides of bowl constantly. Beat 3 minutes at high speed.

By hand, stir in raisins and pineapple. Stir in enough of the 2½ to 3 cups flour to make a soft to moderately stiff dough. Turn out on lightly floured surface. Knead till smooth, about 10 minutes. Place in greased bowl; turn once to grease surface. Cover; let rise in warm place till double, 1 to 1½ hours. Punch down; let rest 10 minutes. Shape dough into Crown Coffee Bread or Fruit Bread Trio.

Crown Coffee Bread

Using Basic Fruit Dough, pat ¾ of dough evenly into a greased 10-inch tube pan. Divide remaining dough in half; roll each to 28-inch strand. Twist together. Place on top of dough; seal ends. Cover; let rise till double, 45 to 60 minutes. Bake at 375° about 45 minutes. Brush with butter; sprinkle with sugar.

Fruit Bread Trio

Using Basic Fruit Dough, divide dough in thirds. Shape each into a smooth ball. Place balls on lightly greased baking sheet, with balls just touching. Cover and let rise till double, about 45 minutes. Bake at 350° about 35 minutes. Cool. Prepare **Icing:** Combine ¾ cup sifted powdered sugar and 1 tablespoon milk; beat till smooth. Spread over bread. Trim with almonds and candied cherries.

Apricot Crescent

Sift together 2 cups sifted all-purpose flour, 1 tablespoon sugar, 1 tablespoon baking powder, and 1 teaspoon salt. Cut in ¼ cup shortening till mixture is crumbly. Beat together 1 whole egg and 1 egg yolk (reserve egg white). Add enough milk to egg to make ⅔ cup. Add to dry ingredients and stir only till moistened. Turn out on lightly floured surface and knead gently for 30 seconds.

Roll to 14x9-inch rectangle. Brush with 1 tablespoon melted butter; spread with Apricot Filling. Roll up like jelly roll, starting with long side; seal edge well. Place, sealed edge down, on greased baking sheet and curve into crescent shape. With scissors, cut 1-inch slices to within ¼ inch of the inner edge. Turn each slice slightly on its side. Beat reserved egg white lightly and brush over dough; sprinkle with sugar. Bake at 425° till the coffee cake is done, 15 to 20 minutes.

Apricot Filling: In heavy saucepan combine 1 cup chopped dried apricots, ¼ cup raisins, ½ cup sugar, and ¾ cup water. Boil until thick, about 10 minutes; stir frequently. Add 1 teaspoon lemon juice; mix well. Cool.

Caramel-Pecan Rolls

      2 packages active dry yeast
   5½ to 6½ cups sifted all-purpose flour
               • • •
   2¼ cups milk
      3 tablespoons shortening
      2 tablespoons granulated sugar
      1 tablespoon salt
               • • •
      1 cup brown sugar
      ½ cup butter or margarine, melted
      2 tablespoons corn syrup
      1 cup pecan halves
               • • •
      ¼ cup butter or margarine, softened
      ½ cup granulated sugar
      1 teaspoon ground cinnamon

In large mixer bowl combine yeast and *2½ cups* of the flour. In saucepan heat milk, shortening, 2 tablespoons granulated sugar, and salt just till warm, stirring occasionally to melt shortening. Add to dry mixture in mixing bowl. Beat at low speed with electric mixer for ½ minute, scraping sides of bowl constantly. Beat 3 minutes at high speed.

By hand, stir in enough of the remaining flour to make a soft dough. Turn out onto a lightly floured surface; shape into a ball. Knead till smooth and elastic, about 5 to 10 minutes. Cover with clear plastic wrap, then a towel; let rest 20 minutes. Punch down.

Meanwhile, in small saucepan combine brown sugar, ½ cup melted butter or margarine, and corn syrup; cook and stir till blended. Distribute mixture in bottom of 36 well-greased muffin pans (or use three 9-inch round cake pans); top with pecan halves.

Divide dough in half; roll each portion to a 16x10-inch rectangle. Spread each rectangle with *half* the softened butter or margarine. Mix ½ cup granulated sugar and cinnamon; sprinkle sugar-cinnamon mixture over dough.

Roll up dough jelly-roll fashion, beginning with the long side; seal the edges. Cut into 18 slices. Place the rolls, cut side down, in prepared muffin or cake pans. Cover the rolls with oiled waxed paper, then with clear plastic wrap; refrigerate 2 to 24 hours.

When ready to bake, remove rolls from refrigerator; let stand 20 minutes. Before baking, puncture any surface bubbles with greased wooden pick. Bake at 425° for 20 to 25 minutes. Invert on cooling racks. Makes 36.

German Stollen

      1 package active dry yeast
   4 to 4½ cups sifted all-purpose flour
      ¼ teaspoon ground cardamom
               • • •
   1¼ cups milk
      ½ cup butter or margarine
      ¼ cup granulated sugar
      1 teaspoon salt
      1 slightly beaten egg
               • • •
      1 cup raisins
      ¼ cup currants
      ¼ cup chopped mixed candied fruits
      ¼ cup chopped, blanched almonds
      2 tablespoons grated orange peel
      1 tablespoon grated lemon peel
               • • •
      1 cup sifted powdered sugar
      2 tablespoons hot water
      ½ teaspoon butter or margarine
         Candied fruits

In large mixer bowl combine yeast, *2 cups* of the flour, and cardamom. Heat milk, ½ cup butter or margarine, granulated sugar, and salt just till warm, stirring occasionally to melt butter. Add to dry mixture in mixer bowl; add egg. Beat at low speed with electric mixer for ½ minute, scraping sides of bowl constantly. Beat 3 minutes at high speed. By hand, stir in raisins, currants, ¼ cup mixed candied fruits, nuts, and grated peels. Stir in enough of remaining flour to make a soft dough.

Turn out on a lightly floured surface. Knead till smooth and elastic, about 8 to 10 minutes. Place in a greased bowl, turning once to grease surface of dough. Cover and let rise in warm place till double, about 1¾ hours. Punch down; turn out on a lightly floured surface. Divide dough into 3 equal parts. Cover; let dough rest 10 minutes before shaping.

Roll each of the 3 parts into a 10x6-inch rectangle. Without stretching, fold the long side of each rectangle over to within 1 inch of the opposite side; seal edge. Place on greased baking sheets. Cover and let rise in a warm place till almost double, about 1 hour. Bake at 375° till golden brown, 15 to 20 minutes. Combine powdered sugar, hot water, and ½ teaspoon butter or margarine. While Stollen is warm, brush with powdered sugar mixture. To match picture, top Stollen with additional pieces of candied fruits. Makes 3.

Cranberry Nut Loaf

Sift together 3 cups sifted all-purpose flour, 1 cup sugar, 4 teaspoons baking powder, and 1 teaspoon salt. Combine 1 beaten egg, 1½ cups milk, and 2 tablespoons salad oil; add to dry ingredients, stirring just till moistened. Stir in 1 cup coarsely chopped cranberries and ½ cup chopped nuts. Turn the mixture into a greased 9x5x3-inch loaf pan. Bake at 350° till the loaf is done, about 1¼ hours. Remove from pan; cool loaf on a rack. Slice to serve. Makes 1 loaf.

Pumpkin Nut Bread

In mixing bowl blend ¾ cup canned pumpkin, ½ cup water, 1 egg, 1 teaspoon ground cinnamon, and ½ teaspoon ground mace. Add one 17-ounce package nut quick bread mix; stir till moistened. Turn mixture into greased 9x5x3-inch loaf pan. Bake at 350° till done, about 50 minutes. Remove from pan; cool. Drizzle with icing, if desired. Makes 1 loaf.

Orange Nut Bread

2¼ cups sifted all-purpose flour
¾ cup sugar
2¼ teaspoons baking powder
¾ teaspoon salt
¼ teaspoon baking soda
• • •
¾ cup chopped walnuts
1 tablespoon grated orange peel
• • •
1 beaten egg
¾ cup orange juice
2 tablespoons salad oil

Sift together the all-purpose flour, sugar, baking powder, salt, and baking soda.

Stir in the chopped walnuts and grated orange peel. Mix beaten egg, orange juice, and salad oil together. Add to dry ingredients, stirring just till moistened. Turn batter into greased 8½x4½x2½-inch loaf dish. Bake at 350° about 55 minutes. Remove the bread from the pan; cool on rack. Wrap the bread and store it overnight. Slice to serve. Makes 1 loaf.

A Christmas bread for gift-giving—German Stollen.

Mint-Apple Jelly, Cinnamon-Apple Jelly, and Apricot-Pineapple Jam.

JAM AND JELLY SPECIALTIES

When your favorite fruits are in season, take full advantage of them by cooking up a batch of jam, jelly, or marmalade. Be sure to make enough so that you'll have a variety of jellies handy for gift giving.

Ladle the mixture into decorative jelly glasses, and add a label that gives the name of the product and the date. Store the jellies in a cool, dry, dark place until you're ready to give them.

For an intriguing addition to the gift, decorate the top of the jar with a cluster of artificial fruits that hint of the contents.

Canning Procedures

Preparing jars: Wash the jelly glasses or jars in warm soapy water; rinse them with hot water. (You can use a dishwasher for this step.) Keep the jars hot until you are ready to use them. This will prevent the possibility of breakage when the hot jelly is poured in.

Jelly tests: To test a jelly made without added pectin, dip a large metal spoon into the mixture; tilt spoon until syrup runs over side. When the jellying stage has been reached, the liquid will stop flowing in a stream and divide in two distinct drops that run together and sheet from the edge of the spoon. Or, use a thermometer. The temperature of the mixture should register 8° higher than the boiling point of water. (Find the temperature at which water boils in your area. The boiling point varies with the altitude.)

Sealing jellies, jams, and preserves: Cover hot jelly (not preserves or soft jams) immediately with enough hot paraffin to make a layer ⅛ inch thick. Prick any air bubbles. (Melt paraffin in a double boiler. Never let paraffin reach smoking temperatures.)

If canning jars with lids are used, omit the paraffin. For jams and preserves, any type of canning jar may be used. Prepare lids following manufacturer's directions. Fill hot, scalded jars with boiling hot mixture. Wipe top and threads of jar clean. Place lid on jar; seal at once. Screw band tight.

Cooling and storing: Let jellies and jams stand undisturbed overnight. Cover paraffined jars, but do not use a lid that makes a tight seal. Label jars with name of the product and the date. Store in a cool, dry, dark place.

Cinnamon-Apple Jelly

    4 cups apple juice
    1 2½-ounce package powdered fruit
        pectin
    Red food coloring
    4½ cups sugar
    3 to 4 tablespoons red cinnamon
        candies

Combine apple juice, pectin, and several drops red food coloring in very large saucepan. Bring to hard boil. Stir in sugar and candies. Bring again to full *rolling boil; boil hard 2 minutes,* stirring constantly. Remove from heat and skim. Pour into hot, scalded jars; seal at once. Label cooled jars. Makes about 8 glasses.

Mint-Apple Jelly

    4 cups apple juice
    1 2½-ounce package powdered fruit
        pectin
    6 drops green food coloring
    1 cup lightly packed fresh mint leaves
    4½ cups sugar

Combine apple juice, pectin, food coloring, and mint leaves in a very large saucepan. Bring to hard boil. Stir in sugar. Bring again to full *rolling boil; boil hard 2 minutes,* stirring constantly. Remove from heat; skim. Remove leaves. Pour into hot, scalded jars; seal at once. Makes about 8 glasses.

Apricot-Pineapple Jam

    6 cups fresh apricots, quartered
    1 20½-ounce can crushed pineapple
    4½ cups sugar
    1 4-ounce bottle maraschino cherries,
        drained and sliced

In a saucepan combine the first 3 ingredients. Bring the mixture to a rolling boil, stirring constantly. Add maraschino cherries. Boil hard, stirring constantly, till syrup sheets from spoon, about 15 minutes. Pour into hot, scalded jars; seal immediately. Makes 4 pints.

Cran-Pineapple Jelly

3 cups cranberry juice cocktail
1 cup unsweetened pineapple juice
⅓ cup lemon juice
1 1¾-ounce package powdered fruit
pectin
• • •
5 cups sugar

Combine fruit juices with pectin in very large saucepan; stir over high heat till mixture boils hard. At once, stir in sugar. Bring to *full rolling boil; boil hard 1 minute,* stirring constantly. Remove from heat; skim off foam. Pour into 6 to 8 hot, scalded jelly glasses, leaving ½-inch space at top. Seal at once. Makes 6 to 8 glasses jelly.

Blueberry Marmalade

Remove peel from 1 medium orange and 1 lemon. Scrape excess white from peel; cut peel in *very fine* shreds. Place in very large saucepan. Add ¾ cup water. Bring to boil; simmer, covered, 10 minutes, stirring occasionally. Remove white membrane on fruit; finely chop pulp (discard seeds). Add to peel with 3 cups crushed blueberries. Cover; simmer 12 minutes. Add 5 cups sugar. Bring to *full rolling boil; boil hard 1 minute,* stirring constantly. Remove from heat; immediately stir in *one-half* 6-ounce bottle liquid fruit pectin. Skim off foam; stir and skim for 7 minutes. Ladle the mixture into hot, scalded jars. Seal the jars at once. Makes six ½-pint jars marmalade.

Gingered Rhubarb Jam

4 cups diced fresh rhubarb
3 cups sugar
3 tablespoons finely snipped candied
ginger
2 tablespoons lemon juice
Few drops red food coloring

Combine rhubarb with next 3 ingredients in large saucepan; let stand till sugar is moistened by juice, about 15 minutes. Cook over medium-high heat, stirring frequently till thick and clear, 12 to 15 minutes. Skim off foam; add red food coloring, if desired. Ladle the mixture into hot, scalded jars or glasses. Seal the jars at once. Makes three ½-pint jars jam.

Peach-Rum Jam

3 pounds fully ripe peaches, scalded,
peeled, and finely chopped
(4 cups)
1 1¾-ounce package powdered fruit
pectin
5 cups sugar
¼ cup light rum

Combine peaches and pectin in a very large saucepan or Dutch oven. Place over high heat and bring to a full rolling boil, stirring constantly. Immediately add all the sugar and stir. Again bring to a *full rolling boil and boil hard for 1 minute,* stirring constantly. Remove from heat; stir in rum. Skim off foam with metal spoon. Stir and skim for 5 minutes to cool slightly and prevent floating fruit. Ladle into hot, scalded jars or glasses. Seal at once. Makes six to seven ½-pint jars jam.

Strawberry-Rhubarb Jam

2 cups thinly sliced rhubarb
2 cups sliced fresh strawberries
2 tablespoons lemon juice
1 1¾-ounce package powdered fruit
pectin
5½ cups sugar
12 drops red food coloring

Combine rhubarb, strawberries, lemon juice, ¼ teaspoon salt, and pectin in large saucepan; cook and stir till mixture comes to a fast boil. Add sugar and stir. Add food coloring. Bring to *full boil; boil hard 1 minute,* stirring constantly. Remove from heat; skim off foam and quickly pour into hot, scalded glasses to within ½ inch of top. Seal. Store in cool, dark place. Makes six ½-pint glasses jam.

Double Berry Jam

Wash and crush 1 quart fresh blueberries and 1 quart fresh red raspberries; measure 4 cups (fill last cup with water, if necessary) into large saucepan. Add 7 cups sugar. Bring to *full rolling boil; boil hard 1 minute,* stirring constantly. Remove from heat. Stir in *one-half* 6-ounce bottle liquid fruit pectin. Skim off foam. Pour into 8 hot, scalded jars. Seal at once. Makes eight ½-pint jars jam.

Cherry-Strawberry Jam

>   1 20-ounce can pitted tart red cherries
>   (water pack)
>   • • •
>   1 10-ounce package frozen, sliced
>   strawberries, thawed
> 4½ cups sugar
>   3 tablespoons lemon juice
>   • • •
>   ½ 6-ounce bottle liquid fruit pectin

Drain cherries; reserve juice. Chop cherries; measure and add enough juice to make 2 cups. Combine cherries, strawberries, sugar, and lemon juice in large saucepan. Bring to *full rolling boil; boil hard 1 minute,* stirring constantly. Remove from heat; stir in pectin at once. Skim off foam. Stir and skim for 5 minutes to prevent fruit from floating. Ladle the mixture quickly into hot, scalded jars. Seal the jars at once. Makes six ½-pint jars jam.

Plum Jam

> 4½ cups plums (about 2½ pounds)
> 7½ cups sugar
>   ½ 6-ounce bottle liquid fruit pectin

Wash plums, cut in pieces, and remove pits. Crush fruit and measure. Combine plums and sugar in large pan. Bring to a *full rolling boil; boil hard for 1 minute,* stirring constantly. Remove from heat; add pectin at once. Skim off foam and alternately skim and stir jam for 5 minutes to prevent fruit from floating. Ladle into hot, scalded glasses and seal at once. Makes eight ½-pint glasses jam.

Cherry Marmalade

>   2 medium oranges
>   1 quart pitted dark sweet cherries
> 3½ cups sugar
>   ½ cup lemon juice

Slice unpeeled oranges paper-thin; discard any seeds. Barely cover orange slices with cold water; cook till soft. Add cherries, sugar, and lemon juice. Simmer till thick and clear. Skim off foam and quickly ladle marmalade into hot, scalded glasses. Seal at once. Makes about four ½-pint glasses marmalade.

Peach Conserve

Combine 2 pounds fully ripe peaches, scalded, peeled, and mashed (3 cups mashed), and one 6-ounce can frozen orange juice concentrate, thawed, in a very large saucepan. Stir in 5 cups sugar. Bring mixture to a *full rolling boil; boil hard 1 minute,* stirring constantly. Remove from heat; immediately stir in one 6-ounce bottle liquid fruit pectin and one 3½-ounce can flaked coconut. Skim off foam with metal spoon. Stir and skim for 7 minutes. Ladle into hot, scalded jars or glasses; seal at once. Makes seven ½-pint jars conserve.

Three-Fruit Marmalade

> 4 medium oranges
> 4 pounds fresh peaches, peeled and diced
>   (8 cups)
> 4 pounds fresh pears, peeled and diced
>   (8 cups)
> 1 1¾-ounce package powdered fruit
>   pectin
> 9 cups sugar

Slice unpeeled oranges in quarters, then in ¼-inch slices. Discard seeds. Measure fruits into large kettle and mix thoroughly. Cover and bring to a boil. Simmer gently 5 to 10 minutes. Stir in pectin and cook gently for 1 minute. Stir in sugar and bring to a vigorous boil, stirring constantly. *Boil hard 1 minute;* remove from heat. Skim and stir about 7 minutes. Pour the mixture into hot, scalded jars. Seal the jars at once. Makes 8 pints marmalade.

Apple-Orange Marmalade

> 1 orange
> 5 cups sugar
> 2 tablespoons lemon juice
> 3 pounds tart apples, thinly sliced
>   (8 cups)

Quarter orange, remove seeds, and slice very thin. Heat 1½ cups water and sugar till sugar is dissolved. Add lemon juice, orange, and apples. Boil rapidly, stirring constantly, till mixture thickens, 12 to 15 minutes. Remove from heat; ladle into hot, scalded jars. Seal at once. After jars cool 30 minutes, shake gently to distribute fruit. Makes 3 pints.

Delightfully bold, reusable pompon gift wrappings.

chapter 10

GLAMOUR WRAP-UPS

All of us at one time or another have received a beautifully wrapped gift, and, just before unwrapping it, have exclaimed, 'This package is almost too pretty to open.' These words are the supreme compliment for the gift-giver.

On the following pages you'll find lots of unusual gift wrap ideas, using materials other than the standard gift wrap paper and ribbon. Some of these ideas result in clever packages; others, pretty ones. All of them are sure to yield many compliments on your cleverness and creativity.

GIFT WRAPPINGS

Style your gift boxes and food containers with flair and care, and see how much pleasure it adds to gift-giving. You'll find that an imaginatively wrapped present is a fun way to tell someone that they're extra special.

An unusual gift wrapping needn't be expensive, especially if you employ a little ingenuity. Don't overlook the potential of little oddments you already have on hand—fabric remnants, aluminum foil, shelf paper, construction paper, sewing trims, stray buttons, yarn, paper bags, and last year's greeting cards.

Anyone can put wrapping paper around a box and stick a ready-made bow atop, but, if you've taken the extra time to make or select a special gift, be a little more dramatic. For example, if you're giving a gift to a sailing enthusiast, wrap the gift in a nautical map. Or, if the receiver is an amateur musician, clad the gift in sheet music. In other words, key the gift wrap to the individual's special interest. Make a splash at the next bridal shower you attend by applying the following suggestion. Watch the local newspaper for the picture and announcement of the bride-to-be. Wrap your gift in this sheet of newspaper, making sure you

position the article of interest in an eye-catching spot so it won't be missed. As a finishing touch for the wrap-up, top the package with a bow.

Or, use a different approach and develop trims that hint at the gifts inside. Treat a box of golf balls to a golf-tee design. Use barbecue mitts as toppers on a package of chef's tools. If you're welcoming a new baby home from the hospital, top the package with a rattle, or better yet, fasten diaper pins to the loops of the bow. These touches not only show your thoughtfulness, they will be useful, too.

If you're going to make a special wrap, consider the possibility of making it reusable. Cover the lid and box separately so the design is not spoiled when the package is unwrapped. By doing this, the recipient can use the box to store gloves, scarfs, handkerchiefs, or jewelry.

The reusable wraps at left are ideal for children's gifts. Cover the lids and the boxes separately, then trim them with cotton ball fringe. It takes 34 one-inch pompons to decorate the 5½-inch-square box with the flower motif. Position the trims on the box, then glue them in place, beginning in the center and working outward. The cat in the center takes 46 cotton balls; the lion, 74. Use black shiny buttons for the eyes, or buy wiggly ones and glue them on. Add chenille whiskers on the cat and lion.

Provocative package wraps from the local office supply store.

You can give any gift an extraordinary lift by using the most ordinary materials. A dramatic gift wrap can be created from an assortment of articles that you probably already have around your house. Try using some colorful shelf paper from the kitchen, yarn from your sewing basket, and office supplies that are lying around in your desk drawer. Arrange and rearrange the various articles into a design appropriate for the gift-giving occasion. You'll be amazed at what interesting designs you can create just by using mailing labels, photo mounts, gummed reinforcements, paper clips, and thumb tacks along with a few dabs of white glue and a foot or two of leftover yarn. Accept the challenge that your desk drawer offers, and your imagination will be your only limitation.

All of the provocative packages above are made from materials commonly found in a home office or purchased from an office supply store. Starting at the left, moving clockwise:

Build a house from mailing labels, then shingle the roof with photo mounts. The flowers are notary seals and gummed reinforcements.

To make the green tree, lace yarn over push pins. You'll need 11 pins and a piece of corrugated cardboard the same size as the top of the box to stick pinpoints into. Glue cardboard to box before wrapping. Trim tree with tassels.

The holiday wreath is made by combining tiny green signal dots and red notary seals into the shape of a wreath. Lightly pencil a circle on the lid of the box, then fill in all areas within the lines. Add a red ribbon bow.

The star design on the next package is made by gluing pencils to the box top in the shape of rays and by adding a silver star seal at the end of each ray. This idea will make a particular hit with a child if you have the child's name stamped on each pencil.

For the snowman, stick gummed reinforcements into circles of graduated sizes. Cut the arms, broom, hat, scarf, and facial features from construction paper and glue them in place.

Lace up a package by coordinating oversized paper clips and yarn from the top to the bottom of the box. Sew the paper clips onto the box with fishing line. Then, lace with yarn.

The stylized Santa consists of a mailing label beard, photo-mount eyes, and a notary seal nose. Make his face and hat from paper. At the bottom of the package, add a yarn bow.

For the pyramid in the foreground, set four inverted candy cups into shallow glue, and then form a square in the center of the box lid with them. (This square serves as a base for the other cups.) Glue additional cups on the top and sides, and trim with circles and dots.

Items from your home office, when teamed with wrapping paper or shelf paper and ribbon, make festively wrapped packages. In addition to their unlimited potential, they are easy-to-find materials. What home office doesn't have paper clips, rulers, reinforcement circles, and other such items?

These package wraps are particularly appropriate for gifts intended for your boss, your husband, your son, your brother-in-law, office exchanges, and retirement parties. Keep them in mind just in case you ever draw the gift-wrap detail for such an occasion.

For best results, wrap your package in a bright, solid-colored paper. This way, your trim will contrast more strongly.

The white pine tree is formed from gummed reinforcement circles. Place the tree toward the top of the package. Then, fill in the free space at the bottom of the package with three strips of ribbon. Use inch-wide ribbon and separate it to the desired widths. (For a different approach to the same idea, use photo mounts on white shelf paper to create the same effect, only in striking black and white.)

Call it a snowflake, a sunburst, or just an abstract design. When used to cover the top of a package, the result you get from a combination of erasers and paper clips is very effective. Add adhesive-backed signal dots and a flower center. For a finishing touch, frame your design with narrow strips of ribbon.

The package in the foreground has several items on it that are usable after the gift has been removed from the box—a pair of small plastic rulers, a clamp to use for clipping papers together, plus a few paper clips. These will delight a school-age youngster. Combine these materials with ribbon, and glue them onto a box. Remember, the design you make up doesn't have to represent anything in particular. It can be just a pleasing arrangement of objects.

Gift wraps from your home office.

A gift wrapping is what you make of it. It can be as quick and easy as placing a sheet of gift-wrap paper around a box and attaching a ready-made bow, or, for some creative people, it can involve many hours of exacting work. Or, a gift wrapping can be anywhere in between these two extremes. The choice is yours.

On these two pages, you'll find some gift-wrapping ideas that will appeal to everyone. Each one is a little out of the ordinary. Look them over to see which ones you have the time and patience to make.

The use of yarn instead of ribbon has saved the day for many an 'all-thumbs' gift wrapper. Now, no one need ever know that you can't make a fancy box. Simply take some of your leftover knitting worsted and wrap it around your package. Tie it in a simple 'shoestring' bow, and presto, you've wrapped a package.

With a little more effort, you can perform all sorts of tricks with the yarn. Make pompons by wrapping yarn around a 3-inch piece of cardboard. Slip the yarn off the cardboard and tie it in the center with another piece of yarn. Clip the loops at each end, fluff, and trim. Tape or staple one or more pompons to the top of the package, or, to further decorate your package, string wooden beads or rings on the yarn. You can get a slightly different effect with the same technique by using chubby yarn. For a little

girl's gift, cut several strands of different-colored chubby yarn into 1-foot lengths, then loop them over the corners of the box and through a wooden ring. After the package is opened, the young girl can then use the yarn for hair ribbons or pretty bows.

These yarn-tieing tricks are suitable for any gift-giving occasion; they'll look absolutely smashing if you combine them with brightly patterned paper or fabric.

Gift wraps that double as toys are possible if you are the type of person who has imagination, time, and energy. The six take-apart toys on the opposite page have gifts cleverly concealed inside. Open the lid, remove the gift, and you have a toy that can be either played with or displayed as an accessory on a child's bookshelf. The makings of these gift wraps are exceptionally easy to come by. The wheels on the train, plane, and car are paper-covered rings made from rolls of tape; the smokestacks on the train and boat, plus the rocket ship's body, are cardboard cores made from paper towels. The airborne 'balloon' is a foam ball held aloft with ⅛-inch dowels; chenille stems form ropes; and a colorful coaster holds the pint-sized presents for some lucky child. Finish the project by wrapping the various shapes in brightly colored wrapping paper and then by assembling the pieces with some white glue.

Yarn-bedecked packages, a lifesaver for the 'all-thumbs' gift wrapper.

Gift wrappings that double as toys are sure to delight all your young friends. Best of all, they are inexpensive, easy to make, and a lot of fun to give.

If you were to take a poll of just what constituted a good gift wrap, you'd undoubtedly find that it was something fast, easy, and that didn't require costly trims.

On these two pages, you'll find gift-wrap ideas that have all these qualities, plus many more. They are attractive, unusual, always suitable for any occasion, and perfect for mailing. As an added feature, it takes little talent to re-create these gift-wrap productions.

The personalized packages below are as easy to make as they are pretty. Begin by wrapping the boxes in solid-colored paper. (Don't overlook the possibility of using shelf-lining papers, which now come in a wide variety of bright and pastel colors.) Next, trim the wrapped box with motifs cut from leftover gift-wrap paper, greeting cards, and magazine illustrations. To personalize each gift, clip letters from magazine advertisements, and rubber cement them to the top of the box. After your first attempt at this type of gift wrapping, you'll probably find yourself hoarding old magazines, cards, and papers of every possible description.

The paper-circle-trimmed packages, above right, are the easiest of all to duplicate. Again, begin by wrapping the boxes in gift-wrapping paper or shelf paper. Then, cut circles from any type of paper that is colored on both sides. (If you don't happen to have any such paper on hand, cut two identical circles from a piece of paper and glue them together back to back so that the one circle looks the same on both sides.) Use rubber cement to attach the circles to the paper-covered packages.

To decorate the cube-shaped packages, cut two circles each of two colors of paper. Overlap the circles and alternate the colors as you

Colorful personalized packages with a hint of Christmas about them.

glue the circles to the box. If you wish to add more decoration, repeat the same design with smaller circles on the sides of the box.

Duplicate the balloon motif by cutting three circles of one color and two of another. Fold the circles in half and cement them together. Roll a small length of paper for the neck. To form the basket, cut a paper muffin cup in half and glue it in place. Cut flags from paper and glue them to toothpicks. Glue the assembled design to package, using white glue.

To make the flowerlike design on the next package, cut four circles from one color of paper. Fold them in half and glue half of each circle to the box. For the center, glue a paper coaster in the middle of the half-circle.

For the design on the tall box, fold 4-inch circles into quarters. On the fold line of one quarter, cut to the center of the circle. Overlap one quarter with another and glue the two together. Make four of these units and cement them together, alternating colors. Repeat the design to complete the package trim.

To trim the box in the foreground, cut four circles of one color, four of another. Fold the circles in half and arrange them radially in pairs, alternating colors. Cement half of each circle to the top of the box.

Patchwork is everywhere—even on gift packages. The packages, below right, were designed from remnants of too-pretty-to-throw-away printed wrapping papers. Except for the two triangular designs shown at the left side of the picture, all of the other packages were covered with the rectangular patchwork.

To begin, cut the various papers into equal width rectangles, whenever possible. Glue all the rectangular pieces of paper to a sheet of tissue paper, and then wrap your package.

To make the triangular-patterned paper, first make cardboard patterns of an equilateral triangle and a 45-degree triangle, and use these patterns as you cut the printed paper. Then, glue the equilateral triangles to one sheet of tissue paper and the 45-degree triangles to another sheet of paper.

Wrap the packages as usual, and trim with rickrack, lace, or braid. To personalize a package, glue on flowers or letters for names.

A collection of paper circle packages.

Patchwork gift packages.

196

Children's oilcloth animal gift wraps later double as toys and wall hangings.

Personalized people-pleasing packages dressed up in paper, yarn, and trims.

Sophisticated wrappings combine tassels, braids, mirrors, and pendants.

Colorful travel poster cover-ups help to create an international flavor.

'In tune with the times' trappings combine mod posters, toys, and games.

Novel burlap package wraps are destined to become all-occasion keepsakes.

Once you get your mind moving on different ideas for gift wraps, you'll find that it's difficult to stop. Every scrap of fabric or paper and every discarded trinket probably will give you a whole rash of new and clever ideas.

The collection of packages on the opposite page may help you conjure up a couple more 'show-off' styles for your special packages.

The oilcloth animal gift wraps, top left, are sure to delight the children on your gift-giving list. Each of these packages comes with a bonus present of either a toy or a wall hanging. The design motif may be of any animal, but for best results, keep the shapes as simple as possible. Trace a pattern from a coloring book or do a freehand outline to fit the size of the gift. Transfer this pattern onto a scrap of ½-inch foam rubber, and cut out the shape. Now, draw the same animal on a double thickness of oilcloth or vinyl and cut it out, allowing an extra 1 inch around for seams. Place the layer of foam rubber between the two pieces of oilcloth, with the shiny sides out, and staple the edges together. Cover the box top with matching or contrasting oilcloth, and glue the animal to the top of the package. Add a nose, eyes, and other features with adhesive papers, tape, marking pens, felt and vinyl scraps, and yarn. For the final touch, make a colorful border from chubby yarn to cover up the staples.

People-pleasing packages are represented by the whimsical trio of gift wraps at the top right.

The beguiling 'lady' package features hair made by gluing lengths of yarn in place, paper eyelashes, and a lace-banded dress cut from striped fabric or paper.

To decorate a small cube-shaped box, transform the box into a flowerpot. Trim the pot with a remnant of braid. And, in the pot, plant a springy, cardboard sunflower.

The bonnet-bedecked box begins with a hat cut from heavy, striped paper. The bonnet is then trimmed with paper flowers and yarn. For a coy touch, also glue on a set of paper lashes.

Sophisticated wrappings, middle left, are created from elegant fabrics and rich papers. Select intricately patterned flocked or foil papers and luxurious fabrics such as silk, crepe, or velvet. The trims are an assortment of tassels, beads, sequins, seals, pendants, mirrors, laces, and fabric braids. For more trim ideas, browse through notions departments, fabric shops, craft and hobby shops, and stationery stores.

Colorful travel posters, middle right, are another source of gift papers. For the perfect final touch, top each package with a trim that is appropriate for the country the package represents. Try gayly colored crepe paper flowers for Mexico or Spain, egg-carton tulips for Holland, chopsticks for China, a tiny plastic flag of a particular country, or a toy plane or ship. This is an exceptionally good idea to keep in mind for bon voyage gifts, going-away gifts, and for all those souvenirs you bring home to friends.

'In tune with the times' trappings, bottom left, will be a hit with many of the children and teenagers on your gift list. Combine mod posters with brightly colored rubber balls, a set of jacks, a record, or a skip rope, or search the variety store toy counter for other novelties that you can use to decorate the package.

Burlap package wraps, bottom right, will become keepsakes long after they have served their original gift-wrap purpose.

For the name package, cut two pieces of burlap to 15x28 inches, and stitch the sides and one end. Then, turn and fringe the ends to a 2-inch depth. Tack on fabric braid. Now, slip the gift inside, and slip-stitch the end shut. Using a felt-tip pen, transfer a pattern and the name onto the top of the box. Following your pattern, glue on felt, braid, and rug yarn.

To make the fringed package, cut the burlap to fit the box. Trim off any excess fabric, and use masking tape to hold the fabric in place while you slip-stitch the corners. With a felt-tip pen, trace a pattern on the top of the box. Using white glue, fill in the pattern with felt, fringe, and rug yarn.

For the tote bag, cut two pieces of burlap to 20x11 inches, and sew the three sides together. Fringe the top and add a cardboard bottom for support. Glue on colorful pompons to accent the tote bag, if desired.

MAKING YOUR OWN GIFT PAPERS

Give that handcrafted gift a special wrap with gift paper you create. With only a small expenditure of time, energy, and money, you can print reams of your own unique gift-wrap paper. Using shelf paper and paper toweling, in both white and pastel colors, print your own designs, using one of several methods—roller printing, string-pulling, vegetable, fruit, and utensil printing, and dip-dyeing.

Use different widths of rollers to decorate rolls of shelf paper. To achieve startling effects, follow these easy directions. Allow yourself an adequate work area—a 3- to 6-foot table (painter's sawhorses with boards are ideal) —pour a variety of water-based paints into cereal bowls or saucers, and lay out newspapers to protect the floor. Then, unroll the shelf paper into 3- to 6-foot lengths, cut it with scissors, and begin painting the design.

One roller is all you need to create bold stripes. Alternate the widths of the stripes by using the roller's edge to make a very narrow stripe. Or, create a checkerboard motif by rolling a roller for a few inches and then lifting it from the paper. The fact that the color blocks are uneven is far from a drawback; it contributes to the primitive look.

Use two rollers of different widths simultaneously to cover the entire area of the paper with contrasting colors. Try using two rollers of the same width, running them crisscross, vertically, or horizontally along the shelf paper. Just experiment with the rollers and see what you come up with.

After you've finished the roller prints, lay the lengths of paper on the floor for a few minutes to let the colors set. While they are still damp, pick up each piece separately and hang it over a basement laundry line. Leave the pieces overnight for drying. When dry, roll them together for future package wrapping.

String-pulling is a very ancient method of decorating paper. Again, use shelf paper or ordinary brown wrapping paper. Cut off one

or two yards of paper (here, shorter lengths of paper are handier to work with). Assemble ordinary postal string, or heavier twine if you wish to make thicker outlines. Cut the string not longer than an arm's length (you will be coiling some of the string on the paper with the rest hanging over). Dip the string in poster paint, squeeze out the excess, and lay it in swirls and loops on the paper, as illustrated in the top center drawing at the right.

Fold a square of newspaper over the coiled string, exerting a gentle pressure with the left hand. Quickly pull the string, which extends from between the newspaper and the shelf paper, toward you with one continuous motion. Remove the newspaper and let the design dry thoroughly. Don't use more than two colors.

Fruit, vegetable, and utensil print paper can feature a wild collection of fruits, vegetables, and utensils that can be found in most supermarkets any time of the year.

To make these papers, use some new variations of the well-known potato printing technique. For potato printing, cut the vegetable in half, and make a few notches with a paring knife. If the potato is not particularly shapely, trim the edges into any desired outline. Dip the potato in paint and press it to the paper. For a striking effect, alternate rows of vegetable print with bands made from a roller.

After you've mastered the potato print, graduate to other fruits and vegetables. Try a cabbage cut in wedges, a Bermuda onion cut in half, or make wagon wheels from lemon slices. Also try designs made with kitchen hardware—wire whisks, cookie cutters, and gelatin molds.

Kitchen paper toweling and liquid dye make simple but sensational shadow designs. The end result will resemble an expensive batik or tie-dyed paper. And, best of all, you can turn out yards of superb-looking paper in a few hours. To make a large amount of this type of wrapping paper, take the cardboard core from the inside of a regular-size roll of paper toweling. Reroll

Roller printing.   **String-pulling.**   **Vegetable printing.**

Kitchen utensil printing.   **Dip-dyeing.**

about ¾ of the roll lightly. Fill a small basin with ½ cup dye and a like amount of water. Repeat the process with another color. Immerse one end in one color, letting it remain in the solution for about one minute. For lighter shades, double the amount of water. Wearing gloves, remove the toweling from the dye and squeeze out excess liquid. Repeat the process with another color at the other end of the toweling. Unroll the paper carefully and loop it over a clothesline for drying.

For shorter lengths of dip-dyed wrapping paper, you'll find that folding six or eight of the squares into a very small, compact square and immersing each corner in a different color of dye for ½ minute will produce a feathery effect. Or, fold paper toweling into triangles, and dip the corners of the triangle.

If you're the kind of person who really likes to get your hands into a project, making gift-wrapping paper provides you with an excellent opportunity. Here are a few fun ideas for your consideration. Dip the palm of your hand in poster paint and make handprints all over shelf paper or brown wrapping paper. When you think you've mastered this, try making bear tracks across the paper. To do this, dip just your palm in the poster paint, make your palm print on the paper, and dip your fingers in the paint and print them just above your palm print. (If you prefer a three-toed bear print, don't bother dipping the fourth finger!) Or, perhaps you or one of your friends has a foot fetish. If so, try making footprints on snow-white shelf paper. This design is created by a clenched fistprint, four fingers, and a thumbprint. Splash them at random all over the paper, or arrange them so that they appear to march over or around the gift box.

These different ideas should give you a few ideas of your own. Put them into action by working on your own personalized gift-wrapping paper. The work will seem like play!

GIFT CONTAINERS

A gift from your kitchen is one of the nicest ways to let someone know you are thinking of them, whether it be during the holiday season, a thank-you for the weekend, or simply a helping hand for the hostess. Chapter 9 should have given you a few new ideas of what food to give, and perhaps you also have some 'tried and true' family recipes that you want to give. By all means, do it, but as you prepare the food, think of how you can present your gift. A clever gift wrapping will make your gift even more appreciated and perhaps more useful.

Decorated canning jars are a clever wrap for your favorite home-canned delicacy. If it is at all possible, let your decoration hint at what's inside. For instance, the jars, below left, contain corn relish and pickled mushrooms, and the jars communicate this idea.

The jars of corn relish were appropriately decorated to resemble ears of corn. To make this trim, roll a circle of heavy paper that measures 6 inches in diameter into a cone to fit the jar's lid. Cut the tip off of the cone and insert yellow yarn 'silks.' Cut crepe paper in an 8x9-inch piece. Then, cut this piece of crepe paper halfway down in the shape of four husk tips. Tape this around the jar, leaving a space to view the jar's contents. Add a layer of 2x8-inch husks, and curl the tips.

To make the mushroom wrap, cut foam balls in half. Add stems, which are slices cut from cardboard cylinders, and glue the two pieces together. Cover the mushroom with narrow strips of tissue paper, and paint with acrylic paints. Secure one or more mushrooms to the top of the lid with white glue. Adorn the side of the lid with narrow strips of gift ribbon.

Inventively decorated canning jars.

Fruit topping adorns apothecary jars.

'Two-for-one' gift wrap.

A bell-ringing gift wrap features stars.

Fruit-topped apothecary jars, left, can hold a cargo of rich candies. Buy inexpensive glass jars, and decorate the lids by adding a top of clay-mâché. Be sure to bring the clay-mâché under the edge of the lid to prevent it from separating when dry. Build up the flower by adding petal-shaped pieces of mâché to the first layer. When the mâché is dry, brush on white glue to seal, then two thin coats of gesso. Paint the lid with acrylic paint.

The 'two-for-one' gift wrap, above left, allows you to wrap one gift inside of another. Bottle up your favorite salad dressing or barbecue sauce and wrap it in a colorful oven mitt—a ready-made one or one you've made yourself from heavy quilted fabric. Bend a coat hanger wire to fit the mitt's outline, starting at the thumb, around the finger section, and to the cuff. Slip the mitt over the wire and bend it to fit around the bottle. Trim it with paper butterflies.

The bell-ringing wrap, above right, can be as useful as it is festive. To make the bell, purchase an inexpensive grater from any house-

wares department. After you've placed your favorite goody inside, cover the bottom of the grater with cardboard. Then, fasten a measuring spoon 'clapper' to the handle of the grater with masking tape. Trim the container with ribbon, a bow, and some silver stars.

While these utensil wrap ideas are ideal for food gifts, don't overlook their potential as kitchen shower gift-wrap ideas.

Instead of giving your special sauce, bottle some of your homegrown herbs, and wrap the bottle in an oven mitt. Or, bottle flower seeds and wrap the jar with garden gloves. Or, fill the grater with lots of little kitchen gadgets. Put in a pastry brush, a wooden spoon, a rubber spatula, a paring knife, a can opener, a sponge, a dish cloth, and a dish towel. Or, easier and quicker yet, pick up a couple of packages of printed recipe cards and place them inside. Other kitchen utensils may also be decorated and used as package wraps. Use your imagination and see what you can come up with when you use plastic containers of almost any kind, juicers, pitchers, sifters, cake carriers, and teakettles.

Raggedy Ann and Andy and their friends are gift-giving food containers made from cardboard tubes and cartons. All of these containers can be used as colorful accessories long after all the edible goodies are gone.

It's really quite easy to duplicate the Raggedy Ann and Andy containers. Simply cut cardboard mailing tubes (3¼ inches in diameter) into 5½-inch lengths. Cut each of these pieces in half for the head and the body. Glue a cardboard lining inside the body section, extending the lining ½ inch above the body.

To trim, cover the heads with pink percale. Make the hair from red yarn, then glue it in place. Next, cut the eyes, noses, and mouths from felt, and glue them in place.

Dress the containers with pieces of leftover fabric. Glue the fabric to the sides of the carton and the dangly legs to the bottom. Trim with buttons, bows, and lace edgings.

For the soldier containers, cover a cardboard tube with white paper. Glue a folded and gathered scrap of red mohair fabric to the top, and add a large white ball fringe.

Glue on sequins for eyes, a pearl for the nose, and felt for the mouth. The chin strap is an old necklace. Glue a 3-inch-wide felt collar to the tube ½ inch from the bottom of container.

For the face containers, spray-paint half-pint ice cream cartons. Cut features from felt and glue them on. Make hair from 8-inch lengths of yarn, and glue it to the top of the lid.

Sprightly Raggedy Ann and Andy food containers made from cardboard.

Inventive, one-of-a-kind suggestions for packaging gourmet food gifts.

Clever ideas for purchased food gifts, left, may be just what you're looking for. Moving clockwise: First, cover the cheese-mouse with clear wrap, then add the felt eyes and ears. Place him atop a wooden cheese board. When you give an unusual blend of tea or coffee, include a set of mugs. For the fisherman, a creel holding seafood snacks and a fish-shaped wine bottle will be welcome. Dress up ham and jelly glasses or jars with owl containers made from paper cups. You'll need two for each jar or glass. Add features cut from paper or cardboard. For the wine connoisseur, add a collection of wine glasses to a raffia-covered bottle. Attach them with colored twine. To make spices look special, dress the bottles in coats of colored burlap or cloth napkins, and attach them to wooden salad tossers. Trim with yarn bows.

Decorated food containers that can be reused indefinitely by the recipient are made to order for the clever cook who likes to share her culinary triumphs with others. These plastic or rubber food containers come in a wide variety of sizes and shapes. You will find a large selection of these containers from which to choose in supermarkets and variety stores.

The 2½-quart rectangular crisper, top, is ideal for pretty arrangements of home-baked pastries and do-it-yourself assortments of gourmet foods. For a hard-to-wrap coffee cake, pie, or fruitcake, use a circular plastic food container. Decorate the tops and sides of the containers with ribbon, yarn, and seals.

The festive six-pack, middle, is great for goodies on the go. To make it, you'll need a 2½-quart rectangular crisper and six 12-ounce boxes to nest inside. Cut colorful felt into letters, and attach to the sides of the large box with white glue. Make gold labels for the lids of the small containers. Wrap the assembled unit in tinted cellophane, and decorate it with a wide ribbon band and stickers.

Decorate a circular food container to resemble a Christmas wreath. First, cover a Styrofoam wreath with live holly, add a bow to the wreath, then trim the sides of the container with ribbon. The recipient now has a holly wreath, a reusable container, and your food gift. If you wish, also include the recipe.

You can easily turn reusable food containers into attractive gift wraps.

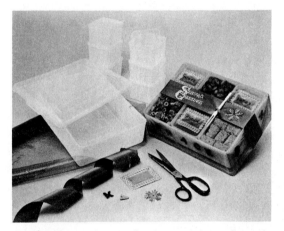

A festive six-pack container that is simply great for goodies-on-the-go.

A circular plastic container that easily becomes a holiday wreath.

WRAPPING PACKAGES FOR MAILING

Have you ever had a friend or relative call from out of town and halfheartedly thank you for the gift that you sent? If your answer to this question is yes, chances are that your handmade gift arrived at its destination either in pieces or otherwise damaged — a victim of poor packaging. This is a sad end for the gift that you worked so hard on for so long.

To prevent awkward situations such as this from happening to you, take the time to learn how to wrap a package properly. So what if it takes you an extra 15 minutes to make sure that the job has been done right! It will be time well spent. Remember that almost anything can be sent safely through the mail if it has been wrapped correctly.

PACKAGING

The single most important thing to keep in mind about packaging is that the container you use must be strong enough to protect its contents during normal mail handling. The strength of the carton that will be required depends, of course, on the weight, size, and nature of the item that you are mailing.

Most stationery stores have packing containers, made from a variety of materials: corrugated or solid fiberboard, kraftboard, chipboard (for small items), and fiber mailing tubes with metal ends. However, if you have some sturdy boxes with the flaps intact, they will accomplish the same purpose. If you can't find a box that is just the right size, cut a larger box down. To do this, first mark the desired height of the box. Then, determine the new size of the top flaps and make a second line. Split the corners to the desired box height. Cut along the second line, shortening the flaps. Fold the flaps down to the new box height.

Another method of utilizing boxes that you have on hand for packaging purposes is to remove the flaps from two similar-sized boxes, pack the gift item in one box, and place the other box over the bottom box, forming a lid. In order to keep the two boxes together, tie twine or string around all six sides.

PACKING

Cushioning material — excelsior, flexible corrugated fiberboard, felt, cellulose materials, cotton, shredded paper, or tissue paper — *must* surround any item that is likely to be broken, scratched, or dented in transit. If a single item is shipped, the cushioning surrounding the item will protect it from outside impact. If two or more items are shipped in the same container, the cushioning will protect the items from damaging one another, in addition to protecting against outside impact. The amount and kind of cushioning again depends on the size and nature of the items being mailed.

To pack fragile articles, individually cushion each piece. Place at least three inches of shredded paper or loose excelsior on all four sides of the box and on the top and bottom. Then, space each piece to avoid the possibility of strain or damage to other pieces.

To cushion a framed picture or mirror, fold several thicknesses of newspaper into long rolls. Wrap these, crosswise and lengthwise, around the front and back of the frame, and pack securely in a strong shipping carton.

OUTSIDE WRAPPING

Theoretically, if a package is in good condition and void of printing or previously used labels, it doesn't need an outside wrapping. However, most people use a wrapping anyway.

You can use a good-quality wrapping paper, if desired, but the ordinary grocery bag performs just as well, and is considerably less expensive. Simply cut the bag open and use as you would regular wrapping paper. Always print clearly the name and return address on the box before wrapping the package.

After wrapping the box, secure the wrapping paper with strong cord, twine, or reinforced adhesive tape. However, don't use masking tape or cellophane tape, as they don't hold well. Then, legibly print the address and return address on one side of the package. Above the address and below the postage, print the words 'Fragile' or 'Perishable' when the terms apply.

INDEX

(Food information grouped under Recipes at back of index.)

RECIPES

We are happy to acknowledge our indebtedness and to express our sincere thanks to the following who have been helpful to us in producing this book:
Arno Adhesive Tapes, Inc.
Bernhard Ulmann
Coats and Clark Inc.
Republic Molding Corporation
Tandy Corporation